The Challenge of Labour in China

China's economic success has been founded partly on relatively cheap labour, especially in the export industries. In recent years, however, there has been growing concern about wages and labour standards in China. This book examines how wages are bargained, fought over and determined in China, by exploring how the pattern of labour conflict has changed over time since the 1970s. It focuses in particular on the city of Shenzhen, where labour conflict and workers' protests have been especially prevalent. This book includes a detailed account of the transformation of labour relations and labour policy in China more broadly from 2004 to 2009, a period when there were significant changes in the labour market, labour regulation and labour relations. The author argues that these recent developments have brought to the fore the class basis of workers' protest in China and have thoroughly undermined the post-Marxist analysis of identity politics. The book makes an invaluable contribution to studies on industry and labour, as well as Chinese studies.

Chris King-Chi Chan is an Assistant Professor in the Department of Applied Social Studies at the City University of Hong Kong, and is an active member of labour NGOs in Hong Kong and on mainland China. He gained his PhD at the University of Warwick, UK and previously worked as a trade union organiser in Hong Kong.

China Policy Series

Series Editor: Zheng Yongnian, China Policy Institute,
University of Nottingham, UK

1. **China and the New International Order**
   Edited by Wang Gungwu and
   Zheng Yongnian

2. **China's Opening Society**
   The non-state sector and governance
   Edited by Zheng Yongnian and
   Joseph Fewsmith

3. **Zhao Ziyang and China's Political Future**
   Edited by Guoguang Wu and
   Helen Lansdowne

4. **Hainan – State, Society, and Business in a Chinese Province**
   Kjeld Erik Brodsgaard

5. **Non-Governmental Organizations in China**
   The rise of dependent autonomy
   Yiyi Lu

6. **Power and Sustainability of the Chinese State**
   Edited by Keun Lee, Joon-Han Kim
   and Wing Thye Woo

7. **China's Information and Communications Technology Revolution**
   Social changes and state responses
   Edited by Xiaoling Zhang and
   Yongnian Zheng

8. **Socialist China, Capitalist China**
   Social tension and political
   adaptation under economic
   globalisation
   Edited by Guoguang Wu and
   Helen Lansdowne

9. **Environmental Activism in China**
   Lei Xei

10. **China's Rise in the World ICT Industry**
    Industrial strategies and the catch-up
    development model
    Lutao Ning

11. **China's Local Administration**
    Traditions and changes in the
    sub-national hierarchy
    Edited by Jae-Ho Chung and
    Tao-chiu Lam

12. **The Chinese Communist Party as Organizational Emperor**
    Culture, reproduction and
    transformation
    Zheng Yongian

13. **China's Trade Unions–How Autonomous Are They?**
    Masaharu Hishida, Kazuko Kojima,
    Tomoaki Ishii and Jian Qiao

14. **Legitimating the Chinese Communist Party since Tiananmen**
    A critical analysis of the stability
    discourse
    Peter Sandby-Thomas

15. **China and International Relations**
    The Chinese view and the contribution
    of Wang Gungwu
    Zheng Yongnian

16. **The Challenge of Labour in China**
    Strikes and the changing labour
    regime in global factories
    Chris King-chi Chan

The Challenge of Labour in China

Strikes and the changing labour regime in global factories

Chris King-chi Chan

LONDON AND NEW YORK

First published 2010
by Routledge
2 Park Square, Milton Park, Abingdon, Oxon OX14 4RN

Simultaneously published in the USA and Canada
by Routledge
270 Madison Avenue, New York, NY 10016

Routledge is an imprint of the Taylor & Francis Group, an informa business

© 2010 Chris King-chi Chan

Typeset in Times New Roman
by Keystroke, Tettenhall, Wolverhampton

British Library Cataloguing in Publication Data
A catalogue record for this book is available from the British Library

Library of Congress Cataloging-in-Publication Data
Chan, Chris King-chi.
The challenge of labour in China : strikes and the changing labour regime in
global factories / Chris King-chi Chan.
p. cm. – (China policy series ; 16)
Includes bibliographical references and index.
1. Labor–China. 2. Labor policy–China. 3. Industrial relations–China.
4. Strikes and lockouts–China. I. Title.
HD8736.5.C36 2010
331.0951–dc22
2009051546

ISBN13: 978–0–415–55703–0 (hbk)
ISBN13: 978–0–203–84975–0 (ebk)

Contents

List of illustrations   vii
Acknowledgements   ix
Abbreviations   xi

1   Introduction: globalisation and Chinese migrant workers   1

2   Labour conflict in Shenzhen: a historical review   18

3   Community and shop floor culture: a prelude to workers'
    protest   46

4   Strikes and changing power relations in the workplace   81

5   Workplace conflict, legal institution and labour regime   122

6   International civil society, Chinese trade unionism and
    workplace representation   146

7   Conclusion: workers' struggle and the changing labour
    regime in China   164

Notes   178
Bibliography   183
Index   194

Illustrations

Map

2.1 An illustrated map of Shenzhen   21

Tables

2.1 Foreign Direct Investment in China, 1990–2004   24
2.2 Reported labour protests of FIE workers in the PRD from 1993
     to 1994   31
2.3 Arbitrated labour disputes in China, 1993–2004   36
2.4 Workers' collective action reported in the PRD from 2002 to 2005 37
2.5 Reported causes of collective actions in the PRD   38
3.1 Size, gender, and place-of-origin attributes of different departments
     in the Sun Factory   65
5.1 The legal minimum wage rate in Shenzhen   124

Boxes

5.1 Petition to the top management about working conditions in the
     Moon Factory   130
5.2 Public letter posted in the workshops before a strike in the Moon
     Factory   132
5.3 Pamphlet circulated during a Strike in the Moon Factory   135
5.4 Letter posted on an internet forum expressing workers' grievances 137

Acknowledgements

I am indebted to many teachers, friends, informants and institutions that have helped me to finish this book, which is based on my PhD research at the University of Warwick.

This research could not have been completed on time without the persistent guidance, encouragement, friendship and help of my PhD supervisor, Professor Simon Clarke. Working with Simon has been among the most enjoyable moments of my study life. Gratitude is extended to my friend Tim Pringle, with whom I worked under the ESRC non-public action project headed by Simon; to Professors Tony Elger and Annie Phizacklea, my teachers, who inspired my further exploration in the sociology of work and labour studies during my MA studies at Warwick; and to other Warwick teachers on the research method courses. Warwick postgraduate research training is unique as it is a collective project in which department members contribute their different expertise. Professor Michael Burawoy from UC Berkeley led inspiring and encouraging discussions in my research seminar held by Warwick IRRU and CCLS. Professor Theo Nicholes, my external examiner, gave invaluable comments on the manuscript. The University of Warwick generously granted me a Warwick Postgraduate Research Fellowship, Overseas Student Research Awards and the departmental bursary so that I could finish the project without financial burden. Much of the book was written in the library facilities of the University of Birmingham, where I lived. The walking path along the Midlands' industrial canals stimulated lots of ideas. I would not have enjoyed my life in England so much without the company of colleagues and friends, including, but not exclusively, Yubin, Huamei, Waiha, Elizabeth, Rosario, Rodrigo, Sole, Claudio, Olya, Nico, Cheng, Jeremy, Jacky, Charlene, Darren, Suki, Anita, Albert, Anne Barrett, Professor Ann Davis and Alex. I also want to thank Ed Shepherd for his meticulous proofreading of this book.

I am especially grateful to my many friends in Hong Kong and Guang Dong. Dr C. H. Ng, Elizabeth Tang and Lee Chuk Yan helped me to embark on my study at Warwick. Dr Pun Ngai, Dr Y. C. Chen, Parry, Jenny, Suet Wah, Mei, Vivien, Ng, Jane, Sophia, Yau, and many others in the CWWN and SACOM offered me friendship, kind assistance and insightful discussions during and beyond my fieldwork. I especially benefited from the China Labour Studies seminars organised by Dr Pun Ngai and attended by many other friends. Pun Ngai continued to provide critical comments on some of my work. My friends in HKCTU, GM, LESN, AMRC, HKCIC, CLSN, IHLO, CLB, WE and CLA, especially Yingyu, Sosheung, Au, May, Juliana, Pingkwan, Apo, Monina, Ling, April, Tat, Yin, Shan, Yuk Yuk, were very helpful in sharing important information, suggestions and reflections during this research. Prior to this project, I learned much from colleagues in HKCTU, who are engaged deeply in the labour movement. My deepest tribute is directed to my anonymous friends and informants in Shenzhen. In particular, the struggles of the workers and their brave pursuit of justice always inspired and encouraged me on my intellectual exploration and praxis. This book is dedicated to them.

I would like to thank the Hong Kong Polytechnic University and the City University of Hong Kong for generously granting me research time to complete this book. Part of the completion was done in Peking University when I was working at Peking U's and Hong Kong Poly U's joint China Social Work Research Centre. Gratitude is extended to friends and colleagues in Beijing who supported my work. Arguments from this book have been presented in a number of international conferences and workshops. I would like to thank Anita Chan, Peter Alexandra, Colin Barker, Yan Hairong, Rachael Cohen, Lu Huilin and many others for their useful comments and discussions.

I would like to express my love and gratitude to my family. The love from my great-grandmother, who passed away in 1981, always encouraged me in every important moment of my life. My parents work hard through difficult times and provide me with infinite love and care. I also have to thank my brother and sister-in-law for their care of our parents while I was away for study; my grandparents, aunts and uncles for their encouragement over the years; and my parents-in-law for taking care of me in Hong Kong. My deepest love is dedicated to Lynn, my wife, for her unlimited spiritual, intellectual, emotional and practical support in our life. Without Lynn's support, I would not have been able to embark on this challenging but pleasurable journey of PhD study.

Abbreviations

ACFTU	All China Federation of Trade Unions
AMRC	Asia Monitor Research Centre
CCP	Chinese Communist Party
CLB	*China Labour Bulletin*
CSR	Corporate Social Responsibility
CWWN	Chinese Working Women Network
FDI	Foreign Direct Investment
FIE	Foreign Invested Enterprise
FOA	Freedom of Association
GM	General Manager
ILO	International Labour Organisation
IT	Information Technology
JV	Sino-overseas Joint Ventures
LSSB	Labour and Social Security Bureau
MOLSS	Ministry of Labour and Social Security
MSI	Multi-stakeholder Initiative
NGO	Non-governmental Organisation
NIC	Newly Industrialised Country
OHS	Occupational Health and Safety
POE	Privately Owned Enterprise
PRD	Pearl River Delta
R&D	Research and Development
SCRO	State Council Research Office
SEZ	Special Economic Zone
SKIZ	She Kou Industrial Zone
SKIZFTU	She Kou Industrial Zone Federation of Trade Unions
SOE	State-Owned Enterprise
SZMFTU	Shenzhen Municipal Federation of Trade Unions
SZMLSSB	Shenzhen Municipal Labour and Social Security Bureau
TNC	Transnational Corporations
TVE	Township or Village Enterprise
UCE	Urban Collective-owned Enterprise
WTO	World Trade Organisation
YRD	Yangtze River Delta
ZHMFTU	Zhu Hai Municipal Federation of Trade Unions

1 Introduction

Globalisation and Chinese migrant workers

Introduction

> The integration of China's 1.3 billion people will be as momentous for the world economy as the Black Death was for 14th-century Europe, but to the opposite effect. The Black Death killed one-third of Europe's population, wages rose and the return on capital and land fell. By contrast, China's integration will bring down the wages of low-skilled workers and the prices of most consumer goods, and raise the global return on capital.
>
> (*The Economist*, 30 September 2004)

'Globalisation' and its impacts and implications have come under a new spotlight in a wide range of academic disciplines as well as among practitioners, policy-makers and social activists. As a common understanding, to usher in the age of globalisation, the boundaries of national borders were broken down and a single global economy was created. As a result, international trade and investment increased dramatically from the mid-1970s. This global transformation was rooted in the economic crisis of 1973 (Wood *et al.*, 1998). Relocation of production to the lower-cost developing world was one of the significant strategies of capital in the West to boost the falling profit rate.

The crisis of capitalism in the West encountered a crisis of state socialism in the East from the 1970s. The reform and opening policy of China since 1978 to some extent has bailed out Western capitalism from the crisis by providing an 'unlimited' supply of low-cost and unorganised labour. From the 1970s, even the newly industrialised countries (NICs), such as South Korea, Hong Kong, Taiwan and Singapore, were subjected to labour cost rises caused by a shortage of labour and rising worker protests and organisation (Deyo, 1989). China then became a new haven of manufacturing investment and global production as soon as it was open to the world. The label 'Made in China' can now be seen everywhere in the world. South China has become a new global manufacturing centre, comparable to Manchester in the early nineteenth century, Birmingham in the early twentieth century, and the Asian tiger economies in the 1970s, but with a much bigger scale and scope. The potential of Chinese workers to change this condition has significant meaning for global labour politics. This study was designed to contribute to the debate on globalisation and labour with reference to China.

Understanding globalisation

Globalisation seems to be taken for granted as the 'common sense' of our era (Munck, 2002), yet its nature is widely contested in different academic disciplines. Regardless of its ambiguity, a common understanding of globalisation is that a rapid increase in international trade and investment from the mid-1970s has broken down national borders and created a single global economy – often called the 'global village'. Neo-liberal economists, therefore, present globalisation as a natural and inevitable process leading to economic growth. Scholars from the left, however, generally take different views. There are two contested understandings of globalisation among those social scientists who were originally attached to the Marxist tradition.

For some of them, globalisation is a 'new historical epoch' in the name of 'new capitalism', 'post-industry', 'postmodernity', 'post-Fordism', 'network society', 'risk society', and so on. The underlying implication of this 'new epoch' thesis is a pessimistic position on labour politics. In 1980, two influential works by continental sociologists were translated into English. Gorz (1980) declared *Farewell to the Working Class* in advanced capitalism, while Frobel *et al.* (1980) pointed out the trend of industrial relocation to the developing world in their notion of the 'new international division of labour'. These authors suggested that a fundamental and qualitative change in capitalist production had universally weakened the power of the working class as predicted by Marx. Their works were sweepingly aped by left social scientists. Among others, another influential book was Rifkin's (1995) *The End of Work: The Decline of the Global Labor Force and the Dawn of the Post-Market Era*, which provoked a theoretical debate about the end of work. This school was generally called 'post-Marxism' in the light of its departure from Marx's class analysis and the notion of the historical agency of the working class in social transformation.

Their position was rejected, however, by neo-Marxist scholars from a wider range. Burnham (2001), drawing on the 'open Marxist' tradition, argued that capitalism from its very beginning has been an international system. Cohen (1987; 1991), influenced by world system theory which categorised the history of capitalism into phases, argued that the division of labour in the history of capitalism is always changing and thus suggested a concept of the 'changing division of labour' to displace Frobel *et al.*'s (1980) 'new international division of labour'. Wood *et al.* (1998) further pointed out that Marx had already perfectly predicted the contemporary phenomenon of globalisation by quoting *The Communist Manifesto*, written by Marx and Engels in 1848:

> Exploitation of the world market [has] given a cosmopolitan character to production and consumption in every country. . . . All old-established national industries have been destroyed or are daily being destroyed. They are dislodged by new industries . . . that no longer worked up indigenous raw material but raw material drawn from the remotest zones, industries whose products are consumed not only at home but in every quarter of the globe. In

place of old wants, satisfied by the production of the countries, we find new wants, requiring for their satisfaction the products of distant lands. . . . In place of the old local and national seclusion and self-sufficiency, we have intercourse in every direction, universal interdependence of nations.

(Wood *et al.*, 1998: 5)

According to Wood, although Marx did not use the term 'globalisation', all of the 'new' phenomena were stated clearly in his writings (Wood *et al.*, 1998: 5). Therefore, Marxism remains a valid and powerful framework to study working-class politics in the age of globalisation. Harvey (2001), however, contended that orthodox Marxism missed the important dimension of 'space' in the study of class struggle. He emphasised the specific cultural and institutional factors in the national and local context in shaping the pattern of labour resistance and rejected the universality of working-class politics. In spite of these sorts of differences, their common ground was that the logic of the capitalist mode of production remained unchanged and globalisation is only the further expansion of capital accumulation from Europe to the world (Cohen, 1987; 1991; Harvey, 1990; Wood *et al.*, 1998; Burnham, 2001; Katz-Fishman *et al.*, 2002; Silver, 2003). According to them, 'global capitalism' is a more accurate and precise rhetoric to portray contemporary globalisation. They argue that the labour and capital relation in capitalism is a continuously changing process, and what has happened in the past thirty years has been another strategy of capital to lower production cost as a consequence of competition and economic crisis.

Crisis of labour and labour studies

The post-Marxist and neo-Marxist theorists, however, had a common under-standing of the historical origin that made this intellectual turn after the early 1980s. According to Gorz (1980: 14), for example: 'There is a crisis in Marxist thinking because a crisis had developed within the labour movement.' Similarly, Silver (2003) pointed out that it was a crisis of the labour movement in the West that gave rise to a crisis of the Marxist school of labour studies. However, the two strains of thought had opposing perceptions on the future of working-class power. The post-Marxists are highly pessimistic, while the neo-Marxists are generally optimistic.

As described by Frobel *et al.* (1980), transnational corporations (TNCs) relocated low-technology industries to developing countries with unorganised and low-cost unskilled labour. The level of productivity in some NICs, then, will 'match or exceed' the metropolitan economies (Frobel *et al.*, 1980; see also Cohen, 1987: 222–27). These phenomena led some labour researchers to comment on a 'race to the bottom' among workers in different countries. The competition is not only between the North and South, but also within the Southern countries; the relocation is not only from the high-wage countries to the lower, but also from the better-organised regions to the countries where workers' rights of association are constrained (Mazur, 2000; Ross and Chan, 2002; Chan and Robert, 2003;

A. Chan, 2003). On the one hand, as workers are to be replaced by computerisation and automation, there will be an enormous loss of job opportunities; on the other hand, the flexibilisation of work, employment and society altered the patterns of work identities (Aronowitz and DiFazio, 1994; Casey, 1995; Rifkin, 1995; Aronowitz and Cutler, 1998; Bauman, 1998).[1] As a result, production loses its significance in generating a movement of resistance, whereas consumption gains its pivotal role. The non-class-based identity movements are the only 'potential subjects of the Information Age', according to the notable American theorist Castells (1997: 354, 360; cited by Silver, 2003: 2). The challenge that globalisation posed to traditional labour studies, nonetheless, is more than the decline of workers' collective power in the West. The state was said to lose its significance in regulating labour relations. Capital, in the form of the TNC, has gone beyond the boundary and limit of the traditional nation-state and reached out to trade and investment at a global level.

This new development brought a challenge to two main streams of labour studies: industrial relations and industrial sociology. The former has a legacy in institutional analysis, but today state, trade union and collective bargaining have lost their importance. The latter was revitalised by Braverman's (1974/1998) labour process studies and Burawoy's (1979; 1985) workplace ethnography, but the new development of the labour process debate, as criticised by Strangleman (2005: 7), has 'a tendency for a very narrow set of [business school centred] interests to emerge which has not always helped define or develop a broader sociology of work'. To be sure, the two traditions had come to integrate or compromise after the 1970s, especially in the UK where Fox (1966) called for absorbing industrial sociology into industrial relations, responding to the popularity of spontaneous shop floor struggles in that period. Now in the face of globalisation, the two traditions come to a similar reflection: linking up the local and global by comparative workplace studies (e.g. Bélanger *et al.*, 1994) or global ethnography (Burawoy *et al.*, 2000).

Marxist sociologists also attempt to break through the limitations of these two mainstream traditions of labour studies by proposing a new paradigm or approach for labour studies. Silver (2003: 5) used the statistics of Western newspaper strike reports to show that 'while labor has been weakened in the locations from which productive capital emigrated, new working classes have been created and strengthened in the favored new sites of investment'. In contrast to Silver's generalised method, Cohen (1991) called for a specific approach: to new international labour studies. According to him, traditions of industrial relations, trade union studies and labour history had all been inadequate to provide a satisfactory answer to the labour question since the 1970s. His 'new international labour studies' paradigm advocated that the agenda of labour studies should depend on the specific conditions in metropolitan, post-socialist and peripheral capitalism. The most common trend of the new labour studies is, however, the effort to broaden the horizon of labour politics and bring in the role of other social movements. A large quantity of scholarly attention has been paid to the rise of social movement unionism in Asia, Africa and Central and South America (e.g.

Moody, 1997; Munck, 1988; 2002; Munck and Waterman, 1999; Waterman, 1999; Hutchison and Brown, 2001). In these studies, the interaction between the traditional trade union movement and wider civil society was extensively discussed and sometimes highlighted.

Regardless of all these neo-Marxist attempts to revitalise labour studies, the sociology of work in general and the Marxist school of labour studies in particular experienced a decline and marginalisation in the discipline of sociology. According to Strangleman (2005; 2007), this crisis was partially a result of the intellectual turn of post-Marxists on 'the end of work'. He condemned the 'end of work' thesis and suggested more empirical studies:

> The working class are seen as passive victims of globalisation, local labour now simply waits to be exploited by all-powerful global capital. . . . It seems to me that the sociology of work stands at an exciting moment in contemporary capitalism, but in studying this moment it needs to draw on its historical rich resources and combine theory with empirical research.
>
> (Strangleman, 2007: 100)

This study, accordingly, attempts to draw and reflect on the new empirical evidence of labour politics in China, the new global production centre in the world, with a connection to the rich theoretical insights of labour studies.

Chinese migrant workers in globalisation

With its population size and unprecedented booming economy, China has become one of the focuses in the debate on economic globalisation in recent years. After open door reform was launched in 1978 by the Communist leader, Deng Xiao Ping, China has risen to become a global manufacturing centre with an 'unlimited' supply of low-cost and unorganised peasant workers. Its impact on the world is striking.

In 2002, China was the top world producer of eighty products, including colour TVs, washing machines, DVD players, cameras, refrigerators, air-conditioners, motorcycles, microwave ovens, PC monitors, tractors and bicycles (*The Economist*, 28 July 2005). Since 2003, China has been the country receiving the largest amount of foreign direct investment (FDI) in the world. In 2005, China became the world's third-largest trading country, surpassed only by the USA and Germany. In 2006, China became the fourth-largest economy in the world in terms of GDP (US$2,226 billion). Alongside the dramatic economic growth in quantity, the manufacturing structure was also moving into high-end goods. Electronic products made up 56 per cent of total exports in 2006 (*China News Net*, 11 December 2006). Its advanced technology exports are second only to those of the US, and China overtook Japan to become the second-largest investor in research and development (R&D) in 2007.

Despite this advance, with 29 per cent of the world's workforce, labour cost in this giant 'global factory' is as low as only one-sixth of that of Mexico and one-fortieth of that of the US (Lee, 2004). The GDP per capita in China increased from 379 yuan in 1978 to 8,959.8 yuan (US$1,090) in 2003 (G. H. Chen, 2004). But in 2006, its GDP per capita (US$1,702) still ranked as low as 110th in the world (*China News Net*, 11 December 2006). This contradiction of rapid growth and cheap labour cost, high total amount and low per capita figure, has attracted comments on China's role in driving a 'race to the bottom' in globalisation from labour researchers, the labour movement, businesses and politicians (Chan and Robert, 2003; *Business Weekly*, 22 December 2003; Izraelewicz, 2005; Au, 2005) as well as eye-catching magazine reports, such as the one quoted at the beginning of this chapter. The potential of Chinese migrant workers to improve their conditions, therefore, has significant meaning for global labour politics. Underlying this phenomenon is the transformation of the form of employment and industrial ownership in China.

On the one hand, from 1990 to 2003, the number of industrial workers employed in state-owned enterprises (SOE) declined from 43.64 million (68.4 per cent) to 13.34 million (36.3 per cent) (National Bureau of Statistics of China, 2000; 2005; cited by Lee, 2007a: 40). In terms of industrial output, the state-owned or state-controlled sector dropped from 75 per cent in 1981 to only 28 per cent in 1999 and 38 per cent in 2003 (Lee, 2007a: 39). The remaining SOE workers also experienced escalating exploitation and labour intensification under the threat of losing their jobs (Lee, 2007a). On the other hand, according to the national census in 2000, the number of rural–urban migrant workers in China, a practice that was prohibited before 1978, was as high as 120 million. Now peasant migrant workers represent 57.5 per cent of the manufacturing workforce (Lee, 2007a: 6). Most of the boom in manufacturing is labour-intensive and export-oriented light industry in the coastal regions, especially the Pearl River Delta (PRD) in the south and the Yangtze River Delta (YRD) in the east.

The subordination of migrant workers was exacerbated by the Household Registration System (*Hukou*), which originated in 1958 as a socialist mechanism to stop peasants moving to the cities. A household-based production contract system (*Jiating Lianchan Chengbao Zerenzhi*) was introduced in 1978 to release peasant workers from the collective and forced labour of communes and allow them to move to the cities. However, although it was loosened, the *Hukou* system continues to deny urban citizenship to migrant workers, who were supposed to settle in the cities only temporarily. Most of them settled in factory-provided dormitories. The rural *Hukou*, however, guarantees them a piece of farming land in their home village.

In short, in the past three decades, the manufacturing centres in China have been moved from the interior and the north to the coast and the south, and young temporary migrant workers, who work in conditions of low pay, long working hours, despotic management and appalling environment, have gradually replaced veteran urban permanent SOE workers with their 'iron rice bowl'.

Labour relations in transition

In the wake of an emerging market economy, the state set up a legal regulation framework to replace the 'socialist' administrative regulation in the mid-1990s (Ng and Warner, 1998; Taylor *et al.*, 2003; Clarke *et al.*, 2004). In 1993, the 'Enterprise Minimum Wage Regulation' was issued by the Ministry of Labour. Under the regulation, local governments are given the autonomy to formulate their own legal minimum wage. More significantly, a Labour Law was legislated in 1994. The law laid down a foundation for workers' legal and contractual rights, a system for solving labour disputes as well as collective contracts and collective consultations between the trade union and management (Clarke *et al.*, 2004). The right to strike has not been recognised by the law since it was removed from the constitution in 1982 (Taylor *et al.*, 2003), and any action to disrupt social order is illegal under Section 158 of the Penal Code.

The local authorities, nonetheless, were passive in enforcing the laws (Cooke, 2005) and migrant workers were usually paid below the legal minimum (A. Chan, 2001). According to the law, all trade unions should be affiliated to the All China Federation of Trade Unions (ACFTU), which is under the leadership of the Party. About 30 per cent of non-state enterprises have established trade unions, and the trade union presidents are typically managers (A. Chan, 2001; Cooke, 2005). As a result, trade unions cannot fulfil their primary role as stipulated in the Labour Law (Chapter 1, Article 7): to 'represent and protect the legal rights and interests of workers independently and autonomously'.

The arbitration procedure, then, became the main channel to solve individual and collective disputes between migrant workers and their employers. The total number of registered labour dispute cases increased from 12,368 in 1993 to 260,471 in 2004 (National Bureau of Statistics of China, various years). In recent years, spontaneous strikes have also been staged by migrant workers in workplaces to show their discontent (Lee, 2000a; A. Chan, 2001; Taylor *et al.*, 2003: 175).

The puzzle

In the face of this spectacular social change in China over the past three decades, the puzzle is to discover the role of workers in this process. Marx (1967; 1977; 1980) allocated industrial workers a privileged historical role in advancing social change in capitalism, which is embedded in the labour process. According to him, exploitation in capitalist production leads to workers' economic struggle within the workplaces for improvement of working conditions and wages, and the consciousness formed from these experiences gives rise to workers' organisations and political struggles based on class interests. In *Poverty of Philosophy*, Marx wrote:

> Economic conditions had first transformed the mass of the people of the country into workers. The combination of capital has created for this mass a common situation, common interests. This mass is thus already a class against

capital, but not yet for itself. In the struggle, of which we have noted only a few phases, this mass becomes united, and constitutes itself as a class for itself. The interests it defends become class interests. But the struggle of class against class is a political struggle.

(Marx, 1982: 36)

Does contemporary China's case, or, in a wider perspective, labour politics in the era of globalisation, further prove the failure of Marxism as an analytical tool? Does it confirm the post-Marxist theorists who forcefully contended that the working class is 'dead' in the new age (Gorz, 1980; Castells, 1997)?

Here my special concern is with the migrant industrial workers rather than the state workers. To be fair, the state workers have staged campaigns and protests against the state's initiative to privatise SOEs or demanded proper lay-off compensation and pensions, the scale and duration of which have never been witnessed among the migrant workers. As a result, more academic attention has been paid to the protests of the state workers (Lee, 2000b; 2002a; 2007a; Cai, 2002; Hurst and O'Brien, 2002; F. Chen, 2000; 2003a; 2006). However, as long as the SOE workers failed to challenge the wave of privatisation, their role as an agency for social transformation was weakened as a result of their numerical decline and the change of labour relations in the SOEs. In contrast, strikes and other forms of protest are emerging among migrant workers in the south.

As far as migrant workers are concerned, the reform began with the liberation of 'labour', but resulted in new forms of bonded labour (A. Chan, 2000; 2003). Exploitation has continuously intensified. For instance, in 2004, the Chinese Ministry of Labour and Social Security (cited by A. Chan, 2006a: 285) announced: 'Studies show the salary of migrant workers in the PRD has grown by a mere RMB 68 (US$8.2) over the last 12 years, far behind the increase in living expenses, and in real terms, wages were declining. . . . Wildcat strikes and other less confrontational forms of resistance have erupted in an increasing number of these factories.'

Working men and women should not be viewed as passive victims of the globalisation process. In fact, ethnographic workplace studies of women workers, who are at the lowest end of the global production chain, have shed light on the micro-resistance strategy of workers (Lee, 1998; Sargeson, 1999; Pun, 2005c). However, as world labour history has shown, without mobilisation and organisation, labour as a social force is unable to challenge the dominance of capital in the workplace, community and society. Why do Chinese workers fail to pose a political challenge to their rivals, global and domestic capital? To answer this question, we should study the (un)making of migrant workers' subjectivity in contemporary China. What is the solidarity base of migrant workers today? What factors have facilitated or impeded the formation of a class-based action strategy?

One may assume that the history of China's integration into global capitalism is short. However, in neighbouring South Korea a significant labour movement arose in the 1980s after thirty years of rapid industrialisation (Koo, 2001). One may also argue that socialist totalitarianism pre-empts any such social force. But as history in many other countries has shown, a democratic government is a consequence rather than a condition of workers' struggle and mobilisation (Collier, 1999). Although historical and political factors may impinge on the formation of workers' subjectivity, we need a sociological account to reveal how these forces do or do not function.

Recent studies have documented migrant workers' activism in China (Sargeson, 2001; Smith and Pun, 2006; Lee, 2007a). While Sargeson and Smith and Pun called for more empirical studies, Lee concluded that migrant workers' protest is more likely to be a legally based citizens' movement which targets the state. Yet media reports and observation in southern China have revealed an emerging form of labour strikes since 2004 in parallel with a shortage of labour in the region (e.g. *Nanfang Ribao*, 7 October 2004). Without independent trade unions in the workplace and the fundamental weakness of non-governmental organisations, if any, in the community, one may consider that all of these strikes were spontaneous stoppages and so not significant in social change. However, studies in the West remind us that all wildcat strikes have had their underground leaders and hidden logic which awaits sociological exploration and explanation (Gouldner, 1954; Hyman, 1989).

Theoretical contexts

The debate around theory or history, structure or agency, and 'class-in-itself' or 'class-for-itself' has continued for a long time with no conclusion in academics or politics. In the field of labour studies, consents and contests coexist among various current intellectual thoughts.

First, it is agreed that workers' subjectivity formation retained its pivotal role. The concepts of gender, race/ethnicity and skill can complement class to better grasp the underlying principles of subordination and resistance and the possibility of emancipation. However, controversy rests on the relation between 'subjectivity' and its material base and economic structure (Berlanstein, 1992; 1993). While neo-Marxism insists politics and ideology are connected with, although not fully determined by, the economy (e.g. Aminzade, 1981; 1993), the post-structuralist school generally downplays the validity of the material factor in favour of contingent 'identities' as a discourse (e.g. Sewell, 1980; 1993).

Second, the labour process, or coercion, resistance and bargaining in the workplace, which are central to the understanding of labour politics, cannot be isolated from workers' tradition, culture, community experience, state policy, stage of capitalist development and location within the uneven development of the global system. Orthodox universalism may assume that the labour movements in developing countries on the way to industrialisation are not fundamentally different to those in Western countries. Contemporary scholarship is generally sceptical of this optimistic position. Katznelson and Zolberg (1986) illuminated that even within the Western world, the process of class formation varied from one country to another. The 'path dependence' theory (Nee and Stark, 1989) argues well that the post-socialist countries' transformation is dependent on state and society structures, historical contexts and cultural practices, in the words of Burawoy and Verdery (1999) an 'uncertain transition'. In this regard, as a post-socialist and NIC in Asia, China does not necessarily follow the Western path of development. Accounting for China's departure from the West, however, two strands of explanation have emerged (Sargeson, 2001).

On the one hand, institutionalists imply that it is the state institution that dislocates class politics in China (e.g. Howell, 1993; O'Leary, 1998; Solinger, 1999; A. Chan, 2001). Developing from the 'path dependence' theory, new institutional analysts view market reform in post-socialist states as a dynamic process of the interaction between state socialism and capitalism. According to Stark and Nee (1989: 30): 'State socialism represents a distinctive social formation that has its own institutional logic and dynamics of development.' They argued that post-socialist states' pathways to global capitalism are influenced by their respective social, cultural, economic and political traditions (Stark and Nee, 1989; Nelson *et al.*, 1999). Similarly, in his study of development models of NICs, Haggard (1983) claimed that the legacy of authoritarianism and the 'state–business' alliance in East Asian NICs such as Taiwan and Korea had prevented the type of opposition force from labour and students which had risen in Latin American NICs.

On the other hand, the culturalists contest that the departure of China and its East Asian neighbourhoods from the Western road of class formation was culturally determined. The base of workers' collective action in East Asia was claimed to be little 'class' oriented (Perry, 1996; Kim, 1997). Perry (1996: 3) argued that workers' activism in East Asia 'is not fully explained by the familiar models of class-consciousness inherited from the analysis of West European and North American capitalism'. She attempted to demonstrate the importance of 'place' over 'class' in the formation of workers' identity in the region. Although her definition of 'place' was wide-ranging, native place is highlighted as the most crucial factor as far as China is concerned (Perry, 1993; 1996; 1997).

Third, workers' struggle is not isolated from the conditions of civil society and international solidarity. In the new millennium, the perspective of 'new international labour studies' (Munck, 1988; Cohen, 1991) was further strengthened by new patterns of cross-border solidarity and cross-class mobilisation. The theory of Polanyi (1957) that the trespass of the market into society would spark off resistance from civil society was borrowed to explain the new rising form of struggle against neo-liberalism (Munck, 2002). The 'old internationalism' was hailed to be European and male-centric and a more progressive 'new internationalism' was optimistically expected (Waterman, 2001; Munck, 2002). However, the optimistic illustrations underestimated the presence of business trade unions all around the world. Lambert (2002: 186–87), for instance, referred to the post-socialist and post-colonial trade unions as authoritarian business unionism that 'fails to acknowledge and confront labour market inequality' and has eroded 'independent organization, ideology and strategy'. The corporate social responsibility (CSR) practice, which was initiated by the consumer movement in the West to improve labour standards in the developing world, was also pointedly lacking workers' participation and deteriorated into a window-dressing strategy for the corporations (Pearson and Seyfang, 2001; Whitehouse, 2003; Pun, 2005a; Sum and Pun, 2005). To what extent can the CSR movement facilitate workers' organising power and class capacity in post-socialist China? The debate continues (Pun, 2005a; A. Chan, 2007).

Ethnographical journal

Bearing these debates in mind, I set out on my journey to search for the subjectivity formation of the new Chinese working class and its structural barriers in contemporary globalisation. I view the strike and its relation to organisation as the best scenario in which to study the formation of workers' subjectivity and its implications for labour as a social force. Neo-Marxist labour historians remind us that the formation of working-class subjectivity is a historical process involving numerous and long-drawn-out struggles (Thompson, 1963/1980). We should put workers in the centre and make visible their 'voice'. Here 'voice' is an action, an articulation of interests and strategy formation in a specific historical and spatial context to combat the business–state complex. For the sake of listening to the 'voice', I chose to conduct participant observation in the workplace and workers' community; for the sake of giving meaning and interpretation to the 'voice', I situated the local ethnography in the broader history and social structure.

I chose the city of Shenzhen, China's first and most flourishing Special Economic Zone (SEZ), in the province of Guang Dong, to conduct my fieldwork. I selected Shenzhen not only because it is a 'powerhouse' of the 'global factory' (Lee, 1998), but because it is the city most prone to labour conflicts. The number of cases handled by labour dispute arbitration committees in Shenzhen was reported to be as many as one-tenth of the total national figure (*Nanfang Ribao*, 28 October 2004).

My research journey echoes Mills' (1959) statement half a century ago that social studies can track back to the researchers' biographies, personal histories and their interactions within wider society. I was born in a rural village in Guang Dong in late Mao's China. The class label of 'political identity' was vital to decide one's fate and opportunities before Deng's reforms. In 1978, the reforms began. The collective farming land was allocated to families according to the number of family members. The class label was then cleared. As soon as the reforms began, my family planned to move out of the village. I boarded with a family relative in town in order to study at a better primary school, where I witnessed serious discrimination against rural villagers institutionally and culturally. I migrated to Hong Kong in the early 1990s. Hong Kong experienced an economic crisis in 1998. The next year I took a one-year sabbatical to be Students' Union president and was deeply involved in the social movement. The crisis inspired me to study globalisation and its impact on workers. After I graduated from university, I became an organiser for Hong Kong Confederation of Trade Unions. During the years I worked there, the global trend of employment casualisation perplexed me and my colleagues. In order to deepen my understanding of the labour movement and globalisation further, I went to the University of Warwick in 2004 to undertake a masters degree in labour studies and then embarked on my PhD research to study the response of Chinese migrant workers to global capitalism in Guang Dong, my home province.

I went back to Hong Kong and Guang Dong to conduct a pilot study in May and June 2005. During the first two months, in order to make more sense of the current labour issues in the region, I visited workers' services centres, factories, workers' dormitories and occupational hospitals in the PRD, and participated in the organising of cross-border labour protests in Hong Kong and Guang Dong. During the summer, I carried out documentary research in university libraries and labour non-governmental organisation (NGO) resource centres to study the pattern of the transformation of labour conflict from 1978 to 1995 in the PRD. This constituted part of the data in Chapter 2.

After the pilot study, I planned to use a service centre as a contact point to get in touch with workers. Fortunately, one of the labour centres had a vacancy for a project coordinator. I formally took up the one-year job from September 2005. My full participation in the CSR training project in the Star Factory provided me with the data that is presented in Chapter 6. The Star Factory case was based on my participant observation in an in-factory workers' training programme and intensive discussion with the chief director, general manager, middle-level managers and workers in the factory over seven months as well as other trainers, multi-stakeholder initiative (MSI) staff and TNC managers.

The data for Chapters 3 and 4 were not gained as straightforwardly as that for Chapter 6. From late October 2005, I paid regular visits to a hospital with my colleagues to provide a consultation service to industrially injured workers. There I encountered many injured workers from the Sun Factory and told them I was writing a paper on strikes. Some of them were thrilled about this and began to tell me their strike stories with a sense of pride, although they did not fully understand my work. They then took me into their community, dormitories and workshops.[2] Finally, I moved into the community in April 2006 to live with a veteran worker of the Sun Factory who was setting up a small shop with his wife in the village. I lived there until my return to Warwick in August. During the half-year, I had numerous opportunities to participate in workers' social lives, observe their work culture and conduct interviews with them.

Before I identified the Sun Factory as one of the main cases in this study and moved into the village, I made investigations into the labour relations of more than ten factories with my colleagues. Strikes had happened in most of these factories. Although I did not document the data in this research, due to the constraints of time and length of this book, they provided me with ample background knowledge to sense the universality and peculiarity of the cases I chose to present.

After I had finished the main part of the fieldwork, I maintained contact with the workers. In December 2006, August 2007 and January 2008, I returned to the field sites to observe the new developments on a half-yearly basis. In August 2007, I encountered another wave of strikes led by the Moon Factory (in the same town as the Sun Factory). Moon was one of the factories my colleagues and I had studied in the first round of fieldwork. Relations fostered with workers in the factory helped me to document the case presented in Chapter 5.

Class struggle and the changing labour regime in China

During my fieldwork, I found that striking was very common in migrant workers' experiences. Despite the rising proportion of peasant migrants in the industrial workforce, migrant workers' protests have been subject to little academic attention. Scholars have concentrated their studies of post-1978 labour protest on SOEs in northern China (e.g. Lee, 2000b; 2002a; 2007a; Cai, 2002; F. Chen, 2000; 2003a; 2006; Hurst and O'Brien, 2002).

Until the late 1990s, migrant worker rebels, if they existed at all, were said to be weak. Lee, for example, compared the labour uprising of state workers with the resistance pattern of migrant workers to argue that the latter was 'less progressive' and 'adeptly and flexibly adjusted to capitalism' (Lee, 2000b: 220; Lee, 2002a). The common paths of migrant workers in southern China to express grievances in the early 1990s included collective complaints or suggestion letters to management or the local Labour and Social Security Bureau (LSSB), unorganised spontaneous work stoppages and finally 'time consuming and pacifying' legal procedures (Lee, 1998; 2000a; 2002a: 210). W. Y. Leung found that 'the working class did not wage large-scale class-based organized actions articulating class-specific demands . . . although there were sporadic but consistent expressions of class-specific grievances by workers' and 'a momentous rise in the number of labour protests . . . during the years 1992–94 [were] scattered, spontaneous and unorganized' (W. Y. Leung, 1998: 15, 44).

In recent years, however, although still limited, the literature has begun to suggest a rising form of labour protest among migrant workers. Lee reported that migrant workers in the late 1990s were more politically active than they had been at the beginning of the decade: 'an emerging element in Chinese labor politics which is likely to play a larger role in the coming years but which was totally absent during the early 1990s' (Lee, 2002b: 63). '[B]y the late 1990s, incidents of worker unrest had become so routine that government and party leaders identified labor problems as the "biggest threat to social stability" . . . accelerated reforms have triggered both a proliferation and a deepening of labor activism' (Lee, 2000a: 41).

Sargeson (2001) and Smith and Pun (2006) have documented stories of women migrant workers' protests developing in dormitories. Sargeson (2001) presented a story of women migrant workers who started a campaign for equal wage and promotion opportunities with their local counterparts. Smith and Pun's (2006) dormitory study also found that kinship, place of origin and peer networks which prevail in factory-provided dormitories supply a base for workers' protests. In their case, hundreds of women workers in an electronics factory joined hands to demand lay-off compensation through a series of actions, including a demonstration outside a government building. According to them, a 'Chinese dormitory labour regime' was a peculiar form of labour process in global capitalism which embedded both control and resistance. Sargeson (2001) and Smith and Pun (2006) urged further study. Sargeson (2001: 66), for instance, called for 'the need to conduct more intensive empirical research into the intentions, patterns and effects of workers' activism'.

A more forceful effort was Lee's (2007a) book, *Against the Law: Labor Protests in China's Rustbelt and Sunbelt*, which compared the patterns of collective protests of laid-off northern state workers with those of migrant workers in southern China. Referring to migrant workers, Lee observed 'three major types of workplace grievances that often lead to labor arbitration, litigation, and protests . . . (1) unpaid wages, illegal wage deductions, or substandard wage rates; (2) disciplinary violence and violations of dignity; and (3) industrial injuries and lack of injury compensation' in southern China (Lee, 2007a: 165). According to Lee, it was only after the 'rationalisation' of the administration and arbitration procedure failed to protect workers' legal rights that the victims were forced into 'radicalisation' and took to the streets. 'Worker solidarity peaks at the point of collective exit from the factory, occasioned by plant closure or relocation,' Lee (2007a: 175) elaborated. Despite the higher level of solidarity workers showed in this sort of case, the migrants would disperse to different places after the protest without maintaining proper contact with each other. Therefore, Lee argued that 'Chinese workers can hardly be described as having much marketplace, workplace, or associational bargaining power' (Lee, 2007a: 24). Alternatively, Lee (2007a: 25) borrowed 'three potential insurgent identities' from Western labour studies – namely, 'proletariat', 'citizen' and 'subaltern' – to analyse both laid-off state workers and migrant workers in protests:

> I have found that class identity is more muted and ambivalent among migrant workers than among rustbelt [northern state] workers, whereas claims made on the basis of equality before the law and of citizens' right to legal justice are impassioned and firm, as in the sunbelt [south]. Workers also identify themselves as the marginalized and the subordinate in society.
>
> (Lee, 2007a: 195)

In short, Lee privileged non-class 'citizenship' over 'class' for migrant workers and implied that laid-off state workers were more class conscious. It is certain that veteran state workers had better organisational resources such as the trade union, workers' congress or a stable urban community so that they could stage a joint factory campaign, which is much more difficult for migrant workers to achieve. Nonetheless, Lee's position on 'class' is unsatisfactory because she has abandoned the material and historical base in favour of an interpretation of class in linguistic terms.[3] In this regard, the theorisation of F. Chen (2000; 2003a; 2006) of the class-consciousness of former state workers and Pun's (2005c) imagination on class formation of migrant workers are more satisfactory.

In Chen's (2000; 2003a) early studies of protests of laid-off state workers, although the memory of Maoism and the language of *Gongren Jieji* (working class) were dominant in the language and slogans of the insurgents, Chen showed high scepticism about their class-consciousness. It was only his recent study, of a campaign by previous state workers working in privatised factories to overrule the privatisation decision and take over the factory by themselves, that made Chen relatively positive about the possibility of class-consciousness (F. Chen, 2006). The language of 'class', which was rooted in the historical memory of the pensioners, did not have any material base. First, they were out of the production centre. Second, they did not have any experience of capitalist relations of production. Third, their target was the state rather than the new factory owners.

Migrant workers, by contrast, were all within the production centre under a capitalist class relation. Except for some extreme cases, their demands can only be satisfied by interest concessions from the capitalists. In spite of this, as Lee (2007a: 195, 204) described, migrant workers rarely used the term *Gongren Jieji* or *Gongren* (workers) to describe themselves, as the state workers did. Instead, they identified themselves as *Mingong* (non-state workers), *Nongmingong* (peasant workers), *Wailaigong* (outside workers) or *Dagong* (selling labour to the bosses). These differences should be understood in their political and cultural contexts. Politically, *Gongren Jieji* and *Gongren* were terms of political rhetoric imposed in Mao's era, while *Mingong*, *Nongmingong* and *Wailaigong* were the social stigma attached to the new workers after the reform. Culturally, *Dagong* is a term more attached to the Cantonese context with a very similar meaning to *Gongren*. Pun quoted a *Dagongzai* (a man selling labour to the bosses) saying:

> We are not treated as human beings. . . . We work like dogs and never stop. When the superior asks you to work, you have to work no matter when and where . . . Who cares who you are? We are nobody, we are stuff. . . . What is *dagongzai*? *Dagongzai* is worth nothing. *Dagongzai* is only disposable stuff (*Feiwu*).
>
> (Pun, 2005c: 23–24)

On the basis of such a self-understanding by workers, Pun (2005c) argued that migrant workers' understanding of class relations was grounded in everyday life. Pun (2005c: 24–25) suggested that 'a new generation of migrant workers has rapidly developed a range of examples of class awareness and understanding in the workplace'.[4]

Although I agree with Pun's equalisation of *Dagongzai*, or in a gender-balanced term *Dagongzai/nu* (man and woman selling their labour power), with *Gongren*, I would put it further. If the migrant workers did not totally hail themselves as workers, would that mean that there is no working class and so no class struggle in the global factories of China? E. P. Thompson's notion of 'class struggle without classes' comes to mind here:

> People find themselves in a society structured in determined ways (crucially but not exclusively in productive relations), they experience exploitation (or the need to maintain power over whom they exploit), they identify points

of antagonistic interests, they commence to struggle around these issues and in the process of struggling discover themselves as classes.

(Thompson, 1978: 49; cited by P. K. Edwards, 2000: 145)

To interpret Thompson's approach in contemporary workplace study, Edwards put it straightforwardly:

Classes exist as a result of the fundamental processes around the system of production, and can thus be identified independently of any beliefs among class actors; and that relations between members of classes are a form of class struggle even when people do not use the language themselves.

(P. K. Edwards, 2000: 142)

For Clarke (1978), class relations and their political and ideological forms cannot be separated from each other in class analysis, although the concept of class as a social relation should be analytically prior to the latter. I prefer this approach as it highlights the importance of the relations of production, but leaves leeway for studying subjectivity formation in a historical context. The meaning of studying workers' identification in struggle and day-to-day life is to disclose how class struggle unfolds in specific contexts. In short, I see class formation as a historical process which departs from a capitalist relation of production (Thompson, 1963/1980; Katznelson, 1986).

On the basis of this theoretical orientation, I attempt to explain the distinctive forms of class struggle in contemporary China, which I call 'class struggle without class organisation'. Through multiple ethnographic case studies, the potentials of migrant workers' protests in challenging global capital are examined. I suggest that the rapid expansion of global capitalism into China has intensified class struggle in the workplace and beyond and has given rise to an emerging form of labour protest in the country. The migrant workers' protests against global capital have become more and more radical, tactical and coordinated. Workers' protest has posed a profound challenge to both the state authorities and global capitalists. Nonetheless, working-class formation has been dislocated by the state strategy of labour regulation and social control. Although workers' class-consciousness has been strengthened, in particular that of the mature skilled workers, the formation of workplace organisation, which can play a primary role in representing workers' interests, was impeded by the lack of institutional and external support. The right to strike is not recognised by law. The function of the ACFTU, the official trade union, is constrained by the state's aspiration to maintain industrial peace and social order. International civil society, despite its active role in promoting CSR and the anti-sweatshop movement, is too vulnerable to provide support to workplace organisation in the context of China. As a result, informal networks prevail in the social and working life of migrant workers and act as an organising base for workers' protest. Despotism still prevails in the labour process, but state regulation, NGO activism, and workers' collective actions exert more and more pressure on the conduct of the management. Without class organisations, the emergence of a labour movement is unlikely, but the unstable workplace relations and labour market also present a challenge to both state and management and lead to steady improvement of general working conditions. In the light of these conditions, I theorise the factory regime in this time-space as 'contested despotism' under 'a changing labour regime' (R. C. Edwards, 1980; Lee, 1999).

Structure of the book

This book consists of seven chapters. Chapter 2 is based on documentary research to develop a retrospective analysis of the transformation of labour disputes from the early 1980s to 2004 in Shenzhen and suggests the research gap should be filled by further empirical evidence.

Chapter 3 provides the findings of my half-year's participant observation in a migrant workers' urban community. The complicated social relations of place, gender, skill and age are revealed in this chapter. These dynamics of the community provoked workers' militancy and solidarity in a large strike in 2004 after the rise of a 'labour shortage'. The strike took place first in one department in opposition to the factory's rationalisation reform, which aimed to discipline the skilled workers, and then extended to the whole factory and other factories in the community. Workers asked for enforcement of the legal minimum wage.

The cause, social formation, process and impact of this strike are outlined in Chapter 4. This chapter also introduces the labour process and labour recruitment in the factory before and after the strike and the transfer of the strike experience to the company's new subsidiary plant in the city of Hui Zhou. Working conditions and the labour process in these two factories are compared.

Chapter 5 presents a development of the strike pattern in 2007 through another case study. After the strike wave in 2004 and 2005, the Shenzhen city government dramatically enhanced the legal minimum wage rate. In 2007, however, it decided to leave the minimum rate unchanged. This, together with a similar rationalisation reform to that implemented on the eve of the 2004 strike, set off a new strike in another factory in the town in which the 2004 strike had taken place. This strike, however, was coordinated to occur on the same day in two factories with the same owners in different towns. Workers' demands went beyond the limit of the law to ask for reasonable wages and improvement of living and working conditions.

Chapter 6 examines the potential and limitations of workplace organisation under the international CSR programme. Data was gathered by the author through intensive participation and interviews.

Finally, Chapter 7 provides an overview of the changing characteristics of workplace struggles in China and their implications for the transformation of labour regime, Chinese society and international labour politics.

2 Labour conflict in Shenzhen

A historical review

Introduction

> As E. P. Thompson reminded us, if we stop history at any particular moment, there is no social context at all, only a multitude of unconnected individuals.
>
> (Dawley, 1976: 4)

The dynamic of China's reform was rooted in labour market reform. A household-based production contract system was introduced to liberate the peasant labour force from the collectives and the forced labour of the communes. Not only did the policy boost productivity, it also released a large number of surplus labourers from rural areas. The urban reform, on the other hand, was initiated in three realms, namely deregulation, marketisation and then privatisation of the SOEs and urban collective-owned enterprises (UCEs), establishment of township or village enterprises (TVEs), and encouragement of Sino-overseas joint ventures (JVs), foreign invested enterprises (FIEs) and later domestic privately owned enterprises (POEs) (Cooke, 2005).

The reform began from the liberation of 'labour', but resulted in new forms of bonded labour (A. Chan, 2000). Exploitation appeared to be consistent, if not consolidated, over two and a half decades. Before 1978, workers were not allowed to move without official permission and wages were all centrally fixed (Meng, 2000). Under the restructuring programme, however, a market-oriented labour relation was fundamentally taking shape by the mid-1990s (Leung, 1998; Taylor *et al.*, 2003; K. Chang, 2004). In order to regulate the labour market, a revised Labour Law was announced in 2004 and was swiftly used by workers to defend their rights (Gallagher, 2005; Lee, 2007a).

Previous research in the region found that labour resistance was individual and spontaneous in the early 1990s, but with a more collective form in recent years (Lee, 2000a; 2002b; 2007a; Pun, 2005c; Smith and Pun, 2006). However, a thorough historical review was absent. Thompson (1963/1980) reminded us that the making of a working class is a historical process. This chapter sets out to explore the pattern of collective labour conflict from 1979 to 2004 in Shenzhen, China's most vibrant SEZ.

As will be shown, the legacy of state socialism has had a strong influence on the formation of workers' discontent and struggle patterns as well as industrial relations as a whole. However, with the constant expansion and penetration of the global market economy in China, the legacy is dwindling and the potential of workers' radicalisation is being created through the accrual of struggle experience and the intensification of exploitation. That a labour movement cannot be moulded at this stage is primarily a result of the fact that the workers' ambition for self-organisation is obstructed by strong state intervention and an unstable labour market. This chapter lays down the context for the ethnographic case studies presented in subsequent chapters, which focus on the social formation of and obstacles to migrant workers' protest in southern China's FIEs. The chapter begins with a review of the history of Shenzhen SEZ and China's economic and labour market reform after 1979. While the key cases studied took place in the western part of Shenzhen, from the first export-oriented industrial zone, She Kou, in the 1980s to its neighbour and thriving industrial district, Bao An, in the 1990s and 2000s, relevant discussion also extends to the surrounding PRD area. Data has been drawn from documentary research supplemented by interviews with veteran workers as well as labour organisers and researchers in the region.

The formation of modern Shenzhen

In 1979, Shenzhen, with a population of a mere 30,000 and a gross domestic product (GDP) of 196.38 million yuan, was a tiny town lying on the border between socialist China and the British colony Hong Kong. A journalist portrayed the town in this way:

> The urban area of the tiny town was only 3 square kilometres; the houses were low and shabby, as its highest building was 5 storeys. The streets were narrow, and the cityscape old and obsolete. It [had] only two little pitiful lanes: 'the pig street' and 'the fish street', along with a crossing street. If you lit a cigarette at one end of the street and walked to the other end, the smoke would just die out.
>
> (H. Chen, 2006: 3)

When I began my fieldwork in 2005, Shenzhen had risen to be a world-class city and one of the symbols of China's reform achievement. At the end of the year, the total population of the city was 8,277,500 (Shenzhen Municipal Statistics Bureau, 2006). Just like any other major industrial city in the world, the rise of Shenzhen as a modern metropolitan city was a result of the extensive inflow of migrants and capital (Lee, 1998; Pun, 2005c) and a series of administrative reorganisations. Official figures showed that the temporary population, which is mainly migrant workers, was as high as 6,458,200 (Shenzhen Municipal Statistics Bureau, 2006).

In January 1979, as a first indication of Deng Xiao Ping's open door policy, the central government approved the proposal of Guang Dong province to establish

Shenzhen and Zhu Hai municipalities, which neighboured capitalist Hong Kong and Portuguese-ruled Macau, respectively. Shenzhen replaced the administrative territory of Bao An county in the restructuring. Half a year later, the central government decided to set up four Special Export Zones, which were later renamed Special Economic Zones, in Guang Dong province (Shenzhen, Zhu Hai and Shan Tou) and Fu Jian province (Xia Men), which faces Taiwan across the strait. Although the formal legislation for the ground-breaking project was not passed until early 1980, the land reclamation project for the first export-oriented industrial zone began in 1979 in She Kou, a peninsula in western Shenzhen.

The idea of the open door policy was a historical innovation of the socialist state and its advance was piecemeal or, in the words of Deng Xiao Ping, 'crossing the river by touching the stones'. The Shenzhen SEZ gained special status in tax and trading policies. Alongside other measures, the profit tax on overseas investment was set at 15 per cent (compared to a national rate of 30 per cent); foreign trade firms were allowed to run their businesses independently of administrative control from the ministries; tariffs were exempted on imported material for export production. Yet, the SEZ status was limited to the southern 396 square kilometres close to the Hong Kong border (now including the districts of Yan Tian, Luo Hu, Fu Tian and Nan Shan) rather than its full 1,953 square-kilometre territory (Shenzhen Municipal Government, 2008). The area outside the SEZ retained the name of Bao An county under the administration of Shenzhen municipality. The industrialisation and urbanisation of Shenzhen SEZ was basically finished by 1992 and spread rapidly to land outside the SEZ. In 1993, Bao An county was abolished and divided into two urban districts: Bao An in the west and Long Gan in the east. The district of Bao An is thus next to the inner SEZ district of Nan Shan in which the She Kou industrial zone is situated (see Map 2.1). The factories of She Kou relocated to Bao An from the middle of the 1990s onwards, because of the higher rent and higher minimum wage within the SEZ. She Kou then became a commercial and logistics centre while Bao An rose as a new industrial cluster. In this process, the local rural villages were transformed into communities where villagers gained the status of urban citizens after their agrarian land was developed for industrial purposes.

Labour reform: a historical review

As a product of the country's reform policy, the economic development of Shenzhen was shaped by the central state policy and political atmosphere within the country and the Party as well as global economic conditions (C. Chan, 2005).

1979–83

During this period, reform was mainly introduced in rural areas. The market-oriented household-based production contract system was introduced to replace the communes and production brigades. From 1978 to 1984, the per capita income

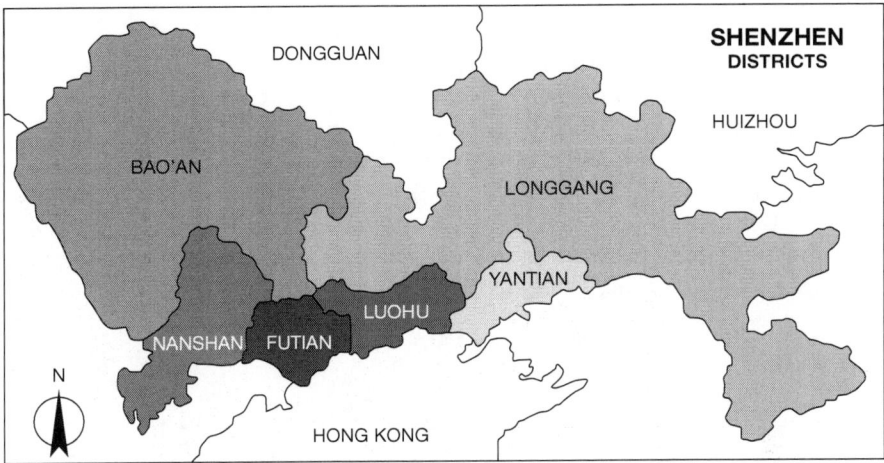

Map 2.1 An illustrated map of Shenzhen

in rural China grew at an average annual rate of 15 per cent in real terms (S. G. Wang, 2000; cited by Pun, 2005c: 72). Export-oriented urban economic reform was limited to the four SEZs. The achievement of Shenzhen SEZ was especially startling. From 1978 to 1983, the GDP of the city increased elevenfold to 1.31 billion yuan. In 1983 alone, more than 2,500 economic cooperation agreements were signed by the government with foreign partners (Yin and Yang, 2004: 80).

1984–88

The urban economic reform was not formally launched until 1984. In January that year Deng Xiao Ping paid his first visit to the SEZs and highly praised the model of the She Kou Industrial Zone. In October, the third Standing Committee meeting of the Chinese Communist Party (CCP) Twelfth Congress passed an eleven-point resolution. The fifth item stipulated that 'the economic reform should focus on urban enterprises', and the final point stated that 'open door is a basic national policy'. As a result of the new political direction, the open door policy was expanded from SEZs to fourteen coastal cities while a flexible wage system was introduced for SOEs in 1984, followed by a labour contract system two years later (Shek and Leung, 1998; Cooke, 2005). The deregulated TVEs were encouraged to grow and compete with SOEs. From the middle of the 1980s the thriving TVEs absorbed a huge number of surplus labourers liberated by the rural reform. It was estimated that a 130-million-strong workforce was transferred to industry, and 70 per cent of them were locally transferred to TVEs (Bai and Song *et al.*, 2002). The agricultural productivity and rural income growth stagnated in the second half of the 1980s (Pun, 2005c). After the spring festival of 1987, the annual 'tidal wave of migrant workers' (*Mingong Chao*) flooding into the train stations of coastal cities was first captured by the media (Lee, 1998).

1989–91

The student-led democracy movement struck the country as an expression of social discontent towards the reform (A. Chan, 1993; W. Y. Leung, 1998). SOE worker activists formed the Workers' Autonomous Federation (W. Y. Leung, 1998). After the suppression of the movement, China entered a period of 'readjustment and restoration' (*Zhili Zhengdun*) (Deng, 1992). The reform and open policy was in stagnation. After the democratic movement, some student activists tried to organise and establish independent trade unions, yet they were all mercilessly suppressed (W. Y. Leung, 1998; Lee, 2007a).

1992–94

Deng Xiao Ping again visited the southern SEZs (*Nan Xun*) and called for acceleration of the reform process. He pledged in Shenzhen that 'reform and open policies must be insisted on for 100 years'. Afterwards, a series of new policies was put forward, for example the privatisation of small SOEs, the institution-alisation of the labour arbitration system (in 1993), the announcement of a Labour Law (in 1994) and the introduction of local state fiscal autonomy (in 1995). FDI utilised in China rose from US$4.7 billion in 1991 to US$11.3 in 1992 and US$26 in 1993. On the other hand, the hardship of rural lives in inland provinces, such as Si Chuan and Gui Zhou, forced more peasants to move across provincial borders to Guang Dong looking for work. According to S. G. Wang (2000), the reform turned from a win–win to a zero-sum situation of a rising unemployment rate and widening wealth gap in 1993 (Pun, 2005c: 72). Official data estimated that the number of migrant workers in Guang Dong was around ten million in 1993 (Lee, 1998: 68). The number of inter-provincial migrant workers in the mid-1990s was estimated to be at least 12.5 times that of the early 1980s.

1995–2000

The privatisation of SOEs was launched in this period, producing millions of laid-off workers (Cooke, 2005: 1). Between 1996 and 2001, twenty-six million manufacturing jobs (40.5 per cent of the total) were lost (X. Jiang, 2004; cited by Au, 2005). Anti-privatisation protests were sparked among the SOE workers over compensation and enterprise ownership (Cai, 2002; F. Chen, 2000; 2003b; 2006; Hurst and O'Brien, 2002; Lee, 2000b; 2002a; 2007a; Yu, 2006). The laid-off workers (*Xia Gang*) joined the peasants to compete for the jobs offered by JVs, FIEs and POEs in the coastal cities. The high unemployment rate in the cities engendered a 'tidal wave of return home' (*Hui Liu Chao*) of migrant workers. The labour market suffered unprecedented dual constraints: the ability to absorb the rural and laid-off surplus labourers in the cities and the growth of rural income both declined (Bai and Song *et al.*, 2002). The growth of FDI fell after 1994 and even experienced an 11.2 per cent decline in 1999 due to the Asian financial crisis.

2001–08

After China was admitted into the World Trade Organisation (WTO) in November 2001, the growth rate of FDI returned to double digits in 2001 (14.9 per cent), 2002 (12.4 per cent) and 2004 (13.3 per cent). Since 2003 China has also surpassed the US as the top FDI inflow country in the world. Export-oriented light manufacturing, such as garments and textiles, toys and electronics, benefited from a tariff reduction and rapid growth of production in the country. With higher tax income from urban areas, the scope of the central government's social policy extended. In this period, the political discourse was also shifted to create a new hegemony of 'harmonious society' under the regime of President Hu Jin Tao and Premier Wen Jia Bao, who took power in 2002, responding to escalating social unrest. At the beginning of 2004 the CCP Central Committee and the State Council issued a 'No. 1 Document' entitled 'Opinions on Policies for Facilitating the Increase of Farmers' Income', in which the government publicly stated that 'peasant-workers are an important component of production workers' and hence deserved state protection and basic civic rights. Under this direction, some provincial governments began to cancel agricultural tax or even provided agricultural subsidies. This policy was extended to the whole country under the central government's campaign of 'building new socialist rural villages' in 2006. The new initiative persuaded some older migrant workers to return to their villages. The dramatic changes in both urban and rural China gave rise to the media-reported phenomenon of 'shortage of labour' (*Mingong Huang*) after late 2003, in Fu Jian province, the PRD and then in the YRD and the country as a whole, in contrast to the 'tidal wave of peasant workers' (*Mingong Chao*) of the early 1990s. Surveys by the Guang Dong provincial MOLSS revealed that the province lacked two million 'skilled workers' (*Nanfang Ribao*, 10 February 2004) as enterprises employed 13 per cent more migrant workers in 2004 than they had in 2003 (*Nanfang Zhoumo*, 15 July 2007). Another survey suggested that the number of workers who had left rural villages for jobs increased by 3.8 per cent in 2004 (*Min Ying Jingjibao*, 8 May 2004). The official source also revealed that there was a shortage of 2.8 million workers in the whole country, 1 million in the PRD and 300,000 in Shenzhen alone (*Nanfang Zhoumo*, 9 September 2004; *USA Today*, 12 April 2005).

Global economy, state policy and workers' strikes

Labour historians have implied that an economic boom can strengthen workers' confidence and lead to proactive strikes (e.g. Franzosi, 1995). Burawoy (1985) introduced a powerful concept, the 'politics of production', to situate labour politics in the workplace into state regulation. This notion was extended to take global 'forces' into consideration in his later study (Burawoy *et al.*, 2000). In what follows, I try to connect the wave of strikes with broader state policy and the global economy.

Table 2.1 Foreign Direct Investment in China, 1990–2004

Year	Utilised FDI (US$ billion)	Change on Previous Year (per cent)
1990	3.5	+3
1991	4.4	+26
1992	11.0	+150
1993	27.5	+150
1994	33.8	+23
1995	37.5	+11
1996	41.4	+9
1997	45.2	+8
1998	45.5	+1
1999	40.4	−11.2
2000	40.8	+0.94
2001	46.9	+14.9
2002	52.7	+12.4
2003	53.5	+1.5
2004	60.6	+13.3
2005	72.41	+19.42

Source: Ministry of Commerce, various years

By looking in detail at the 'worst strike' to take place between 1981 and 1986, we will see how workers' discontent was constrained in the early stage of reform. While 1989–92 was a period of reform stagnation where no significant development was seen in the export-oriented economy, 1993–94 was a turbulent time within which a tidal wave of strikes arose in the twin SEZs of Zhu Hai and Shenzhen. Strike cases will be presented to illustrate how they were different from those in the 1980s. After 1995, the Labour Law and the labour arbitration mechanism provided workers with channels to express their dissatisfaction in a time of high unemployment. However, after China was admitted into the WTO, the export-oriented economy was further expanded and more job opportunities were available. The reported phenomenon of a 'shortage of labour' has given those in privileged job market positions the courage to rebel through semi-organised strikes in Shenzhen and the surrounding area since 2004.

1986: a silent strike[1]

> I hate the rural village. I can't forget that my father was discriminated against by the production team leaders and allocated the hardest tasks. After land was contracted out, our lives improved, benefiting from the hard-working habit of my father. But I dreamed of life in the city, and moved out to work in foreign invested factories in 1983 and never went back.
>
> (Lian,[2] a female migrant worker in the 1980s)

Workers' stories

Lian, like most of the first-generation peasant workers, was a local migrant from outlying Guang Dong. In 1988, the number of rural migrants working in the PRD was estimated at 0.9–1 million, 80 per cent of whom were from other parts of Guang Dong, and 20 per cent from other provinces (Wong, 1989: 37).

During her eight years' work in Hui Zhou and Dong Guan, two cities adjacent to Shenzhen, Lian experienced two strikes. One was when workers protested about an unreasonable unpaid task in 1986; the other was against the management locking the doors of workers' dormitories during work time. In Lian's memory:

> Most of the workers came from the same village in the county of Hai Feng. We chose the day the Hong Kong boss was in the factory to take action. Some of us threw stones and bricks[3] into the boss's office even though he had accepted our demand. The boss was afraid of us. You know, Hai Feng is near Hui Zhou. They [the Hong Kong bosses] were newcomers to our land, and would not know what would happen in the next step.

Except for these two incidents, Lian did not hear of any other strikes in the industrial zones in which she worked.

Although Lian was determined to stay in the cities, one of her friends, Fong, was more frustrated by working life. It was 1987 when she first arrived in Dong Guan, where she worked for several small factories. In her experience, there were no strikes. She could not get used to the strict discipline in the factories: 'I always cried . . . and tried to change factories for better conditions. . . . Finally I gave up and returned home three years later.' Unlike Lian, she chose an individual 'solution' – returning to her home village in the face of hardship.

Complaint as a channel of grievance

These two women's stories gave us some hints that the strike, with strong rural and local components, was not a common phenomenon in the 1980s. The features of industrial relations in the SEZ were best reflected in She Kou Industrial Zone (SKIZ). According to the Shenzhen Municipal Federation of Trade Unions (SZMFTU), they received 976 complaint cases from workers in 1986, of which 791 were resolved, 63 rejected and the remainder unresolved or withdrawn (W. Y. Leung, 1988).

One of the complaint cases in SKIZ took place in a Hong Kong-invested toy factory, Kader.[4] The factory employed 1,600 workers in 1983. Workers were discontented with the long working hours and lodged a complaint with the trade union. The She Kou Industrial Zone Federation of Trade Unions (SKIZFTU), with the support of the local state, advised the factory to restrict overtime work. Twenty workers supported the union by refusing to work overtime on the first evening after the negotiation between the union and management, but the management fired one of their leaders. SKIZFTU demanded that the company re-employ the dismissed worker. Kader responded by threatening to withdraw investment. Supported by the SKIZ government, SKIZFTU represented workers to sue Kader and finally forced the management to accept their request.

In this case, the trade union and the local state took a very proactive role in protecting the workers, while the workers were relatively passive in defending themselves.

Rise of stoppages

Direct workplace confrontations did not escalate in Shenzhen SEZ until the late 1980s.[5] According to an estimate by SZMFTU, there were nine small strikes in 1986 in Shenzhen, all of which took place in FIEs and lasted for only a few hours each. The *China Youth News* also reported in July 1988 that there had been at least twenty-one strikes in FIEs in Shenzhen SEZ during 1986 and 1987. The official newspaper claimed that both the number and scale of strikes had escalated since 1987 and called for labour law legislation to prevent more strikes (*South China Morning Post*, 30 July 1988; *Hong Kong Standard*, 30 July 1988; cited in W. Y. Leung, 1988: 157–58).

SKIZFTU officials revealed a number of strike cases in 1986:[6]

> A group of more than 20 women workers (most of them from the same village) . . . walked off the job for two hours because they found the attitude of the foreman unbearably rude and harsh. The union went to mediate and advised the foreman to improve his manners. The workers resumed work shortly after. . . .
>
> Several hundred workers . . . struck for a day over low wages. The union went to mediate and persuade the workers to return to work. The management of the factory had always resisted having a union at the plant. . . .
>
> Twenty-six workers . . . struck for six hours in protest against their low wages. The management fired them all. After the union mediated, twenty-five workers were reinstated, but the strike leader remained laid off.
>
> (W. Y. Leung, 1988: 156)

A leaked secret action

A strike in June 1986 was especially notable.[7] As described by AMRC (1995: 33), it was 'a small-scale strike that shocked She Kou (at that time, strikes were rare in SEZs; moreover, Sanyo was regarded as a model factory)'. The Sanyo Semiconductor Factory, then the biggest employer in She Kou, was a wholly Japanese-owned FIE that employed over 2,000 workers. The company had experienced another strike in the same factory earlier in the year. According to SKIZFTU, around 600 workers struck for paid holidays in Spring Festival on 5 January 1986. But they withdrew their demands and returned to work soon after holding discussions with trade union cadres.

The strike in June 1986 resulted from management breaking a contract. The twenty-one workers who staged the strike had all been recruited by the management committee of SKIZ from their homeland, Rao Ping county in northern Guang Dong. They worked together and lived in the same dormitory. Before they came to Shenzhen, they were told that their salary would be increased after three months, but this still had not happened after ten months.

At midnight on 11 June 1986, the group gathered together to write a petition letter to the management. Zheng and Chen acted as coordinators. In the morning, they went to work like everyone else. But after one hour, they left the workshop collectively without informing anyone and returned to their dormitory.

The trade union had been aware of the discontent in the factory. Two officials from SKIZFTU had visited the plant on 10 June, but the workers had refused to reveal anything. Meanwhile, at 4 p.m., the company had pinned up a notice to inform workers that their monthly salary would be increased by twenty yuan, backdated to 1 April. Nonetheless, the workers did not give up their strike plan, even though the pay rise was their central demand.

Trade union and party intervention

It was reported by a trade union official in 1986 that 'industrial relations in wholly foreign-owned enterprises were much [tenser] than in joint ventures' as Chinese partners and trade unions were able to intervene in the latter cases (W. Y. Leung, 1988: 155). In Sanyo factories, over 50 per cent of the workers were members of SKIZFTU.

Two trade union cadres, as well as officials from the Party Committee and SKIZ Labour Service Company, a government body that monitored employment issues in the zone, appeared in the workers' dormitories immediately after the 'wildcat' action took place.

During the 'ideological work' of the officials, the workers did not say a word. Their conversation was recorded as follows:

'Why don't you go to work?'
Silence.
'It's no good to set up an issue. Our law will not allow it to happen anyway. Please go back to work because the consequences may be serious if you don't. If there is any problem, you can raise it with the union. The union can approach the company and help to resolve . . .'
Silence.
'What you are doing is against Section 158 of the Penal Code. In the name of the union, we demand you go back to work immediately.'

(W. Y. Leung, 1988: 162–63)

The officials' strategy turned from 'soft' persuasion to 'hard' threats as time went on. The workers seemed frightened, especially by laws about which they had no idea. The workers' right to strike had been abolished in the 1982 version of the constitution. Now, strikes were not illegal (K. Chang, 2004), but any action to disrupt social order *was*, under section 158 of the Penal Code.

The workers finally backed down and started to return to work one by one. However, one of their leaders, Cheng, suddenly shouted out: 'Hey! If anybody can beat me in arm-wrestling, they can go back to work' (W. Y. Leung, 1988: 163). All of the twenty-one workers then rejoined the strike with Cheng. In response, the cadres resumed their 'ideological work'. The strike ultimately lasted for over ten hours. Trade union, Party and administrative officials talked with the workers throughout that time.

The day after the strike, the workers' leaders, Chen and Cheng, were fired and sent back to their homeland. According to a cadre of SKIZFTU: '[They were] handed in to the local labour department, [which was] informed not to arrange jobs for these two persons again. [It is] a piece of mouse faeces to stir up a bowl of soup' (AMRC, 1995: 33). According to the union incident report, which suggested more training for union officials and education for workers, it was the 'worst strike' in the industrial zone between 1981 and 1986 (W. Y. Leung, 1988: 164).

Weak workers' subjectivity

The basic characteristics of the Sanyo strike were in line with Lian's experience and the accounts from SKIZFTU officials. An outline of labour relations in the 1980s can be sketched accordingly. As a response to harsh conditions, some of the workers kept silent or chose to quit ther jobs, while a few complained to the trade union. Wildcat strikes were increasingly adopted by workers later in the decade. Still, they were very locally orientated and lacked any strategic planning. The ten-hour strike at Sanyo was the 'worst strike' in six years because others were even shorter and more easily pacified by trade union cadres. But even in this 'worst' case, the workers expressed their discontent about 'being cheated' in a very passive manner. Unlike a mature strike, they did not have formal demands, did not negotiate with the management or trade union and Party Committee cadres, but kept silent throughout the day. With little education, they knew nothing about the legal status of a strike. The crucial element in organising the strike was the fact that the participants all hailed from the same place. They had no intention of informing workers from other counties and dormitories about what they were planning to do.

The strong legacy of state socialism

As can be seen in Sanyo, Kader and other cases described by SKIZFTU, the official trade unions played a key role in constraining workers. The SOE model of labour control, where the CCP Committee and trade unions worked with the administration to accommodate workers, still prevailed in the SKIZ. The techniques of trade union intervention in the case also stemmed from the state socialist ideology. On the one hand, they suggested that the company made concessions;

on the other, they did 'ideological work' among the strikers. This dual role caused problems.

There were lots of arguments and suspicions within the CCP on the direction of the reforms before 1989. As an example, the establishment of Shenzhen SEZ was criticised by the *People's Daily*, the CCP institutional newspaper, in 1985 as 'getting rich on the back of the rest of the country' (cited in W. Y. Leung, 1988: 130). At this stage, under the discourse of the 'socialist market economy with Chinese characteristics', the market economy was not an alternative, but supplementary to the state-planned economy and therefore subject to interference from the state under the ideology of socialism.

1992–94: a wave of strikes

> Farming back at home was a declining business. The harvest was not enough to cover expenditure, never mind produce a profit. From the early 1990s onwards, most of our villagers went to Guang Dong to look for a job. My husband followed them in 1994, while I came two years later and left behind my two children with my parents-in-law.
>
> (A worker from Si Chuan province)

Unlike in the 1980s, workers crossing provincial boundaries to arrive in the PRD outnumbered local migrants in the early 1990s. This new phenomenon was called 'a tidal wave of peasant workers' (*Mingong Chao*) or an 'unchecked flow of population (from the countryside to the cities)' (*Mangliu*). After the Spring Festival of 1992, two million migrant workers from inland provinces flooded into Guang Dong (Xie, 1997).

Escalating workplace conflicts

The working conditions in the region were appalling. The upward potential of workers' salaries was restricted by the unlimited supply of labour and the local state's labour-unfriendly policy. For example, enterprises in the PRD needed to pay a wage adjustment tax to the local government for monthly salaries over 600 yuan. This policy naturally restricted wage rises (Liu *et al.*, 1992).

According to a survey by the Guang Dong Federation of Trade Unions, among 1,500 workers in twenty FIEs, 25.4 per cent had their identity cards, temporary settlement certificates (in the city) and SEZ passes kept by their employers to limit their mobility. Two workers commented on this phenomenon:

> 'I joined the factory like a beggar, worked there like a prisoner, and lived like a thief' (a male worker who escaped from an electronics factory). . . . 'This [the factory] is an invisible prison, and we are prisoners without trials' (a female worker from a shoe factory).
>
> (*Gongyun Yuekan*, 1994: 3)

During 1993 and 1994, the media in Hong Kong and China reported widely on the stories of long working hours, infringement of the minimum wage rate, physical abuse of workers, poor workplace safety, disastrous industrial accidents, and workers' protests.[8]

Li Bo Yong, the head of the central state MOLSS, expressed his concern:

> This year's labour and employment condition is very bad, and the labour conflict cases have a trend of rapid escalation; last year the number of strikes, work stoppages, collective administrative complaints (*Shangfang*), petitions, marches and demonstrations was not lower than ten thousand, among them the foreign invested enterprises were most evident. At the same time, the problems of occupational diseases and industrial accidents were also very common, and needed to be resolved as soon as possible. . . . The MOLSS is actively preparing for legislation and setting up related policies. There will be a series of regulations and policies announced. It is hopeful that the above problems can be controlled or regulated to a large extent.
>
> (*Kuai Pao*, 14 March 1994)

Strike tide[9] in 1993–94

W. Y. Leung (1998: 38) reported 'a momentous rise in the number of labour protests such as strikes, sit-ins and street demonstrations waged by larger numbers of workers during the years 1992–94'. Table 2.2 illustrates the cases concerning FIE workers in the PRD.

In the words of K. W. Jiang (1996: 139), there was an 'unprecedented strike wave in FIEs concentrated in south China' in the early 1990s, while Taylor *et al.* (2003: 175) described it as 'the third wave of strikes' in the history of the People's Republic.[10] A labour activist who investigated labour relations in industrial zones in the PRD in 1993 and 1994 commented: 'From the phenomenon of workers' self-organisation and the fact that a strike in one enterprise can inspire workers in other enterprises to form a strike tide, the potential capability of networking and organisation among workers in different enterprises is gradually manifested'(*Gongyun Yuekan*, 1994: 12).

One of the typical strike chains occurred in Zhu Hai. Although the wage level in Zhu Hai was second only to Shenzhen in the early 1990s,[11] workers suffered from a high inflation rate. The official national inflation rate was 20 per cent,[12] but it was even higher in Zhu Hai (AMRC, 1995; *Gongyun Yuekan*, 1994). A series of strikes was staged by workers for a reasonable wage adjustment: 'During the 75 days from 9 March to 23 May, 12 strikes took place in 10 foreign-owned factories [in Zhu Hai], 7,263 workers participated directly, with an accumulated stoppage of 18,147 working day shifts' (*Gongyun Yuekan*, 1994: 9; AMRC, 1995: 32). The following three strikes, which took place during 1993 in Zhu Hai, provide a glimpse into the general pattern.[13]

Table 2.2 Reported labour protests of FIE workers in the PRD from 1993 to 1994

Year	Organisation	Participants	Location	Goal
1993	Strike; formation of independent union	Workers (about 800)	Zhu Hai: Japanese-owned Canon factory	Pay rise; improved benefits
1993 January to June	Strikes (nineteen incidents)	Workers	Zhu Hai	Terms of employment
1993 January to June	Strikes (ten incidents involving 4,135 people)	Workers	Shenzhen	Terms of employment
1994 March to April	Two-day strike	Workers (300 at a Hong Kong-owned plant)	Hui Zhou, Guang Dong province	Wage payment
1994	Independent union	Three leading organisers	Shenzhen	Independent union; bulletin; educational and other service to workers

Source: W. Y. Leung, 1998: 331–35

Canon strike

In March 1993, workers in a Japanese-owned factory, Canon, demanded a 30 per cent wage increase and provision of living dormitories. The management agreed to increase wages by about 7 per cent, and said the extra money would be deducted if workers arrived late or left work early. Over 800 workers staged a strike. The Zhu Hai Municipal Federation of Trade Unions (ZHMFTU) intervened in the case. On the one hand, they criticised workers' demands as unreasonable; on the other, they suggested the management should withdraw the punishment for late arrival and early leaving. Finally, workers returned to work and the company withdrew the new rule. At the end of the strike, labour activists who did not accept the arrangement resigned (Shek and Leung, 1998).

San Mei strike

One and a half months later, workers in another Japanese FIE in Zhu Hai, San Mei, staged a larger-scale strike. They complained that the wage adjustment did not compensate for the inflation rate. At eight o'clock on the morning of 11 May, 700 workers walked out of the workshops and staged a sit-in at the entrance of the factory. Zhu Hai municipal LSSB officials came to mediate in the afternoon, and the police guarded the factory and warned the workers not to tell Hong Kong journalists about the strike the next day.

Two days later, the workers contacted the ZHMFTU and requested approval to organise a trade union in the factory. The ZHMFTU responded that the trade union should be directly led by itself and a planned discussion should be held with the management before such a union could be established. The trade union was not formed, but workers elected a representative committee to negotiate with the management. One to three delegates were sent from each workshop or office, covering the levels of supervisors, group leaders and workers. The first negotiation was held on 18 May, in the presence of the municipal LSSB, the Foreign Investment Service Centre and the police.

The management tried to divide the workers by promoting three workers' representatives in the first negotiation meeting. Workers responded by electing new delegates. 'What is worth mentioning is the dispute in San Mei stirred up a comprehensive strike among 3,000 workers in two nearby shoes factories' (AMRC, 1995: 37). A joint strike was organised in the two factories, which were owned by the same Taiwanese investor.

Ya Pu Luo strike

At the end of 1993, over 1,000 workers in Ya Pu Luo, a toy factory in Zhu Hai, went on strike for a wage rise. The organisers circulated handwritten pamphlets outside the factory calling for others not to work, and displayed a *Dazibao* (poster) demanding improvement of working conditions and increased wages. The *Dazibao* was also posted outside the factory, on recruitment and notice boards in the industrial zone, to publicise their action. The factory announced that the daily wage would be increased from 8 to 10 yuan, still lower than the Zhu Hai municipal minimum wage rate of 12.5 yuan. The strike continued, and some of the strikers even staged a sit-down protest outside the factory. On the third day, the hundreds of workers who were still on strike were dismissed.

Strike in Shenzhen, 1994

One year after the 'strike tide' in Zhu Hai, a strike occurred in Yong Feng, a Taiwan-invested shoe factory in Bao An, Shenzhen.[14] The factory was notorious for its cruel management: for example, workers who failed to walk along the special lines marked on the floor were subjected to a fine or physical punishment. Workers in the factory, who had lodged a complaint with the Shenzhen Municipal Labour and Social Security Bureau (SZMLSSB) as their salaries were lower than the legal minimum wage, were shocked to find that 150 yuan had been deducted from their salaries for meals and other living fees, which had been provided for free before. Workers' discontent intensified when a safety guard beat a woman worker. On the evening of 13 March 1994, the day they received their salaries, a strike began: 'They created uproar, struck objects [to make noise] and expressed outrage' (AMRC, 1995: 38). The strike was initiated by male workers in the assembly workshop where work was most intensive and low paid. The next morning, a notice was posted calling a strike in the name of a 'temporary trade union'. Over 3,000 workers followed the appeal.

The strike lasted for three days. The dormitory and factory were next to each other but separated by a wall. During the daytime, the police were patrolling within the factory while the workers stayed quietly in the dormitory. However,

> As soon as the night came, workers created uproar, struck objects and threw sundries down to the floor or towards the factory. According to a worker, as it was easier to be recognised and punished during daytime, they kept silent in the day, but voiced agitation at night, as it was hard to recognise workers, and the management or police dared not catch workers in the dormitory at night (because the dormitory at night was the world of workers, catching workers might lead to violent conflict).
>
> (AMRC, 1995: 38)

Workers were so worried about revenge that there were no volunteers to act as representatives to negotiate with management during the dispute. So an 'agreement' was reached between the management and officials from the LSSB without any involvement of or consultation with workers. The factory returned the deducted 150 yuan to the workers, but the latter had to sign new contracts with the factory, formalising the charging policy. The exchange 'concession' from the management was to increase the overtime wage rate from 1 yuan per hour to 2.1 yuan, the minimum standard set by the Shenzhen municipal government. The LSSB also announced that the 'temporary trade union' was an illegal organisation. Some of the leaders quit their jobs in fear of punishment. But most of the workers did not even know who the initiators of the 'temporary trade union' had been.

'Socialist' control mechanism in decline

The traditional form of labour control ceased to be effective. F. Chen (2003a) commented that the official national trade unions faced a contradiction between their roles of representing (workers), mediating (conflicts) and pre-empting (independent trade unionism) after the reform. But we saw in southern China that workplace trade unions significantly lost their position in pacifying workers and mediating workplace conflicts in the private sector; although, in some cases, the municipal or district trade unions still played a role in accommodating workers. The Party Committee was also absent from FIE, TVE and POE workplaces. As early as 1986, when strike activities were still minimal, a trade union report on the Sanyo strike revealed that trained cadres were insufficient to tackle such incidents (W. Y. Leung, 1988). When the open policy accelerated and FIEs and JVs flourished after 1992, it was impossible for the traditional model of intensive workplace intervention from the trade union and Party Committee, a residue of state socialism, to be maintained. Indeed, the SKIZFTU model, featuring trade union cadres' close relationship with rank-and-file workers and their successful mediation role, was one of the four models promoted by the ACFTU (ACFTU, 1995; Feng, 2001). Nevertheless, it was never successfully followed by other industrial zones.[15] As Howell (1993: 8) pointed out, the 'ideological dilemma' of trade unions had increased the tension between the unions and their members, which accounted for the emergence of autonomous trade unions in 1989. Thereafter, the role of trade unions among workers was further eroded. In order to ease tense labour relations, the state encouraged the ACFTU to establish trade unions in FIEs. A new version of the Trade Union Law was also announced in 1992 to consolidate trade union collective consultation rights, while heightening control of higher-level trade unions over their affiliates. In 1994 alone, 17,293 trade unions were set up in FIEs, nearly double the total figure of the previous ten years. But, as pointed out by many researchers (e.g. K. W. Jiang, 1996; Cooke, 2005; A. Chan, 2006b), most of them were organised and fully manipulated by the management and were not even able to perform the socialist 'transmission-belt' role. Without consent from the management, the higher-level trade union would not approve an application from workers to register a trade union (AMRC, 1995). The LSSB then replaced the trade union in mediating between workers and management.

The repressive state apparatus

The legacy of socialism declined, but the state apparatus became more repressive towards workers. China's export-oriented developmental trajectory seemed to follow the path of Korea and Taiwan, where labour and political opposition was ruthlessly suppressed by the state and business nexus (Haggard, 1983). In the face of the emergence of large-scale workplace protests, the police and LSSB, which had tended to be neutral in the 1980s, became very active in cracking down on workers' activism. Their suppression impeded but could not eradicate the wide spread of workers' collective action. A new control ideology, legality or rule by law, was therefore created (Lee, 2002a). In 1993, the 'Rules on Handling Enterprise Labour Disputes' were introduced, followed by the more comprehensive Labour Law in 1994.

Why do workers become radical?

Workers made great progress in terms of their demands, collectiveness, strike duration and strategies compared with the strike in 1986. They elected representatives and even attempted to organise independent trade unions. In some cases, their actions were well organised (e.g. in San Mei); in others, they adopted passive but wise tactics to escape suppression and lengthen the struggle (e.g. in Yong Feng). What are the reasons for this development?

First, exploitation intensified. As wage levels did not increase in line with inflation, real wages declined. Labour abuse cases were also very common. In 1993, eighty-three young workers died in a fire in a Hong Kong-invested toy factory, Zhi Li, in Shenzhen. The case was reported widely in China and Hong

Kong.[16] Hong Kong labour NGOs and activists began to initiate labour rights campaigns in the region. The ACFTU also took a pro-labour stance on this issue.[17] FIEs' illegal abuse of Chinese workers' rights became one of the main discussion topics in the media. The social atmosphere was positive in encouraging workers' struggles.

Second, as Xie (1997) found, migrant workers' temporary communities had emerged in the PRD and were developing into civil forces.[18] According to his study of Zhe Jiang in Guang Zhou: 'migrant workers' communities (*Mingong Cun*) have their own internal organisations, regulated by the market and maintained by locality, and solve problems through a variety of strategies' (Xie, 1997: 199). A labour activist in Hong Kong who conducted surveys in the PRD in 1993 and 1994 suggested a knock-on effect of strikes: 'Strikes were just like flu, which infected one factory after another. Workers had linkage with each other.' Another labour activist I met in Shenzhen said that 'after every big strike, there were follow-up strikes in the surrounding area. Workers knew each other through the network of *Laoxiang* [people from the same place of origin].'

Third, the background of workers was different from that of the 1980s generation. A labour activist who had interviewed striking workers in Zhu Hai in 1993 told me that most of the workers were fresh graduates from secondary school. According to him, there was also a boom in workers' literature (*Dagong Wenxue*) during the early 1990s. In contrast, those working in She Kou in 1986 were described by trade unions as having 'not enough education' (W. Y. Leung, 1988: 164). In the above strike cases, workers' knowledge of the law had greatly improved. They also had different working experiences. The early 1980s migrant workers had worked or witnessed the tightly disciplined working system in the communes. The 1990s generation had not grown up under such a strict regime. An employer, on the other hand, credited the media and internet for the enlightenment of workers: 'There are even internet bars in rural villages, not to mention the TV and newspapers. You cannot cheat them any more.'

2004: strike for a union

> I suddenly remembered some data. . . . The number of strikes in Shenzhen and Dong Guan involving more than 1,000 workers in enterprises this year [2004] was as high as over thirty, but most were eventually defeated. . . . Why? The key point is that we did not organise ourselves. Basically we, the higher-positioned staff, did not stand up.
>
> (An engineer in the Uniden strike, quoted in a workers' blog)

Legal mobilisation and its limitations

The capacity of the new generation of workers to defend their interests and rights was evidenced not only in the spread of strike experiences, but in their legal mobilisation strategy. As shown in Table 2.3,[19] the labour laws were promptly exploited to express workers' grievances as soon as they came into effect

Table 2.3 Arbitrated labour disputes in China, 1993–2004

Year	Arbitrated labour disputes	Workers involved in arbitrated labour disputes	Arbitrated collective labour disputes
1993	12,368	35,683	684
1994	19,098	77,794	1,482
1995	33,030	122,512	2,588
1996	47,951	189,120	3,150
1997	71,524	221,115	4,109
1998	93,649	358,531	6,767
1999	120,191	473,957	9,043
2000	135,206	422,617	8,247
2001	154,621	556,230	9,847
2002	184,116	608,396	11,024
2003	226,391	801,042	10,823
2004	260,471	764,981	19,241

Source: National Bureau of Statistics of China, various years

(Gallagher, 2005), while trade unions ceased to play a significant role in workers' lives and wildcat strikes were constrained by the state strategy of suppressing independent workplace organisations. In Shenzhen, the number of cases handled by the labour dispute arbitration committee accounted for one-tenth of the total national figure (*Nanfang Ribao*, 28 October 2004).

Lin (1998) observed that after 1994 the number of strikes in the PRD was stable as the labour laws provided a base for conciliation. This was the central state's effort to absorb workers' radical actions into administration-managed legal channels. A. Chan (1993) argued that corporatism emerged after the insurgency in 1989, yet the basic underlying logic of transformation was social 'stability' and 'development',[20] rather than Western-style state corporatism or social partnership (Clarke and Lee, 2003; Clarke et al., 2004). Thus, in the experience of workers, although awareness of the law continuously increased, reliance on the law soon demonstrated its weaknesses and limitations.

One of the main constraints was the time-consuming nature of litigation. As soon as they lost their jobs, the workers also lost the accommodation provided by the factory. If they found another job, it was difficult to obtain leave from their new employer to attend labour arbitration court and so on. (No boss likes their employees to be in conflict with another factory.) If they did not join a factory, accommodation and other living expenses were a costly burden.

The *China Labour Bulletin* (CLB, 2005a) in Hong Kong reported stories of jewellery workers' struggles for compensation for silicosis. In one of the cases, a worker by the name of Chen Xing Fu took almost three years to win 172,293 yuan compensation through labour dispute arbitration. But his huge expenses of 40,000 yuan, including lawyers' fees, transportation to and from his home village, and living expenses in the city, were totally neglected by the court.

Moreover, after years of legal procedure, even though workers won the lawsuit, the factory might close down or move to another city under another name to evade responsibility (CLB, 2005b), especially in cases involving huge compensation and small-sized factories. The limitations of the legal protection forced workers to use other, usually more radical, means of protest, such as petitioning high-level authorities (*Shangfang*), demonstrating on main roads and even requesting assistance from overseas NGOs.

A new tidal wave of strikes

Alongside the widely reported phenomenon of 'shortage of labour', labour NGOs and media paid attention to the increased frequency of wildcat strikes after 2004. In 2005, I was told by an NGO organiser who had worked in the PRD for eight years that at least half of the workers she met had experiences of striking. One of the cases which struck Shenzhen residents and the media occurred in the Meizhi Haiyan electronics factory. On 6 October 2004, one of the city's main highways was blocked by more than 3,000 workers for four hours. The workers were employed by a Sino-Hong Kong JV, Haiyan. They complained of low wages and long working hours. Their monthly salary could be as low as 230 yuan for a twelve-hour working day, while the legal minimum monthly salary for an eight-hour working day was 610 yuan. Besides, the company did not pay the social security insurance required by law. After representatives negotiated with government officials, 1,000 workers left the scene of their own volition, while the remaining 2,000 were driven off by the police (*Nanfang Ribao*, 7 October 2004). The workers' average salary was soon increased to about 900 yuan. Two months later, the factory was fined over 1.96 million yuan by the Labour and Social Protection Bureau for violating the Labour Law (*Nanfang Ribao*, 7 December 2004).

Workers' protest in the region has progressed in both scale and radicalisation since 2004, as is shown in Table 2.4. However, further analysis found that more than half of the collective protests involved delayed payment or deduction of wages. It showed that workers' protest was still a response to the intensification of exploitation.

The most eye-catching case from the data is that of a workers' strike demanding a trade union in a Japanese electronics factory, Uniden, in Shenzhen. As discussed above, Yong Feng workers in Shenzhen had tried to organise a trade union in 1994

Table 2.4 Workers' collective action reported in the PRD from 2002 to 2005[21]

	2002	2003	2004	2005
Incidents reported	3	10	22	35
Incidents involving in excess of 1,000 workers	0	2	9	13
Incidents resulting in physical conflicts with police	0	2	7	12

Source: P. Leung, 2005

Table 2.5 Reported causes of collective actions in the PRD[22]

1 Delayed or deducted wage	39
2 Long working hours	7
3 Abuses such as body searches or physical punishment of workers	6
4 Unreasonable dismissal	6
5 Rights and interest violations resulting from SOE privatisation	6
6 Occupational diseases	4
7 Anti-Japanese	2
8 Wage rise demand	1
9 Bad food quality	1
10 Demand of a trade union	1
11 Pension insurance	1

Source: P. Leung, 2005

but this had been declared 'illegal' by the state. I chose the Uniden case for further investigation in order to gain an insight into the extent of material progress of workers' self-organising, management strategies and state policy in Shenzhen. Overseas media, labour NGO documents and internet blogs written by workers provided ample information on this case.

The Uniden strike in 2004

The Japanese factory, which was set up in 1990 in an industrial town in Bao An, Shenzhen, had 16,000 Chinese employees in 2004, of which 1,000 were mostly male managerial and R&D staff and the remainder were female production-line workers aged between sixteen and thirty. For many years, the company had a policy of 'R&D in Japan, production in China, and sales in the United States'. In 2004, the top management changed the strategy by transferring the R&D base to China. As a result of this expansion, the company relocated part of its production to the province of Jiang Xi to the north of Guang Dong. The physical size of the Jiang Xi plant is double that of Shenzhen with a long-term strategy to make the former a manufacturing centre and the latter an R&D base. The factory in Shenzhen recruited hundreds of engineering professionals for this reason. According to one of its managers, the main reason for the new strategy was market pressure: 'Without extending our product variety, we cannot get big retailers, such as Wal-Mart and Best Buy,' he said.

When the factory unfolded its ambitious plan in China, a strike occurred in late 2004. It was the fourth significant strike since the establishment of the factory. The three earlier strikes were mollified by the management with cooperation from the local government. 'Disobedient' workers were sacked in each instance.

The immediate cause of the strike in 2004 was that the company had dismissed without any severance compensation a worker who had served in the factory for nearly ten years. On a Friday morning in December, a suggestion letter (*Changyi Xi*n) was sent to the company-provided email address of all administrative and technical employees. The letter set out fifteen demands, which included realisation of the promise to establish a trade union and a permanent contract for workers who had served for ten years. It ended: 'Hope the above points are responded to by 16:00 of XX(day) XX (month) [the same day the letter was circulated]. Otherwise, we will take action as soon as possible.'

At 4 p.m., workers began to walk out from the production building. Employees working in the technical and administrative departments had not yet joined the strike. The officials from the district LSSB arrived at the factory soon after the gathering of workers to talk with the management. At 9 p.m., a pamphlet was circulated among rank-and-file workers. Its message was more or less the same as the email message, but with an extra call for workers to elect representatives on a group basis in order to negotiate with 'the Japanese'. 'Now we need to negotiate with the legal representative (*Faren Daibiao*) from Japan, we don't recognise any Chinese mandated by the Japanese. . . . We will hire a lawyer and interpreter to negotiate with them,' the paper read.

The next day was Saturday. After a morning meeting of all the production department heads, the factory announced to the production workers that the day was a factory holiday and work would resume on Monday morning. Staff in non-production departments still needed to work as usual from 8 a.m. However, contrary to the management's expectations, the staff working in the technology building came out to join the strike from 11 a.m. onwards. The pamphlet which had circulated among production workers now also reached the technical staff. At noon, management announced that the technology building would also be closed in the afternoon.

Some technical staff held a meeting to reach a consensus that all demands of the production workers should be supported. Workers tried to call the media on Sunday and Monday, but there was not any response. From 6 a.m. on the Monday, thousands of production workers first rallied on the drill ground of the factory and the pavement outside. By then, representatives had been elected. The workers were joined by technical staff at 8 a.m. To draw public attention, 600 to 700 women production workers walked towards the highway. However, they were stopped by well-equipped police and security guards.

At 10 a.m., some representatives took to a stage to brief the assembled workers. Among others, the formation of a trade union was a key issue. One of the representatives recalled the speech of a representative:

The factory had promised to set up a trade union during the strike in 2000. Why had they not done so by now? The factory can dismiss workers casually, deduct and keep wages, set up unequal regulations, conduct body checks when [workers are] getting on and off work and even bring in the security guards to grab the women workers who were sacked but still working in the factory. Why [could these things happen]? It is because workers are a weak community. Now we should protect our own rights. We should form our own trade union to protect our workers, and protect the legal rights and interests of us all.

Workers were encouraged by their representatives to speak on the stage. One of them suggested forming a trade union preparation committee. The idea was hailed by the assembled mass. More than fifty workers, recommended by their workmates or pushed forward by them, became committee members. Among them, Tom and Henry, who were both working in technical departments, rose to be natural leaders. They announced:

> Now our trade union preparation committee is established. Those standing above are temporary members of the trade union preparation committee. We are now going to negotiate with the Japanese. Please go back home now and return here again tomorrow morning at 8 a.m. We will report back to you any new progress by then. We should not agree with anything spoken by the government or the factory people.

Police, trade union and labour bureau: pro-management?

Police officers recorded the whole assembly on camera. Some workers tried to stop them, but the policemen simply focused their camera on these workers and threatened to arrest them.

After the end of the assembly, the preparation committee members contacted the SZMFTU and asked if a spontaneously organised workers' trade union was legal. The city trade union responded that it was legal and asked them to contact the town-level trade union branch for advice. They did so and arranged a meeting at the village Party office for 2.30 p.m. A committee lunch meeting was held to elect twelve negotiators. These representatives were those who had been elected by the workers before the morning rally. Other members arranged to stay with the workers and report the scene outside to the negotiators.

The town trade union cadres came, but their meeting with the committee members was eventually held in the human resources office of the factory. Before the arrival of the trade unionists, government officials had already arrived at the factory to talk with the management. When the twelve representatives entered the meeting room, twenty government officials and factory managers walked out of the building and headed to the drill ground, where some workers had gathered. When officials from the district LSSB were about to address the workers, representatives outside the negotiation room informed the negotiators. Henry, an engineer, emerged and told the workers: 'Our negotiation is now under way, and we have not reached any agreement at this moment. Please act according to what we said in the morning.' The police camera followed him throughout this speech. The labour bureau official continued his address, but the workers started to disperse. The police camera was directed not only at the representatives, but at other workers gathering inside the factory grounds, especially those standing in groups. Representatives heard that during their meeting at noon at least four women workers had been forced to sign documents agreeing to return to work.

The negotiation went well, and several dozen points were agreed. Representatives who came out of the meeting tried to calm the emotions of workers who had still not dispersed and said they should go back to work as soon as possible.

Workers' representatives and union rights

Following the resumption of production, some unlawful policies were abandoned by the factory, but the main part of the agreement was not implemented. One item in the deal stated: 'The implementation of the above rules is to be monitored by the workers' representatives.' However, the management said that they did not recognise the representatives, as they had no legal status. Another item stipulated that a trade union would be set up in July 2005 through the collaboration of the management and workers' representatives. Again, though, the management ruled out the role of the workers. In addition, the factory used a variety of excuses to force the resignation of some activists.

Tom, the financial manager of the information technology (IT) department, was one of those subjected to revenge from the top management. The IT department was undergoing restructuring under a manager dispatched from Japan. Tom and other managerial staff who took part in the strike were removed from their posts. Because some other representatives were also forced to quit their jobs, the pressure on Tom mounted.

In April 2005, Tom once more asked his Japanese manager for rearrangement of his workload. The manager replied that a letter of guarantee should be signed in exchange for the work. Tom rejected this and argued with him. In the afternoon, Tom went to the human resources department for further negotiation. To his surprise, two policemen were waiting for him and they told him not to 'exacerbate the issue'.

Several days later, Tom was sacked. A factory-wide strike was staged to demand his reinstatement as well as a wage rise in accordance with the law. The strike lasted for four days and ended without any significant promises from the management. According to the workers, on the third day, the police began to bother the families of the organisers. It seems this was a major factor in persuading the strikers to return to work.

After the strike, the company decided to reactivate its previous production base to reduce risk in China. On the other hand, the factory announced that it would abide strictly by Chinese law. A trade union was set up. A department-based union committee election was held, but the management tried to manipulate the election by asking managers and supervisors to stand as candidates. Still, at least two rank-and-file workers outside the management list were elected in production departments. These two, however, could not withstand the pressure from management and soon resigned from their union posts. They were repeatedly scrutinised in a bid to link them with the strike leaders.

Significance of the 2004 strike

The Yong Feng strike of 1994 and the Uniden strike of 2004 were both characterised by demands for a trade union to represent the interests of workers. They both occurred in the Bao An district. In both cases, the legal minimum wage rate was implemented, at least superficially, after the strike. The leaders of the strikes were more or less forced to leave their factories. And each of the two strikes occurred amid a wider tidal wave of labour conflict. Nevertheless, there were some differences too.

First, in the Uniden case, a trade union was formed with support from the local state and ACFTU branch. When workers telephoned the city trade union branch, the latter's response was unambiguous: it *was* legal to form a trade union. In 1994, LSSB officers and the local ACFTU branch did not appear to support the establishment of a trade union in Yong Feng. In Uniden, representatives sought help from high-level trade unions and formed a twelve-member negotiating team; in Yong Feng, workers did not declare their status as strikers or temporary trade union leaders, and consequently no worker was involved in the negotiation process.

Second, while workers in Yong Feng internalised their struggle within the dormitory, Uniden workers tried their best to externalise their campaign by calling the media, attempting to block highways to gain public attention, and writing blogs and launching a web forum to inform the outside world.

Third, there was a difference in leadership. In Uniden, well-educated technical professionals joined in to lead the struggle. By contrast, the Yong Feng strike was led solely by production workers.

The strike of San Mei workers in Zhu Hai in 1993 might have been better organised than Yong Feng. However, comparing San Mei with Uniden, the key similarities and differences stand out. In the same way as we saw the progress of Yong Feng workers compared with their predecessors at San Yan in 1986, Uniden workers had advanced in terms of their organising capacity, struggle strategy and the duration and scale of the strike. This advance was related to the expansion of capitalism in China, workers' accumulation of experience, and the modification of Chinese state policy.

The power of the state and trade union

Despite this progress and advance, a common limitation underlies the workers' organisation. Even though workers in Uniden were 'successful' in forcing the management to form a trade union, that union was still manipulated by management, which was supported, or at least acceptable, to both the ACFTU and the local authority. In the Uniden case, the follow-up strike in 2005 was defeated after the police allegedly put pressure on the families of the leaders. Subsequent compliance with labour laws and establishment of a trade union were responses of the factory management to hidden state and ACFTU pressure. In fact, the ACFTU has urged giant FIEs to set up trade union branches since its 2003 Wal-Mart campaign. A worker in Uniden wrote in a blog: 'Recently the news reports widely that the Chinese government is urging Wal-Mart to set up trade unions. When workers read [the circulated email of fifteen demands], all felt faintly that something should happen in the afternoon.'

In this regard, the 'socialist' state still holds enough power to exert authoritarian social control and a 'socialist' trade union still functions as an arm of the Party state, although a softer strategy has been applied in the post-Mao era. In fact, the state kept on adjusting its labour policy and ruling strategy during the reform period under the pragmatic ideology of 'crossing the river by touching the stones'. The landscape of labour relations was therefore a reflection of dynamic relations of economic development status, management response, state intervention and workers' collective struggle strategy.

Shortage of labour

In early 2005, the State Council requested the State Council Research Office (SCRO) (*Guowuyuan Yanjiushi*) to coordinate a national project team to conduct 'comprehensive, systematic, and in-depth' research into the 'problem of peasant workers', in order to inform a policy paper on the issue (SCRO Project Team, 2006: 11). The nationwide study by central and provincial experts lasted for over ten months and laid down a foundation for the central government's guideline document, 'Some Opinions Regarding the Solution of the Problem of Peasant Workers from the State Council'. According to the study, 61 per cent of the migrant workers were between sixteen and thirty years old, 23 per cent between thirty-one and forty, and 16 per cent over forty-one. Sixty-six per cent were educated to junior middle school (nine years), but only 24 per cent had received skills training. The SCRO report concluded that 'nowadays and in the near future, the supply of labour force in our country is still more than the demand in general' (SCRO Project Team, 2006: 9). As evidence, the project team concluded that there was a huge number of surplus labourers, 150 million in rural regions, which was still escalating at a yearly rate of six million (SCRO Project Team, 2006: 94). For the project team, the trend in the long run will be 'aggregated surplus and structural shortage' (SCRO Project Team, 2006: 9). Based on this assumption, the project team suggested ten policies, in order: training and job match service; wage and employment management; occupational health and safety (OHS); social security; education of migrant children; public sanitation and family planning services; housing; farming land contracts; legal rights of migrant workers; and administration of migrant workers' household registration. As can be seen, in spite of being far reaching, the project prioritised skills training, matching service and improving wages and working conditions as the answer to the labour 'problem'.

The implication of the SCRO study for the pattern of labour conflict is twofold. First, skills are scarce and they matter. The relocation of Uniden's R&D department to China created a big range of technical employees in the factory, and these then took leading roles in the strike. Skilled workers with better market positions generally took the lead in workers' collective struggles. Second, the reported 'shortage of labour' and high turnover rate were, to some extent, reflections of workers' general discontent towards alienation, exploitation and appalling working conditions. The 'shortage of labour' and the new tidal wave of strikes are actually twin effects of an expanding and transitional stage of global capitalist production in China.

Concluding remarks

The period from 1979 to 2004 evidenced China's integration into a global capitalist economy. At the frontier of the transformation, Shenzhen experienced rapid and dramatic industrialisation, which produced and reshaped the landscape of class conflicts in the region.

In the 1980s, when the open door policy was in the experimental phase, industrial relations were placid in the city. Migrant workers, who had been members of communes or peasants in rural Guang Dong, were under the intensive management of the administration, trade unions and Party Committee. Their knowledge, experiences and subjectivity for resistance to unfair treatment and poor working conditions were very limited. The legacy of state socialism, including the land system, *Hukou* and official trade unions and the Party Committee, all took key roles in pacifying the workers.

From 1992 onwards, a new wave of urban reform was initiated, symbolising the all-round expansion of the open door policy. The PRD was subjected to competition for FDI from other parts of China as well as other developing countries, which in turn led to an intensification of exploitation in FIEs. Economy in the rural areas was declining and gave rise to a new generation, an educated 'tide of migrant workers' to the PRD.[23] As a result, workers began to stage strikes and other forms of struggle against capital. These struggles were limited by the absence of the right to free association, and hindered by state intervention in favour of capital. However, their actions were successful in influencing both state policy and management behaviour. The traditional control mechanism was not enough to settle the escalating class conflict, so the state was forced to initiate legal reform. While legality provided workers with new instruments and a strategy to defend their interests and rights, it also had limitations.

After China joined the WTO, the country's integration into the world economy entered a new phase. The expansion of capitalist production provided workers with new opportunities for jobs and rebellion. Although there was some progress through the new tidal wave of strikes from the mid-1990s, the impediments remained unchanged. The making of a new working class in China is, therefore, a tough and long process. However, the Chinese society and state seemed to transform their own logic. Various aspects of the nature and prospects of this transformation are worthy of deeper study. Concerning labour politics and labour conflict, which are the main concerns of this research, a number of key questions which could not be fully answered in this chapter await more detailed exploration:

1   How is a migrant workers' urban community formed? What is its role in workers' collective actions?
2   How is a strike organised?
3   How is workers' experience of struggle spread out and accumulated?
4   What are the characteristics of the organisers or leaders of workers' collective action?
5   What is management's strategy to combat workers' protests?

6 What is the impact of the workers' struggle on state, management and society?
7 What are the potential and limitations of the new Chinese working class to challenge global capitalism?

3 Community and shop floor culture

A prelude to workers' protest

> Kinship, neighbourhood and community have long been central, not just to the academic concerns of social scientists, but to the everyday attempts of ordinary people to understand and interpret their lives.
>
> (Benson, 2003: 117)

Introduction

This chapter is a prelude to the next chapter, which illustrates the development of labour conflict in the Sun factory. Drawing from the perspective of new labour history, which emphasises the role of community life in the formation of workers' class-consciousness alongside the workplace structure, this chapter sheds light on migrant workers' social and cultural life in one of their villages (*Mingong Cun*) and its impact on the labour process in the Sun factory. It is argued that the bases of power domination and subordination in community and workplace are reinforced by, rather than separate from, each other. The politics of locality, gender, age and skill are exploited as mechanisms of oppression, as well as being, as will be shown in the next chapter, a starting point of solidarity. This argument is complementary to both contemporary ethnography on the role of place and gender in the formation of women migrant workers' subjectivity (Lee, 1998; Sargeson, 1999; Pun, 2005c) and the function of gender, skill and place-of-origin-orientated gangs in the rise of manufacturing workers' struggles in the 1920s (Hershatter, 1986; Honig, 1986; Perry, 1993). My departure from their positions comes in the attention paid to labour market and community dynamics (Hodson, 2001).

The chapter begins with a sketch of Militant village, where the Sun factory is situated, and the attempt of Liao Lin, a worker at the factory, to run a corner shop in the village with his wife. The prevalence of gangster activities forced the couple to close the shop. The place-of-origin-based gang and workers' social life in the community will be outlined. This is followed by an introduction to the labour process and work culture in the Sun factory and how they are shaped by community social life and power relations. The construction process of industrial masculinity and its relation to skilling will be specially examined.

Factory, community and locality

The Sun factory, which produces small domestic appliances, such as coffee pots, toasters and fans, was set up in 1992 as an FIE by a Taiwanese businessman in Shenzhen. At its outset, the factory employed only twenty to thirty workers. In the late 1990s, a Taiwanese listed company, the United Group, acquired 51 per cent of the shares of the factory's holding company. The original sole investor, who kept the remaining 49 per cent of shares, acted as the general manager (GM) running the factory; United, on the other hand, contributed its global distribution and sales network to the joint venture. In this way, the factory was expanded into a giant producer with three plants. The oldest plant consisted of premises that had been rented from the local village government since the early 1990s. The second plant, which workers in Shenzhen called the 'new factory', is the company's own property and was launched in 2001. In 2004, the joint venture invested a total of US$150 million to build a new factory in Hui Zhou, a city on the eastern side of Shenzhen. Eighty per cent of the factory's products are exported to US and European markets, with Wal-Mart the biggest customer. There were 2,000, 4,000 and 5,000 workers in the old, new and Hui Zhou factories, respectively, at the time of my fieldwork. In the Shenzhen operations, 60 per cent of workers were male. They came mainly from the provinces of Gui Zhou, Si Chuan, Hu Nan, He Bei and He Nan, with those from Si Chuan and Chong Qing[1] the biggest group.

The production, social life and informal networks in a migrant workers' village (*Mingong Cun*) have been well outlined by Zhang (2001), who revealed that the Zhe Jiang village, one of the best-known migrant workers' villages in Beijing, was a result of negotiation and interaction between local authority officers and place-of-origin-based social elitists, who were employers, and the agency of the migrant workers in the urban villages. The village was finally shut down under the state's policy to maintain a tidy capital city and proper social control, implying the vulnerability of the migrants' temporary settlements in cities without urban citizenship. Within these villages, power relations were based on social relations and informal networks originating from their original home counties. As we saw in Chapter 2, Xie (1997) studied Zhe Jiang in Guang Zhou and found that the village had its own internal organisation and problem-solving mechanisms.

As a major migrant metropolitan city which rose after 1979, Shenzhen is second to none in the size and proportion of its migrant population as well as the phenomenon of *Mingong Cun*. At the end of 2005, out of its 8,277,500 total population, 6,458,200 were temporary settlers, mostly migrant workers (Shenzhen Municipal Statistics Bureau, 2006). As most of the factories in the city were built within or near a residential area, workers lived in either dormitories provided by the factories or in private houses in nearby communities. According to a survey in the PRD in 2006,[2] 60 per cent of the employed migrant workers lived in collective dormitories or workplaces, 35 per cent in private houses rented from local citizens, and only 5 per cent with family, relatives and in self-owned houses. Kinship and place-of-origin networks prevailed in both dormitories (Smith and Pun, 2006) and villages. Police statistics revealed that there were 290 villages of more than 1,000 temporary migrants in Shenzhen, which were termed *Cheng*

Zhong Cun (village within a city) or *Mingong Cun*, while two million migrants (in 643 groups) lived as '*Tongxiang Cun*' (the same place-of-origin village) (*Southern Metropolitan Daily*, 16 November 2005).

With a territory of 9.8 square kilometres, the community that I call Militant village is one of the biggest *Mingong Cun* in Shenzhen. Official data in 2002 showed that more than 50,000 temporary residents settled in the 4,500 letting flats in the village, with 180 registered enterprises and 2,200 permanent residents. According to the community Party secretary, the residents originally from the provinces of Si Chuan, Gui Zhou and Hu Nan accounted for the majority of the migrant occupants (*Southern Metropolitan Daily*, 16 November 2005).[3]

Production capacity expansion of the existing factories and new investment since the turn of the century had drawn a huge number of migrant workers into the village. Workers told me that the area I lived in was a new development, built since 2003. About 100 multi-storey blocks had been built in an area of less than 0.25 square kilometres.[4] Each building was composed of dozens of small flats or rooms. The rent for our fifteen square metres *en suite* with one bedroom and one lounge was 220 yuan per month. I shared the flat with Xiao Lin, a veteran Sun factory worker. Our neighbours were two couples. One bed was installed in the bedroom and the other in the small lounge.

A young couple's journey in the community

While Marx tended to explain proletarian class-consciousness by common production positions and workplace experience, labour historians have stressed the role of the working-class community behind workers' militancy and solidarity (Dawley, 1976; Richards, 1996; Benson, 2003). As Hayter and Harvey (1993) put it, relocation of industrial capital caused the deconstruction and reconstruction of workers' communities around the world. However, in China, the formation of an urban community was more problematic. For millions of young rural migrants, the struggle to live in the urban area was driven by the material aspiration to improve living conditions and a cultural desire to escape the social stigma attached to being a rural villager (Tam, 1992; Pun, 2005c). Their dream of modernity was, however, brutally impeded, if not virtually shattered, by the rural–urban segregation under the *Hukou* system.

The story of Xiao Lin and his wife, Xiao Ying, was just one example of the new generation's hopes and frustrations in the struggle to sustain family life in the modern city.

Xiao Lin's family

Xiao Lin was a twenty-four-year-old male worker from Gui Zhou province who had grown up in an impoverished family. As farming was not sufficient to support his five-member family, his father set off to the province of Zhe Jiang in eastern China to work in the construction sector as early as 1993, leaving Xiao Lin's older sister, younger brother, stepmother and Xiao Lin himself at home. He had helped his parents' agricultural work since he was in primary three grade. Xiao Lin well remembered undertaking a long walk along a mountainous, slippery pathway to a cigarette factory carrying sixty kilogrammes of tobacco on his back when he was in secondary school. As soon as he graduated from junior secondary school, he followed his father to Zhe Jiang and worked in small factories. Two years later, his parents asked him to return home to marry Xiao Ying.

Just before XiaoYing gave birth to a boy in the middle of 2003, Xiao Lin left his wife and followed one of his *Laoxiang* (people from the same place of origin) to Shenzhen. Two years on, Ying still could not forgive her husband for leaving her alone to give birth to their child. While Xiao Lin and his siblings had all come out to *Dagong* (sell labour power to a boss), his fifty-year-old father had returned home to run a small business. He bought a vehicle to deliver vegetables from town and sell them in their village. He also planted his own vegetables to provide a supplementary supply. By then, the family's finances were much improved. By living frugally, his parents could save 500 yuan per month and help raise their grandson. Xiao Lin had stayed in Militant village since arriving in Shenzhen.

Xiao Lin's pride

Xiao Lin had first worked as a temporary worker in a small toy factory with eighty workers for three months. By working thirteen to fourteen hours a day, seven days a week, he earned 800 yuan per month. However, after the peak season, he was dismissed without any compensation. Then he found a job in a small plastics factory with only twenty-six workers where he was paid twenty yuan per day. As the pay was too low, he resigned. However, the mainland Chinese boss refused his resignation 'application' and withheld his salary, so Xiao Lin was forced to stay on. Before long, the boss planned to relocate his factory to an outer industrial zone with lower rent. After a trip to the new site, Xiao Lin and his workmates found that the new factory, which was near the airport, was horribly noisy. As lack of sleep would affect their daytime performance, they refused to move, then filed a collective complaint with the district LSSB, and finally forced the boss to settle their wage arrears in full.

Xiao Lin was very enthusiastic to share this experience with me. In recalling the story, he emphasised the role of one of his female workmates. One day, the young woman, from Guang Xi, was weeping in the dormitory after a severe reprimand from the boss over her repeated requests to resign. Xiao Lin and two young men from Guang Xi and Hu Nan were motivated by the young woman's plight and joined her to discuss the possibility of regaining their salaries. Complaining to the LSSB might be a good strategy, but none of them knew how to write a letter of complaint. The young woman then asked her friend, who was working in another factory, to send her a sample letter. Thirteen workers from the factory then signed their own version of it. Six of them, including the four letter-drafters, submitted the complaint to the LSSB the following day. Officials in the LSSB issued a notice and asked them to hand it to the factory. At night, the wife of the boss came to the dormitory to inform them that their boss would negotiate with them the next morning at nine o'clock. A preparatory meeting was then held among the thirteen signatories. Disputes arose. Most of them were excited and believed that their boss had given in, so it was a good chance to negotiate with him. Three female workers, however, were scared of retaliation from the boss's family and wanted to give up the complaint.

The Guang Xi worker insisted that the negotiation should be held in the LSSB rather than the factory: 'What bullshit the negotiation is! Whenever [we] resigned from him, he said OK. I have resigned many times, but still not successfully. Let's go directly to the labour bureau. Don't delay any more, the factory will move very soon, next week.'

'She also encouraged us, "It is still worth a try, [even if we are] pottery pots crashing with an iron pot,"' Xiao Lin recalled.

The young woman's determination again impressed her workmates, who agreed to wait for the boss only until 8.30 a.m., rather than his specified 9 a.m., before setting off for the labour bureau. From this critical moment onward, a sense of justice and confidence drove Xiao Lin to act as one of the negotiators with the boss. He told himself: 'The factory must be a "black factory", without legal registration, otherwise the boss would not be so scared. We, the stirrers outside (*Zai Waimian Hunde*), must get back our money. There is no point in letting him keep it!' By this time, Xiao Lin had developed a connection with some 'big brothers' from his home province, although he declared that he never formally joined their gang.

The next day, the workers left their dormitory on time at 8.30 a.m. and arrived at the LSSB at 9.50 a.m. As officials would not allow all thirteen workers to enter the office, they chose Xiao Lin and a young man from Guang Xi to be their representatives. A written agreement was then signed between the representatives and the boss, and stamped by the LSSB for verification: 'As XX factory will move to YY town, workers who are willing to move to the new factory will be properly settled; others will be paid their wages.' Xiao Lin and his mates were thrilled. To celebrate their victory, they did not return to work, instead spending the day together. However, with no money in their pockets, they had to entertain themselves by wandering the streets and climbing a hill in a park.

The next day, the boss called the two representatives into his office and told them that, according to the rules of the factory, absence from work would lead to the deduction of three days' wages. As the thirteen had been absent for three days by that stage, nine days' wages would be deducted from each of them. Xiao Lin recalled:

> I told him, 'If you do so and only give us back twenty yuan, we will use the twenty yuan to take a bus to the labour bureau.' The boss was mad at me: 'F**k!' I turned my eyes to a fruit knife on the table. If he humiliated me again, I would fight with him. But I thought he should be scared of me. 'Insult me again?' I said. He replied: 'Who has insulted you?'

The boss continued to withhold the workers' wages until the day before the factory was moved. A supervisor called in the workers one by one to collect their wages, leaving Xiao Lin to the end. He was annoyed to find that the supervisor deliberately put the three days' absence on his time card and intended to deduct the claimed nine days' wages from him alone. Obviously this was revenge for his row with the boss. Workmates calmed him down and persuaded him to talk with the supervisor peacefully. He made a gesture that he was ready to fight with the supervisor who then gave him his full wage.

During the days we lived together, this incident was mentioned repeatedly in detail. You could see the smile on his face and the pride in his eyes whenever Xiao Lin talked about it.

After leaving the factory, Xiao Lin joined the Sun factory in July 2003. He never considered moving out of Militant village, where he enjoyed cheap rent, food, entertainment and numerous *Laoxiang* and peers. On our walk to a shopping mall five minutes from home, he would stop to talk with four or five mates. Before he moved to stay with me, Xiao Lin and his wife, Xiao Ying, lived in a building in which almost all of the thirty rooms had been occupied by people from his original village and surroundings.

Xiao Ying's dream

When their son was two years old, like many married women in the country, Xiao Ying left her parents-in-law to take care of the child and joined Xiao Lin in Militant village in 2005. She found a job in a Taiwanese electronics factory next to the Sun factory. Unlike the Sun factory, which preferred males for heavy work, Xiao Ying's factory was a more typical electronics factory, where 90 per cent of the workers were young women.

She earned as much as 1,800 yuan per month, a satisfactory income as it meant she could save some money to support her parents. Yet, she complained of exhaustion and hated the drudgery of working in the factory. Also, as workers had to touch toxic chemicals in some of the work procedures, the couple were very worried that it would be harmful to her health in the long term. Xiao Ying quit her job in April 2006 and took over a small corner shop from a local businessman with a transfer fee of 2,000 yuan. The rent for the shop and an attic to be used as the couple's bedroom was 500 yuan per month.

It was around this time that I moved into Militant village. Xiao Lin moved in with me because the attic very small and Xiao Ying's younger brother (who was involved in the local gang as a 'little brother') lived there with them. Xiao Lin was worried that I would be a target for robbery or something similar if I lived with the family above the shop.

There were more than ten corner shops in my local neighbourhood. None of them had any registration or permission to trade from the local government, so the shopkeepers did not pay any fees or taxes. Although selling items such as wine, soft drinks, cigarettes and cooking sauces could generate a little profit, their main income came from service fees for hosting *Majiang*, a traditional Chinese game for four players. Players had to pay twenty yuan for each *Majiang* table.

In the first week, Xiao Ying found that her profits were higher than she had expected. The service fees from the *Majiang* tables was as high as 100 yuan each day. 'People usually get only 100 yuan or a little bit more and run out [of money] very soon. Then others will come to gamble. It is quite easy to earn their money,' Xiao Ying told me happily. Xiao Lin explained the initial 'success' of their business was through his good interpersonal relations in the village. Benefiting from his long time in the community, he was well known among many *Laoxiang*, workmates and neighbours. Their shop became a meeting point for a network of his *Laoxiang* and friends.

As time went on, however, the couple encountered two main difficulties, which finally forced them to close the shop in August 2006. On the tenth day after taking over the shop, some gangsters came to ask who was now running the business and hinted that a 'protection fee' was necessary. They were followed by another group a couple of days later. Xiao Lin sought protection from one of his influential (*You Shili*) *Laoxiang* in the community. This entailed treating his *Laoxiang* to dinners and offering gifts from time to time to maintain a rapport. According to Xiao Lin:

> Those stirrers (*Chulai Hun De Ren*) will see you as a good man and help you if you get along well (*Wan De Hao*) and have meals with them from time to time. They don't need to eat so expensively; the food they eat back home is quite enough. Then, when you need them, you give them a ring and they will ask people to come over. They are also well acquainted with 'big brothers' from other provinces, for example Si Chuan. If people from Si Chuan make trouble for you and you seek his help, he can tell the 'big brother' from Si Chuan that this person is one of us (*Ziji Ren*), please don't bother him. Or, if you don't like one person (*Kan Yigeren Bushunyan*), he can ask those Si Chuan guys to 'do business' – extort him. If you don't buy him meals, no way, he won't help you at all.

Xiao Lin informed his *Laoxiang* about the gangsters. The *Laoxiang* asked about the original background of the groups who came to their shop, but Xiao Lin could not give an exact answer. The shop was robbed twice the next week. One Monday morning, the burglars rushed into the shop, held up one of their relatives, who was keeping an eye on the shop, and escaped with 500 yuan in cash. Xiao Lin then stayed overnight with Xiao Ying in the shop for security. However, two nights later, thieves cut the iron guard on the window, raided the shop and stole almost all of the couple's valuable personal belongings.

These attacks were obviously related to the couple ignoring the gangsters' demands for a protection fee. But Xiao Lin did not give up. He immediately asked his 'influential' *Laoxiang* to sit in the shop from time to time. After the appearance of this *Laoxiang*, the gangsters did not reappear. However, another problem arose.

The *Laoxiang* belonged to the Gui Zhou gang who smuggled drugs (*Baifen*) in the village. His job was to recruit 'little brothers' (*Xiaodi*) or followers (*Mazai*) to distribute the drugs for the gang. He had repeatedly invited Xiao Lin to join his gang and promised to pay him 2,400 yuan per month. Xiao Lin knew that involvement with drugs was a serious crime, so his strategy was to keep a certain distance from this kind of activity while maintaining a personal rapport with the *Laoxiang*. By contrast, Xiao Ying's younger brother seemed vulnerable to the temptation of such a highly paid job, even though drug traffickers faced the death penalty if caught.

To avoid any more trouble, Xiao Ying and Xiao Lin closed the shop in August 2006. As Xiao Ying did not want to return to the factory, she went back to the countryside. Xiao Lin also left the community in frustration.

The gangster network, which was very influential in Militant village, had a dual effect on these migrant workers' lives. Benefiting from an active gangster network originating in their home county and their social relations with 'influential' people in the gang, Xiao Lin and Xiao Ying gained protection. But harassment from the gang and its criminal nature eventually forced them to close a shop which initially had seemed so promising and profitable. Xiao Ying's dream was shattered, but Xiao Lin's continued. He said that he would not return home unless there was 'no way to go' (*Beipo Wulu*) in the city.

Xiao Lin, Xiao Ying and her young brother also all resigned from the local factory, not because their wages were too low, but because of the boredom, alienation and inhumanity of factory work. As Xiao Lin often told me, they did not expect to earn much money by running a small corner shop. Rather, they took that path to regain freedom and humanity by taking control over their working bodies and labour process. The history of capitalism is also a history of resistance to capitalism (Holloway, 2002).

To what extent can Chinese workers break away from the process of proletarianisation? There are some hints in this family's story. Xiao Ying's younger brother's turn to violence, gang allegiance and crime in rebellion against factory life was typical of what has happened in other industrialised societies, especially immigrant countries like the US (Padilla, 1992). Xiao Ying's return to her parents-in-law and son suggested the uniqueness of Chinese industrialisation, which separates the reproduction and production of labour power (Pun and Ren, forthcoming). However, when I visited Xiao Lin in January 2008, Xiao Ying had returned to work in her old electronics factory and Xiao Lin had moved back to Militant village. Xiao Lin was determined to live in a city, and he was lucky to find one of the very few jobs in a labour NGO.

Locality, gangsters and the informal economy

As Ostercher's (1986) study of US workers suggested, in an immigrant society workers are highly divided by age, skill and place of origin. Most significantly, place-of-origin-based gang networks played a pivotal role in the labour market and community life in the early twentieth-century United States (e.g. Thrasher, 1927; Padilla, 1992). In the context of China, Perry (1993: 245), in her seminal study of strikes in 1920s Shanghai, indicated a similar phenomenon: 'Denied the security or status of the skilled worker, such individuals often resorted to gang networks in search of protection. Gangs helped rural immigrants make the difficult transition to urban life.' The resemblance of China to the US in the early stage of industrialisation is a result of similar recruitment patterns that rely on migrant workers (Perry, 1993). In contemporary China, Xiao Lin and Xiao Ying's story reminds us that gangsters continue to play a significant role in workers' social and working lives. Militant village was an active gangster community in Shenzhen. The comparatively cheap rent in the village was at least partially due to its notoriety for criminals and disastrous social order. There were at least ten homicides between 1993 and 1995 in the village.

Robbery and the Gui Zhou gang

Local newspapers reported that a network of unemployed workers from a village in BJ, a county of Gui Zhou, depended on robbery for their livings:

> People are robbed almost every day. . . . They [the criminals from BJ county] will not think about what they will do tomorrow . . . just simply rob as soon as they run out of money. . . . After they get a mobile, they will sell it for several hundred yuan, and then go to a cinema or an internet bar for entertainment, until the money runs out again.
>
> (*Southern Metropolitan Daily*, 16 November 2005)

Yet my experience suggested that such criminal activities were not unorganised and unplanned. I was robbed by a group of gangsters. Four teenagers pushed me into a construction site when I was walking in the street late at night. All my possessions were taken: glasses, money and mobile phone. I noticed that a taxi was waiting close by while the teenagers searched me. As soon as they had finished, they asked me to turn around and then got in the taxi.

Why did gang activities thrive in this community? An informant from BJ who had committed robbery himself explained it to me:

> Many big factories are clustered in this community. The wages in these factories are comparatively high. Workers usually introduce *Laoxiang* to work in the village. However, after their *Laoxiang* came, it was not guaranteed that they would get a job. Those who are unable to get a job have nowhere to live. As soon as their money is spent and some gangsters contact them, it is natural for them to join their activities. Of course, you can also look for jobs in small factories, of which there are quite a lot in the surrounding area. But working conditions there [in the small factories] are pitiful and wages are much lower. Generally speaking, those who come out [from a home village] for the first time are more obedient. They do not easily join [the gang]. But those who have been out for a long time and are more rebellious are more likely to join.

He also defended his past crimes: 'You have never experienced having no money and being hungry. If you had had that experience, you would understand. For three consecutive days, we [three *Laoxiang*] could eat only watermelons stolen from the farm land. It is impossible for anyone to be very full, but I had nothing else to eat.'

He stopped robbing after being arrested by the police and subjected to torture in prison. Afterwards, he worked in several factories, the last of which being the Sun factory. After he left the Sun, he vowed never to join another factory. 'It is too hard and boring to work in a factory,' he told me. He acted as a fence for several months. Through the gangster network of his *Laoxiang*, he bought TV sets and mobile phones from burglars and muggers and sold them for big profits: 'I could buy a TV set for 350 yuan and sell it for 500 yuan while the market price is 800. I lied to the buyers that it was acquired through my *Laoxiang*'s *Guanxi* (connections) in the factory.'

He introduced me to one of his *Laoxiang* from BJ, who had also worked in the Sun factory for several years and had then joined a small electronics factory run by a local mainland owner in 2005. His salary in the small factory was only 700 to 800 yuan, but his main income came from robberies and extortion of his 'littler brothers' at night.

The number of residents, in general, and gangsters, in particular, from Gui Zhou has declined in recent years due to the government's campaign against the Gui Zhou gang's drug smuggling and robbery. This paved the way for the hegemony of the Si Chuan clique in Militant village.

Protection fees and the Si Chuan gang

While the Gui Zhou gang was notorious for robbery and drug smuggling, its Si Chuan counterpart was well known for collecting protection fees from businesses and individuals. Xiao Ying's shop was allegedly threatened by the Si Chuan gang, and many Guang Dong-born businessmen complained that the Si Chuan gang had demanded protection fees from them before they formed their own protection network.

I recognised many shopkeepers who originally came from my home county by their accent, and struck up conversations with them. They reminded me to be careful of 'outside provincial' gangsters (from other provinces), especially the Si Chuan gang.

Laoxiang: You are not working here, then why do you come to live here? It is a very dangerous place, you know, it is an 'outside provincials' nest'. They are very rude. But fortunately, we also have many people here. Some years ago, some 'little outside provincials' attempted to extort money from us and it was almost impossible to do business here. In several cases, we beat them without mercy. We had to do that so they would not bully us again. You know, we, the LF [county] people, are not to be bullied.

Author: How did they extort money from you?

Laoxiang: By collecting protection fees.

Author: How much did they want?

Laoxiang: It varied, from hundreds to thousands of yuan. If one group suc-
             cessfully got it, another group would come too. It was impossible to do
             business if we did not fight back. Now, if one of our people has an
             incident, others will come in a minute [to help]. No one dares to bully
             us now.

Author: Which is the most powerful group of outside provincials?

Laoxiang: Those from Si Chuan. They have the most people, and are also the
             most violent.

During the period I lived in the village, at least one 'big brother' from Si Chuan
was killed in the street by a group of gangsters supposedly from another community. Workers told me that he had provided protection to a skating rink and
nearby businesses. After his death, a temporary shrine was set up beside the
skating rink to make his 'little brothers' show tribute.

The workers offered three reasons for the prevalence of the Si Chuan faction.
First, the largest number of migrants in the village and probably in the city was
from Si Chuan province and Chong Qing municipality.[5] Second, they were united.
A worker from Hu Nan told me that he preferred to have friends from Si Chuan:
'Si Chuan guys are doing well (*Hun De Hao*) because they are more united. We
need to learn from them.' Third, they came out to *Dagong* first. The outflow of
the first generation of Si Chuan workers can be traced back to the mid-1980s.
Some of them gained technical or managerial skills in that earlier period and were
then promoted to higher positions in the factories.

Like those from BJ in Gui Zhou province, migrants originally from the city of
NY in Si Chuan formed extremely united, violent and militant groups. One
interviewee from NY told me:

Our city had been an industrial one. From when I was in secondary school
[mid-1990s], factories began to close down, and lots of workers lost their
jobs. The society was polarised. The corrupt officials became more and more
affluent, while the poor people got poorer. Then the social order became
terrible around 2000. There were acute gangster activities. In our town,
the head of the police station unashamedly stated that he had connections with
both the 'black' and the 'white' sides. He had no alternative, he said: he
had to protect his family. His son at primary school had the services of a
bodyguard. The clique of shoulder-pole (*Biandan*) bearers, which was active
in the city of Chong Qing, originated from our city. . . . Today, the economy
of our city is flourishing, the rich officials have huge purchasing power,
and the outgoing peasant workers send back billions of yuan every year to our
local economy as well.

Small business and the 'local' gang

Migrant workers rarely had the opportunity to meet with original local residents in Militant village. According to a locally born university student, he and his friends steered clear of the migrant workers. They had all been taught by their parents from childhood not to contact the strangers because 'outside is unrest'. Most of the indigenous locals worked in local state institutions or relied solely on rental income for a living. For instance, the director of the community government was said to have rental income of millions of yuan per year. He owned most of the street shop properties in the village. Many other locals, with lesser rental income, were employed by the police to keep up-to-date records of temporary residents in the community.

However, when the migrant workers talked of 'locals' (*Bendi Ren*), they meant more than the indigenous people who had lived on the land before urbanisation. Also included in this description were the new migrants from other parts of Guang Dong province. The 'locals' ran businesses, from small stalls in the street to huge, modern shopping arcades. Workers kept a certain distance from this group of people because they were ferocious. One interviewee told me that 300 'brothers' were mobilised by a 'local big brother', who controlled the collection of industrial waste in the village, against another place-of-origin group in order to take over their business. Further investigation showed that the 'locals' were in fact intra-provincial migrants from eastern Guang Dong, especially from LF county.

As Honig (1993) revealed, the tradition that migrants from one place found jobs in the same occupation still holds in contemporary China. Although a few petty businessmen had worked in factories for a period of time, generally people from LF, who are notoriously militant, preferred to run small-scale businesses, operate in the black economy or even engage in smuggling rather than seek employment in factories. Many of the storekeepers and street hawkers from LF in Militant village had rented farming land for years from local villagers to plant vegetables. After the estate development project was initiated on the farming land, they stayed on in the community to run small-scale businesses or bought a small piece of land from the local government or villagers to build houses for letting. The flourishing economy of the community continued to attract people from their towns and villages to join their businesses.

A hawker from LF county asked me: 'Are you *Dagong* or do you run a business?'

'*Dagong*.'

'*Dagong* [with surprise]? How come you don't do business? It is not difficult to earn a living here. Almost all of us people doing business here are from LF.'

The hawker seemed quite satisfied with the situation in the village. He operated a mobile fruit stall in front of a big shopping mall, which itself was run by someone from LF. His daughter, aged twelve, helped him.

Structure and relations in a gang

Besides the Gui Zhou, Si Chuan and 'local' networks, other provincials, such as those from Hu Bei, Hu Nan and He Nan, also formed their own cliques. The structures of those cliques were homogeneous, although their main income sources and activities were heterogeneous.

Normally a gang had a 'biggest brother' (*Laoda*) or boss, who had a decent status and source of income in the village. He was the bridge between those under his umbrella and the outside world. The Si Chuan boss ran a market; the Gui Zhou boss engaged in smuggling; the 'local' boss was a very rich man who owned many houses and controlled the industrial waste business; the Hu Bei boss worked in a police station; the He Nan boss was the chief security guard in one of the biggest factories in the village.

The 'biggest brother' had a number of 'big brothers' below him in a strict hierarchy. The higher the position, the more power and respect the 'big brother' enjoyed. The distribution of the ranking position was according to his 'face' (*Mianzi*), status and social relations in the society. The 'big brothers' declared loyalty to each other in a ritual and thereafter it was very hard for them to withdraw from the group. One of the workers who had quit a gang told me that he had to join the army in order to convince his 'big brothers' to allow him to leave.

Each 'big brother' had a number of 'little brothers' (*Xiaodi*) or followers (*Mazai*). This relationship was not as strict and rigid as that between the boss and his 'big brothers'. 'Big brothers' with a high ranking position normally hailed from the same place of origin, but 'little brothers' came from a variety of places of origin, and they could be male or female, although males from the same place of origin were dominant in the groups. 'Little brothers' were sometimes unemployed and their lives depended on the 'big brothers'. In the morning, when day-shift workers were working hard in factories and night-shift workers were sleeping, many teenagers wandered the streets or played snooker in the corner shops. Young men far outnumbered young women. One interviewee told me:

> These 'little brothers' have free dinners in specific restaurants which are paid for by their 'big brothers' on a monthly basis. As soon as their 'big brother' calls, they should show up immediately to [do something like] fight with another group or kidnap somebody. If they run out of money, boys rob and girls are persuaded to become prostitutes. The 'harvest' is confiscated and redistributed. Say a group got several hundred thousand yuan through a kidnapping, each 'little brother' who participated would get only a few thousand yuan, with their 'big brothers' keeping the remainder. The 'big brothers' normally only show up for very big deals. But if a 'little brother' is arrested, his 'big brother' will bail him out; if a 'little brother' is in conflict with another, their 'big brother' will call the other 'little brothers' to help.

There was more than one group of gangsters from each province. Si Chuan, for instance, had at least three well-known bosses in the village, each of whom led a clique. Most of the workers were not formal members of the gang but many, like Xiao Lin, were loosely attached to a 'big brother' to gain protection through friendship. Such friendships were maintained both materially and culturally. Treating a 'big brother' to dinner and then relaxing with him was a very common way to sustain the relationship.

Workers' social lives: Laoxiang network and peer group

The place-of-origin network

The clustering of social life around the network of *Laoxiang* was obvious. Xiao Lin and his mates from Gui Zhou, for example, gathered together at the home of one of their *Laoxiang* to cook good food almost every weekend. 'It is *Jiacai* [home cooking].[6] When we were at home, we ate four meals per day, as farming work is very hard. There, during weekdays, we ate very casually. It was a good chance for us to relax and use our home dialect,' Xiao Lin explained.

In Xiao Ying's corner shop, most *Majiang* players were male workers in their late twenties to early thirties who knew the couple well. Some women came but usually as observers to support their husbands or just for a chat with Xiao Ying. Workers sometimes came in groups, and sometimes as individuals looking for suitable game partners. People of Gui Zhou origin were dominant, but there were also peer groups made up of colleagues from the same factory and friends who knew each other through social events.

Language, food preference and living habits of each province or intra-provincial region explained why workers lived in place-of-origin clusters. Not every worker can speak standard Mandarin well, even though many had lived in Shenzhen for years. When *Laoxiang* spoke their own dialects with each other, they described others in specific terms, which reflected a sense of exclusion. People from LF county labelled all of those from other provinces as *Waisheng Zai* (little outside-provincials). When workers from one province talked with each other, they described workers from other provinces as *Waisheng Ren* (outside-provincials) and Guang Dong people as *Bendi Ren* (locals). The Hu Nan people played a version of poker which was not understood by those from other provinces. In He Nan, the host should give a guest a full cup of tea to show hospitality; in Gui Zhou, if the teacup is full it is a sign that the guest is no longer welcome. Such regional differences seemed to be barriers to inter-provincial connections among workers.

However, place of origin was not the only base within many intra-provincial groups. Age, gender and position in production which reflected workers' experience and skills were also essential factors in social life. When men had collective dinners together, usually they would not bring their wives or girlfriends. Men in their early thirties found it hard to develop a rapport (in the workers' own language have fun – *Wan De Hao*) with a worker of eighteen or over forty, even though they knew each other. The above-mentioned group of Gui Zhou workers who had regular dinners together comprised a network of current or previous male workmates in one department of the Sun factory and their previous schoolmates.

Cross-provincial peer groups

Moreover, not all of the workers limited their social life to the circle of their place of origin. There were lots of peer groups or networks among workers in which place of origin was not a crucial factor. Groups could be formed primarily on the basis of age, gender, position in production, economic status or consumption practice. Two such groups will be used as examples for comparison and discussion.

The first comprised four young male workers between the ages of nineteen and twenty-one. These four men came from Chong Qing, Hu Bei, Jiang Xi and Hu Nan. They worked in different factories, but their salaries were roughly equal – about 800 to 900 yuan. They met in hospital when they were being treated for industrial injuries. They all missed their lives in Militant village and complained about the boring nature of the town centre, where the hospital was located. They were allowed to leave the hospital, but they could not afford to do anything in the relatively expensive town centre. After they were discharged, they started to spend time together in the village. They went to the skating rink, internet bar and cinema. Here the prices were cheap: one yuan for a karaoke song, two yuan for surfing the internet or skating, and three yuan for a movie. All of these entertainments were very tempting for a group of rural-born teenagers.

The second group comprised three skilled workers from the Sun factory: a repair technician in the metal department, aged thirty-three from Si Chuan, who was earning 1,500 to 1,600 yuan; a truck driver, aged thirty-one from Guang Dong, with a 3,000-yuan income; and a fork-lift truck driver in the warehouse, aged twenty-five from Hu Nan, who earned 1,800 yuan. All three of these men therefore earned higher-than-average salaries. They ate out in restaurants, rather than at food stalls, and spent their leisure time in the hair salon, massage shop, skating rink or disco. Each driver rented a single room from a private landlord, while the technician lived in a factory dormitory but frequently stayed overnight with one of the others. After a night out with the three men, Xiao Liu, the fork-lift truck driver, invited me to stay in his flat and chatted with me overnight. I asked how the three men had become friends. Xiao Liu told me:

> Over a period of time, we often saw each other at the skating rink. Then we began to say hello one night, and arranged to wait for each other the next night at the factory entrance before going skating together. When we were skating the next night, we met a group of seven to eight. One of them stared at us. We asked him what he was looking at. They responded by inviting us to fight outside. I called my friends to support us. When they arrived by motorbike, the group ran away immediately. One of them, from Guang Xi, was grabbed by our group and brutally beaten. On the third day, we went to the rink again, but with more friends. I crashed into a girl and picked her up, but her

boyfriend insisted that I should apologise. I did not agree. Then we battled. We had more people than them and they called others for help. But after the men came, I found that I knew some of them. As [they] were 'our people' (*Ziji Ren*), we did not fight any more. From then onwards, the local boss of the rink knew us well, and we did not have to pay the entrance fee again.

After our chat, they also got me into the rink for free. As Cockburn (1983: 138) pointed out: 'Male solidarity is not only a way of excluding women, it is a way of assuring a more secure presence within the dangerous world of other men.' The three friends shared a catchphrase: 'We never mind other people's business, but if other people make trouble for us, we should not be afraid, we must fight back.'

Gender, sexuality and masculinity

Male workers were more represented than female workers in most of the entertainment sites, from internet bar, cinema, snooker halls, restaurants, skating rink, dance hall and *Majiang* shops to the hair salon and massage shop. Women workers, on the other hand, spent their time in free or cheaper activities as well as at home. Window shopping in the streets or shopping mall was a typical way for the women to spend their leisure time. Department stores installed big screen TVs in their windows to attract customers. Sometimes, usually at weekends, they also sponsored a show or a singing competition. From time to time, the circus came to give a performance in the plaza outside the mall. All of these free events entertained hundreds of workers, especially the young women, who stood hand in hand and laughed together. In rural villages or small towns in China, it is only at New Year or other traditional festivals that people can enjoy such performances.

Sexual activity was generally very casual in the village. I heard many stories from the male workers of having more than one girlfriend or extra-marital affairs. And when I visited the subsidiary plant in Hui Zhou, one young woman worker told me that the workers in the Shenzhen factory, both male and female, were very open. They engaged in casual sexual relations to alleviate the boredom of routine and hard work. I rode in a factory truck to Hui Zhou with a male machine technician and a female worker. Both were in their mid-thirties. It was the first time they had met each other, but they talked about sex for the whole journey. After the woman got off the truck, the man said: 'If you talk about sex with a woman, and she responds, then you have a chance. If she does not want to talk, there is no way.' Private leasing rooms provided spaces for the workers to escape the rigid control over their private lives that was enforced in the factory-provided dormitories. In the Sun factory, male workers lived in the dormitories of the new plant, while women slept in the old plant. Visits between the dormitory buildings were strictly forbidden, as was any sexual activity in the dormitories.

Pollert's (1981) study of a British tobacco factory found that women often responded to looser disciplinary control by flirting with their male colleagues. Yet, when women in Militant village tried to play this game, trouble often ensued. Some of the men's 'flirting' was actually closer to sexual harassment. And while the men's engagement in casual sexual relations was basically for pleasure, the women were sometimes economically pushed into such behaviour. One male worker told me that a young woman who had lost her job came to him in a 'black' (unregistered) internet bar and asked him for help in topping up her internet card. He topped up fifty yuan for her and as a reward she agreed to spend the night with him.

One evening, a girl dancing in a disco handed a paper bird to one of my friends and they began to chat. The girl said that she had a boyfriend, but he was unemployed, which my friend took to mean that the girl was looking for a richer partner.

It was very common for men to refuse to use a condom. One worker said: 'Girlfriends are my private cars, not [public] buses. Only I can get on. So I don't need to use [a condom].' Consequently, many abortions are performed in private clinics, and sexual diseases are rife. A six-day treatment for venereal disease can cost more than 600 yuan.

The difference between the male and female workers' social lives was due primarily to the cultural construction of gender roles for men and women in the family, industry and society.

First, they had different consumption power which was determined largely, if not wholly, by the gender division of labour in industry. The skilled and managerial positions were all dominated by men.

Second, the gang, whose activities had a great influence on the workers' social lives in the community, was highly patriarchal. No woman could become a 'big brother'. While the male workers who did not want to work in a factory committed robberies to pay for sex, women in the same situation were forced to sell their bodies.

Third, the consumption pattern was male-centred. The massage shop, hair salon and other underground locations provided sexual services for men at prices that were affordable for skilled workers.

Fourth, the commercial interests reinforced the masculine culture of objectivising women. To promote their businesses, some private hospitals and clinics distributed complimentary magazines for workers which advertised their services and published pornographic articles and pictures.

Fifth, the division of labour within the family created more space for the men to indulge in casual relations. One worker told me about the advice given to him by his wife, who had worked in Shenzhen for ten years but had then returned home to raise their children. Jokingly, she had said that if he had affairs, he should choose married women, rather than young girls who would ruin their marriage.

The subordination of women in workers' social lives and the subordination of women in the workplace reinforced each other through the construction of an industrial masculinity. The other side of the pride, militancy and violence of male skilled and supervisory workers in Militant village was the obsession, timidity and quiescence of ordinary female workers. As we will see, masculinity, alongside place-of-origin politics, exerted effects on labour relations in the Sun factory. On the one hand, it helped pacify the discontent of a large number of ordinary workers; on the other, it created a culture of militancy and solidarity against the management in the interest of general workers at critical moments.

Politics of gender and place in the labour process

Taiwanese management team

The GM of Sun was the factory's fifty-year-old founder, who held 49 per cent of the shares after selling 51 per cent to United. He spent two or three days in the factory each week, leaving four deputy GMs to manage the day-to-day operation of the business. Below the deputy GMs there were a number of assistant GMs who each oversaw two production or administration departments. Then a departmental manager was responsible for the administration of each department. All of the managers, from GM to departmental managers, were from Taiwan, until four mainland Chinese department superintendents were promoted to assistant GM status in 2005.

The GM and his family lived in a luxury house in the central district of Shenzhen. All of the other forty-plus Taiwanese managers lived in purpose-built apartments within the new factory estate with a canteen specially servicing them. Local employed managers, even though they were in the same positions as the Taiwanese, were not entitled to live in the apartments. The Taiwanese were socially exclusive towards the local community. The apartments were en suite and designed for professional singles, as only a few managers brought over their families from Taiwan. During weekdays, they would stay within the factory to work; at the weekend, they might drive their company cars to the city centre for shopping or entertainment.

The world of local supervisors

The factory director was a Guang Dong local who was responsible for dealing with the local government departments and had little role in production. Each department manager had a corresponding department superintendent under him. The division of labour between the manager and superintendent in a department was that the former was responsible for administration and coordination with the top management team, and the latter for internal production operation and communications. Department superintendents were assisted by a couple of vice-superintendents, or commissioners when the post-holders were not experienced enough to be vice-superintendents. Under the department supervision team was the workshop supervisor or line supervisor, heading a workshop or production line.

The factory, with its two plants, consisted of five administrative departments – personnel, finance, production control, quality control and production planning – and nine production departments – lacquering, casting, painting, aluminium processing, metal, plastics, processing, assembling and warehouse. The supervisors and superintendents in the production departments had all been promoted from the rank-and-file workers, while the professional positions in the administration departments were mainly staffed by university or college graduates.

With the top management all from Taiwan, and all superintendents and supervisors local insiders, shop floor management and the production process tended to rely on the front-line team. Some supervisors had been brought over from Taiwan when the factory was first established, but they were replaced by locals after their retirement. The turnover rate of Taiwanese managers was high, as they could not adapt well to the local context and sometimes claimed to be manipulated by the local superintendents. In early 2005, around half a year after the outbreak of the strike, the Taiwanese management sent a department superintendent with industrial experience in Taiwan to work alongside the local superintendent (from Hu Bei) in the metal department. He, however, quit after a few months. 'As he did not understand the situation below, it did not work at all,' a skilled worker in the department said.

The local supervisory staff were highly gender and place-of-origin-biased. Men occupied almost all of the posts and half of the department superintendents were from Hu Bei province. The Hu Bei originals had a good reputation for their wisdom and sophistication in management. Many workers quoted a traditional saying, 'The sky has nine-headed birds, and the earth has Hu Bei guys (Hu Bei *Lao*),' when answering my questions about the disproportionate number of Hu Bei provincials in supervisory or managerial positions in Sun and other factories in Shenzhen. Furthermore, as the department superintendents tended to promote their *Laoxiang* as workshop supervisors, most of the shop supervisors were from Hu Bei as well.

However, as the number of Si Chuan workers overwhelmed other provinces and Si Chuan people had better interpersonal networks and skills, most of the line supervisors came from that province. 'They like to buy superintendents and supervisors their dinners. It costs a hundred yuan or more per meal. Over time, the superintendents would feel indebted to him and give him a post,' a worker from Gui Zhou commented. Among ten line supervisors in the aluminium processing department where he worked, eight were from Si Chuan until 2005, when four of them were replaced.

Among the production departments, the metal department was located in the old plant while all other eight departments had operations in both plants. The size, gender and place-of-origin attributes of the departments are illustrated in Table 3.1, according to workers' interviews and my observations within the factory.

The management's strategy to manage and control the workforce was through a division of labour on the basis of gender, age, skill, a reward-and-penalise piece-rate system and strict disciplinary punishments.

Table 3.1 Size, gender and place-of-origin attributes of different departments in the Sun Factory

Department	Supervisory staff	Workers
Lacquering	Superintendent: from Hu Bei; male. Supervisors: all male.	500: almost all middle-aged male.
Casting	Superintendent: from Hu Bei; male. Supervisors: all male.	200: predominantly male.
Painting	Superintendent: from Jiang Xi; male. Supervisors: all male.	350: predominantly male.
Metal	Superintendent: from Hu Bei; male. Supervisors: all male.	600: predominantly male.
Aluminium processing	Superintendent: from Hu Nan; male. Supervisors: all male.	600: predominantly male.
Assembling	Superintendent (old plant): from Si Chuan; female. Superintendent (new plant): from Hu Nan; male. Supervisors: predominantly male.	3,000: predominantly female.
Plastics	Superintendent (old plant): from Hu Bei; male. Superintendent (new plant): from Hu Nan; male. Supervisors: predominantly male.	500; predominantly female.
Processing	Superintendent: from Hu Bei; male. Supervisors: all male.	300: predominantly female.
Warehouse	Superintendent: from Hu Bei; male. Supervisors: all male	45: all male, except clerical staff.
Personnel	Superintendent: from Jiang Xi; male.	
Finance	Superintendent: from Si Chuan; female.	
Production control	Superintendent: from Hu Bei; male.	
Quality control	Superintendent: from Si Chuan; male.	
Production planning	Superintendent: from Hu Nan; male.	

Gender segregation of skill and power

The plastics and assembly departments, where work was routine and simple, employed predominantly female workers, while men outnumbered women in all other departments. The preference of the management for men with physical strength was obvious. When Xiao Lin was interviewed for a job in the aluminium department, his hands were inspected. The calluses on his palms indicated that he had experience of menial work and helped him pass the interview. 'We need people with strong fingers,' the manager told him. At a recruitment fair in a job agency in May 2006, personnel officers emphasised that they needed people who could work very hard in the Sun factory. They made this point especially to younger and female candidates and urged applicants to consider carefully whether the higher pay at Sun would compensate for the hard work they would be expected to put in. Nevertheless, many young workers quit the factory soon after joining, unable to adapt to the harsh working environment. As a result, workers in the factory were mainly in their late twenties or thirties. While the job advertisements of many electronics factories stated an age requirement of eighteen to twenty-eight for women and eighteen to twenty-five for men, the Sun factory specifically requested older workers and accepted a wider range of ages: from twenty to thirty-eight for women and twenty to thirty-five for men.

In the peak season, the factory initiated a large-scale recruitment programme, when it could hire as many as 600 workers in one round. The only pre-work training was a half-day orientation with a talk on factory discipline and a guided visit to the various departments. The new workers were then sent to specific departments on the basis of gender, age, physical condition and skill level. The least experienced workers were more likely to be dismissed during the low season, with the factory retaining its skilled and experienced workers throughout the year. As a result, resignations from skilled workers, who could easily find jobs in other factories, were often 'not approved' by the management. By contrast, those who most needed to keep their jobs were vulnerable to being sacked.

Time-rate and piece-rate

Although the labour contract guaranteed a time-rate payment, in reality a combination of piece-rate and time-rate was implemented. The factory set up an output target for each worker, somewhere between the maximum capacity of an experienced worker and that of a new worker. For instance, if an experienced worker could make 150 pieces in one day and a newcomer 100, the official output target would be set at about 130. If a worker failed to make up 130 pieces, her or his time-rate wage, which was based on the legal minimum salary plus overtime, would be reduced. Meanwhile, those whose output level was more than 130 were paid an extra 'output benefit' (*Chaobanfei*). In the aluminium processing department, for example, the most experienced and industrious workers could earn an extra 400 yuan per month. Meanwhile, a new worker could have her or his wage reduced by 260 yuan in one month.

This reward-and-penalise system created two worlds among the rank and file: the stable veterans and the unstable temps. In the period of my fieldwork, a hardworking veteran could earn 1,800 yuan per month, which was very close to what the line supervisors earned (generally 500–600 yuan on top of the legal minimum rate plus overtime). In the Shenzhen plants, which were different from the Hui Zhou factory (discussed in the next chapter), workers had more control over their pace of work. A conveyer belt was not installed even in the assembly department, where workers sat and worked at small desks. After finishing their task, they put the product into a box on the long table on their left-hand side. Therefore, there was less peer pressure to work hard, so some employees worked slowly in order to enjoy a more relaxed working life. For the experienced workers, even though they did not work very hard, their income was still attractive. By contrast, if the inexperienced employees worked equally slowly, they could be dismissed or not earn enough to live on.

As an exporter to US and European markets, quality was always the most essential concern for the management. Customers frequently visited to conduct quality audits. A limited number of experienced, senior workers were promoted to be quality controllers. The appeal of a quality controller job for workers was not the power or the salary, but the free and easy work. Skilled workers were paid an extra technical subsidy on top of their basic wage dependent on department and skill level. Without the extra output benefit, their salaries were not necessarily higher than those of an ordinary worker. Their main advantage over the rank and file was to escape the intensive piece-rate routine work; in the language of the workers themselves, the controllers' work was 'lighter' (*Qingsong*). The more powerful skilled workers in the factory were the machine repairers. They were all men, aged between twenty-five and thirty-five. There were no female machine repairers even in the departments where most of the ordinary workers were women, such as plastics.

Line supervisors were also promoted from the ranks of skilled or experienced workers. Although they had supervisory responsibility, they did not enjoy much decision-making power or economic advantage. Just like the veteran ordinary workers and the skilled workers, they lived in the factory-provided dormitories, or shared privately let rooms with partners, friends, workmates or *Laoxiang*.

Discipline and punishment

The disciplinary rules in the factory were strict and based on fines. Common disciplinary issues included dozing off, leaving the factory without an off-duty permit (*Ligangzheng*) and absence from work.

If workers wanted to take leave, they had to submit an application form. The form would be signed first by the supervisor and then sent to the personnel department for final approval. These applications rarely won approval in the peak season. New workers dared not take leave without permission and were forced to stay at work even when they were sick. Veteran workers, however, might leave work even if their application was not approved.

Twenty-seven-year-old Qi, a *Laoxiang*, workmate and good friend of Xiao Lin, was one of the longest-serving workers in the aluminium processing department. He had worked in the factory since he first left home in Gui Zhou in 1999. We lived on the same floor, and his wife worked in the same factory with Xiao Ying. The couple shared a small flat of thirty square metres with another couple for a rent of 350 yuan per month. They had a son at home with their parents. They had tried to bring him to Shenzhen in 2005, but financial pressure and inconvenience forced them to send him back to Gui Zhou. Qi complained that he should not have married so early, as he now felt great pressure. From his point of view, eighteen to twenty-five is a man's golden age, and the essential period for career development. He wanted to learn some skills, but that was difficult when he had to support his wife and child. One day, his wife was sick. Qi wanted to take a day's leave to accompany her to hospital, but, as usual, his application was turned down. Nevertheless, he took the day off anyway. The next day, a major warning (*Daguo*) was issued against him, together with a fine of fifty yuan. However, his line supervisor told him: 'This is a lesson for you. The fine will be returned to you. You can get five yuan more extra output benefit each month for ten consecutive months.' According to Qi: 'The supervisors will only respect (*Gei Mianzi* – 'give face to') us veteran workers, as we are very familiar with each other and spend time together often. New workers are very different. Punishment is punishment (*Shuo Fa Jiu Fa*).'

Usually there was only one off-duty permit[7] available to each production line. Workers who wanted to be excused to go to the toilet or for other purposes had to obtain the permit from the line supervisor before leaving. Being found away from duty without the permit resulted in a minor warning (*Xiaoguo*) and a twenty-yuan fine. Dozing off was seen as a more serious mistake and led to a major warning and fifty-yuan fine for three levels, which meant the worker involved, her or his line supervisor and the workshop supervisor were all punished for the worker's error.

Relations, recruitment and promotion

As the biggest factory in the village, the Sun plant had a 9,000-strong labour force before the outbreak of the strike in 2004. But the workforce had declined to about 6,000 by the time of my fieldwork as a result of production relocation to the Hui Zhou factory and outsourcing. The factory had recruited workers by posting an advertisement outside the main entrance until June 2005, when an independent job agency took over. Under the old system, the power to hire a worker rested with the personnel department in consultation with the relevant department superintendent. As the wages in the Sun factory were higher than in other factories in the surrounding area, competition for jobs was intense. As soon as an advertisement was posted, hundreds would show up. This provided opportunities for corruption. Although announced as an open recruitment, many workers I interviewed were admitted to the factory by introduction from a *Laoxiang* or friend already working in the factory, or by paying an introduction fee of 400 to 800 yuan to an intermediary. The introduction fee paid by male workers was more than that paid by female workers. The intermediaries were active in the village and had good social networks. They might or might not work in the factory. In the latter case, they usually had close relations with a department superintendent or personnel officer. In the peak season, when the factory might hire as many as 600 workers in a single recruitment drive, even those without connections had a good chance of being hired without paying an introduction fee. In general, workers were very critical of the unfairness of the recruitment process:

When I joined the factory, the introduction fee for women was 400 yuan, and for men 800 to 1,000 yuan. If there was a Taiwanese present at the interview, people like us [those who had no connections with supervisors] had a bit more of a chance; if it was totally the mainlanders' responsibility, the intermediaries would bring their people in directly and we would only be admitted after them.

(A worker in the aluminium processing department)

This factory relied on connections. Many workers entered through connections. Workshop or line supervisors might introduce their *Laoxiang* with the permission of the department superintendent. If the department superintendent agreed, the people in personnel would not object.

(A worker in the lacquering department)

A factory is just like a government: everybody wants to build up their own power and influence (*Shili*). The department superintendent has to draw the workshop and line supervisors to his side and use their men in order to win their support.

(A worker in the plastics department)

As a result of the manipulation of workers' recruitment by the supervisors, a high proportion of the workers in one department, workshop or production line came from the same province as their head. Moreover, the department superintendent had the power to promote supervisors, and the workshop supervisor could appoint line supervisors. Those who joined through relations or introduction fees enjoyed an advantage in gaining promotion. But the appointment of a new department superintendent would usually lead to dismissal of supervisors loyal to his predecessor and promotion of the new superintendent's relatives or *Laoxiang*.

Accordingly, the superintendent and supervisors in one department were usually related and the trend was towards homogeneity in province background over time. Most of the workers and line and workshop supervisors in the old plant's assembly department were from Si Chuan province, as was the superintendent. As a common practice, if a supervisor was unable to perform their duties satisfactorily, the factory would continue to pay them for the grade of supervisor even if they were downgraded to the status of ordinary worker. In the metal department, both the superintendent and commissioner were from Hu Bei, as were half of the line and workshop supervisors and those who enjoyed the benefits of the supervisors. During 2004 and 2005, the superintendent sacked many supervisors, most of them from Si Chuan, and replaced them with friends and relatives from Hu Bei.

In the aluminium processing department, the head was from Hu Nan. Four of his five subordinate workshop supervisors were his cousin, a brother-in-law and two *Laoxiang*. Qi, who had been working in the department since 1999, explained:

Normally the department superintendent appoints relatives or *Laoxiang* as supervisors. The aim is to control workers. If the supervisors are the superintendent's own people, when workers play up (*Naoshi*), they can help persuade the workers, calm their anger and channel their discontent. Then unrest will be avoided. Otherwise, if supervisors themselves lead the disturbance, and the issue is widespread, the superintendent himself would be removed too.

Having worked in the factory for seven years, Qi said that he had a chance to be promoted to supervisor as his skill was comprehensive. But, as was the common practice, he had to pay at least 2,000 yuan to the department superintendent, followed by regular gifts of 300 yuan or so on occasions such as May Day, National Day, the New Year and the birthdays of the superintendent's children and wife. Qi described himself as an 'unsocial' person, as he did not want to pursue promotion in this way.

He also explained why there was no significant labour dispute between 1999 and 2004, except for one short stoppage in his department that arose from workers' misunderstanding the law in 2001: gangsters pacified the workers.

Gangsters and workplace control

In Shenzhen, it was very common for managers to recruit and promote workers from their own home place for the sake of easy control. If there was a sign of potential collective action, the manager or supervisors would call their *Laoxiang* who were influential among workers to 'give face' (*Geimianzi* or pay respect) by staying away from the action and even persuading other workers to do so. In the Sun factory, the penetration of gangsters from the community into the workplace made the patron–client relations between the supervisory staff and their 'influential' subordinates, and its pacifying effect on shop floor rebellion, even more apparent.

Most of the superintendents and supervisors had worked and lived in the village for many years. Some of them, especially the department superintendents, had worked in the factory as ordinary workers from the plant's early days. Now they were generally aged between thirty and forty. Superintendents earned salaries ranging from 3,500 to 5,000 yuan with an additional, unknown income; the supervisors earned between 2,000 and 3,000 yuan. Their consumption power was obviously better than that of an ordinary worker, and some superintendents had bought houses to settle their families in the village. However, they were not rich enough to live in Shenzhen's metropolitan city centre as their Taiwanese managers did. Moreover, their background as manual workers also determined their consumption tastes and preferences, which were perfectly satisfied in the village. Accordingly, they developed their own social networks and peer groups in Militant village.

The 'influential' people in the village and the gangster 'big brothers' were usually men of similar age, taste, consumption power and place-of-origin background to the factory superintendents and supervisors. They interacted with each other by living in the same housing estates and relaxing in the same entertainment places. Like Xiao Ying and the other small shopkeepers, the superintendents and supervisors were ideal targets for blackmail, burglary and protection rackets. Since their careers, and sometimes their families and property, were located in the village, they were too vulnerable to resist gangster threats. Xiao Ying was forced to close down her shop, businessmen from LF county protected themselves by forming their own *Laoxiang* network and fighting back, while superintendents would forge friendships or become directly involved in 'brothering' with the gangsters.

Consequently, 'mutually beneficial' relationships between the superintendents/supervisors and the 'big brothers' developed. The 'big brothers' introduced their subordinate 'brothers', *Laoxiang* and relatives into the factory, while the superintendents and supervisors gained protection and cooperation from the gangsters. Those introduced by the 'big brother' would then be promoted quickly to supervisory or skilled positions and so became 'influential' in both the community and the factory. I encountered one of them at a party. He was a thirty-five-year-old workshop supervisor in the assembly department and hailed from Hu Nan. Besides his job in the factory, he also ran a shoe shop in the village. I did not ask him too much about his background, but one of my friends had already told me that the supervisor had joined the factory three years previously and that he had fought with his colleagues from the very first day. Yet he was promoted very quickly from line supervisor to workshop supervisor. Men like him, introduced to the factory by 'big brothers', did not perform their duties properly, and they often bullied the other workers, especially the women. My friend reported that he had heard one of them saying with a loud laugh: 'We came here for amusement, not for work!'

A worker in the aluminium department told me he had been seriously bullied by his line supervisor, who had links with a gang. Luo was a thirty-six-year-old honest man from Gui Zhou. He came to the village in 1993 as his first stop in *Dagong* life. He first worked as a casual worker in a small factory in the village, where he earned 500–600 yuan per month. After a year, he was sacked by the factory and worked on a construction site for three months before he returned to Gui Zhou. Soon he headed for the provinces of Zhe Jiang and Fu Jian, where he worked for a total of six years. During that time, he changed from one job to another frequently in the manufacturing and construction sectors. He said: 'Wherever I could earn money, I would go.' He had worked in the Sun factory since returning to Guang Dong in 2003.

Workers like Luo, who came out to *Dagong* in the late 1980s and early 1990s, were described by the Chinese media as the 'first generation of migrant workers', in contrast to the second generation – people like Xiao Lin and his peers. The first generation was less adapted to city life and tended to cling more emotionally to their home villages (Pun and Ren, forthcoming). Hence, 'generation' here focused on culture more than age. The first generation did not imagine that they would stay long in a factory or a city. As their wives or husbands usually stayed at home farming, they would quit their jobs and go back home in harvest season to help their partners. Most of them also ultimately returned to their home villages permanently after several years of *Dagong*, although some, like Xiao Lin's father, remained in the city. Their fates were varied. Some became skilled workers, supervisors or middle-level managers in the factories, but more had to work as delivery, cleaning or construction workers due to age discrimination in the labour market. In the Sun factory, the demanding physical requirements discouraged younger workers and provided opportunities for those like Luo. In the aluminium processing department, more workers were aged over thirty than under, and there were more men than women.

Luo had usually quit jobs in order to visit his family at home, but he abandoned that practice after joining Sun. If he wanted to go back to his home village, he always applied for holidays. His wife followed him to Shenzhen and worked in another factory in the village. They rented a small room near me. After his wife became pregnant, she returned home to bear their child. Then the whole family depended on Luo's income. Generation, age and family pressure were all factors affecting Luo's status in the community, labour market and workplace.

In 2004, an ancillary worker from Si Chuan was promoted to be a supervisor on Luo's production line. He was a ferocious man. One day, he asked Luo to check a batch of irregular items from the casting department. Luo would not be paid for doing this work as it was not one of his normal duties. Furthermore, his wage might be deducted if he could not reach his work target set by the factory, so Luo was understandably reluctant to do the additional work. The Si Chuan man's immediate response to Luo's complaint was to punch him brutally twice and he was seriously injured. 'My chest was too painful for me to speak,' he said. He bought some medicine and applied for half a month of unpaid leave. The line supervisor turned down this leave application. Finally, though, the former line supervisor and the workshop supervisor persuaded the new supervisor 'not to act in this way' and Luo was permitted to take his leave.

Author: Why did this Si Chuan man become so angry with you?

Luo: He knows many gangsters outside, so he is too impudent in the factory. Even our department superintendent is scared of him, and worried about him asking those [gangsters] outside to bother him. He was an ancillary worker responsible for delivering materials with a trolley before he was promoted. It is very light work. Before he was promoted, I had been bullied by him several times. After his promotion, it became even worse. For example, one month before he was promoted, he deliberately threw material on my feet. The skin of my foot was quite grazed. But as it was not very serious, I did not take leave.

Author: Did you file a compliant to the factory?

Luo: No. He would beat you as soon as you said anything to him (*Duo Shuo Jiju*), never mind filing a complaint. But after I was beaten by him so seriously, I really thought that I did not want to work here any more. I also wanted to pay somebody to take revenge, but finally I gave up. If I had done anything, I would have put myself in trouble, and, you know,

I have a wife and children at home. Of course, money was also a consideration.

Luo was oppressed not only by the formal factory regulations, but by an interactive network of factory supervisors and gangsters in the community.

Women workers in the factory were even more quiescent than the men. Wang was a thirty-two-year-old woman who worked in the plastics department. She carelessly cut her wrist in 2002 when she was working. The law states that industrial injury compensation is available for collection until one leaves the factory. It was arranged for Wang to do some lighter work after she got injured. She planned to claim her compensation and then go back home to take care of her children in 2006. But the Social Insurance Bureau found that she had used her sister's identity card to work in the factory, so her legal entitlement to the part of the compensation paid by the Social Insurance Fund was revoked, although the factory was still obliged to pay their part of her compensation. However, Wang was then informed by her supervisor that the factory did not want to pay her any compensation because using another person's identity card was an offence. She broke down immediately and was sent to hospital. Her reaction highlights the dual physical and mental trauma that is so common among Chinese *Dagongmei* (see Pun, 2005c).

I interviewed Luo and Wang just one week before Wang collapsed. Both of them complained about unfairness at work, but neither had ever seriously considered filing a complaint.

Luo: [We have to] rush to finish work targets throughout the year. No matter how much they are, we must make them up. It is very exhausting!
Author: Did you think of filing a complaint?
Luo: How could we complain? For people like us it is not easy to get a job. It is good enough so long as things are not bad and a job can be kept (*Chabuduo Jiu Suanle, You Fengong Jiu Suanle*). Moreover, there is more overtime work here, so the pay is a bit higher.
Wang: Our department tells us to have a self-funded health check every year. Some years ago, a young worker refused to do it and he was immediately sacked. Who would dare to make a complaint after that?
Luo: More than 200 yuan was deducted from some workers' pay as they could not reach their work targets. None of them dared to show discontent.
Author: That deduction is illegal. Did you inform the labour bureau about it?
Wang: No courage. And we did not know how to do it, either. They [the management] use money to bribe the labour bureau. They [LSSB officials] would not speak with the managers on our behalf.
Luo: Right. They [LSSB officials] wouldn't help *Dagongde* (people selling labour power). It was useless to go there.
Author: But then the strike happened. So things changed. Do you know about the strike?
Luo: Yes, of course. It was for higher wages.

Place-of-origin-aligned gangsters were used by the management to control the ordinary workers. It might not have been the intention of the top Taiwanese management to use gangsters in the workplace, but without sufficient knowledge of the local context and production process, they had to rely on the local supervisory staff, who retained personal contacts, loyalty, traditions and customs from their places of origin and brought them into the factory.

Skill, shirking and construction of industrial masculinity

Through the network of place, gender and seniority within and beyond the factory, peaceful workplace relations were maintained. Although female and unskilled workers were very unhappy about their supervisors and there were many infringements of the Labour Law, no significant management and labour conflict occurred in the factory until October 2004. By contrast, horizontal tensions among male skilled and experienced workers were abundant. Violent battles took place often along the lines of place of origin. Gui Zhou and Si Chuan provincials were especially notorious for their militancy and violence.

Chen was a thirty-four-year-old worker from Si Chuan. He first came to Guang Dong as early as 1990, and then travelled frequently between Yan Jiang city, where he worked on various construction sites, and his home town in the first decade of his *Dagong* life. He came to Shenzhen to work in a small factory in Militant village in 1998 and joined the Sun factory the same year. His wife and two children remained in his home town and were fully dependent on his income. Chen had learned motor maintenance in his home town, and this skill equipped him to become a machine repair technician in Sun's metal department. However, his expertise was not the sole factor in obtaining and maintaining his privileged status in the factory.

In 1998, he paid a 600-yuan introduction fee to join the aluminium processing department. But he quit one month later as the work there was too exhausting. One year later, he entered the assembly department. By then, he had developed a better network in the community, so it cost him only 100 yuan to buy some friends a dinner in order to rejoin the factory. After working there for nine months, he resigned again after a row with a supervisor. In 2003, he joined the metal department, having been introduced by one of his brother's friends, who worked in the personnel department and knew the metal department superintendent. This time Chen did not pay any money to get the job, but he did unpaid work for a month in a new restaurant run by his brother's friend, who was clearly part of the 'influential' network. Chen was hired as a welder, but was promoted to repair technician on the first day because of a shortage of technicians in the factory. He well remembered how he became a skilled repair worker:

> I met our department superintendent on the first day of my work in the metal department. The superintendent asked me what I had done at home. I replied: 'Repair vehicles.' He then asked me if I could repair machines. I said no, I had never even seen the machines. The superintendent, however, asked me to

observe how other people did the repair work and learn from them. I said OK. On the second day, when a machine broke down, one of the technicians took me to repair it with him. One week later, I was able to work independently.

Working in the factory as a skilled worker was like being in 'paradise'. Chen took me for a walk through the workshops and dormitories to interview workers and supervisors, although this was strictly forbidden in the factory regulations. According to Chen, he spent most of the working day sleeping or having fun around the factory. He had nothing to do when the machines were working properly. However, most of the machines in his department were decrepit, so they broke down a lot. If this happened, a bell would be rung to inform the technicians. Yet they might not start the repair until an hour before their finishing time. Chen revealed: 'No one disciplines us. As days pass, there is not any achievement.'

The mechanics' privileged position was not unique to the Sun factory. Workers from the Moon factory, a German-invested electronics factory whose strike story will be presented in Chapter 5, told me of the same situation there. According to them, the repair mechanics would talk and flirt with the women workers on the production lines. Yet the supervisors still treated them very well. One of the Moon workers said: 'A machine can be repaired in half an hour or an afternoon. If they [the supervisors] treat the repairers badly, they work slowly, and then you would find it difficult to finish the work target on time. That is why the supervisors have to buy them dinner from time to time, even though they hate them at heart.' It was also why the repair workers were allowed to come to the production line and have fun with the women. However, there was an element of superiority in this, as one of the production workers explained:

> We are different. They come to talk with you just because they are bored and want to kill time with somebody. Outside the factory, some of them don't even want to say hello to you. . . . I've got a *Laoxiang* who is a machine repairer. . . . He is a good man. . . . He comes to talk with me and help me with my work from time to time . . . and he would say hello to me when we meet in the road . . . but that's all.

Chen classified the machine repair technicians in the Sun factory into two types: the 'real' skilled workers, like himself; and the 'false' skilled workers, who were attached to a gang and possessed little skill. Although shirking at work was common among both groups, the latter, who were more directly involved in the gang and/or had a closer links to the superintendent, took it to extremes. This aroused discontent among the 'real' skilled workers towards the management. Chen complained about the 'worthlessness' of skill and the value of *Guanxi* (connections) in the factory. The personnel officer who introduced him into the department in 2003 left the factory, so his interpersonal connection with the superintendent was dramatically weakened. He was also unhappy about the superintendent's dismissal of three supervisors from Si Chuan in 2004. According to Chen, although he had better skills, he was also paid much less than the superintendent's relatives, *Laoxiang* and those who 'never worked in the workshops' (meaning the gangsters).

The 'false' skilled workers were clustered in the metal, lacquering and painting departments, and, to a lesser extent, in processing. Chen estimated that there were several hundred workers of this kind within the factory. As salaries were paid by the factory, keeping so many slackers in the workshops would not directly hurt the interests of the mainland superintendents and supervisors. Meanwhile, the Taiwanese managers, who worked in the office, depended on the locals to control the workers and manage production, so they had no choice but to turn a blind eye (*Yiyan Kai Yiyan Bi*) to what was happening on the ground. But I was still curious about the Taiwanese owner's attitude to these deceptions.

Author: Many workers do not perform their duties properly, so why doesn't the GM take action on it?

Chen: He cannot see all of this happening.

Author: Is it because he spends most of his time in Taiwan and hardly shows up at the factory?

Chen: No. He is in the factory most of the time.

Author: He must never patrol the workshops, then?

Chen: No. He goes to every department. But [it is] very rare for him to go to the assembly department [where the workers are most docile]. In fact, all of the departments fear his visits. As soon as he comes to a workshop, people there tremble. He condemns people very fiercely. Department superintendents are blamed by him on every Monday and Friday morning meeting. One time, when he came to our department, he approached a pile of rubbish on the floor and two workshop supervisors ran to pick it up almost as soon as they saw him.

Author: What would happen if someone was found sleeping by the GM?

Chen: They would be sacked immediately (*Ji Chao Bulun*). But normally he cannot find them.

Author: Why not?

Chen: Someone would tip them off! (*Tongfeng Baoxin Ma!*) If the GM goes to a department, those people [who are slacking] will go to other departments.

When I visited the shop floor with Chen in November 2006, some of the workers still gathered together to chat casually, although it was said that most of the 'false' skilled workers had left after the strike in 2004.

Fights were very common among the workers, especially those with skills or outside connections. Chen shared an example. A line supervisor asked a worker to take a tool from another production line. Another worker who had previously used the tool became enraged when he could not find it. The supervisor kept quiet, but one of the workers challenged his rival to a fight outside the workshop. The two men then battled in the corridor. They were found by the security guards and reported to the manager. Both were immediately dismissed, which was standard company policy for fighting. But often fights occurred within the workshops, the Taiwanese managers would not find out, and the supervisors would ignore them.

Violence frequently erupted after a supervisor distributed duties to skilled workers. As their jobs were non-standardised, if one worker saw that another's duties were easier than his own, he might feel unfairly treated (*Bushunyan Bufuqi*) and fight back. Workers from Si Chuan and Gui Zhou formed the two most powerful rival groups. The latter said of the former: 'Good at flattery, but can only be small, not big, officials (*Hui Pai Mapi, Daguan Dangbuliao, Dang Xiaoguan*).' Meanwhile, Si Chuan workers described those from Gui Zhou as 'paper tigers'.

Chen was involved in a quarrel with a supervisor in 2005, but he never fought with him within the factory. Rather, he resigned from his job and left for Guang Zhou for three months. After he returned to Shenzhen, he beat up the supervisor when they met in the street. The latter asked his friends to have dinner with Chen, and asked Chen to 'give face'. Chen accepted his apology and returned to work in the factory.

Although he could resort to violence in this way, Chen had a very strong sense of justice and fairness. He said he could not bear the fact that some of his Si Chuan *Laoxiang* bullied the minority in his workshop. That was why most of his good friends were from other provinces and other workshops. 'They [his Si Chuan workmates] knew several stirrers outside. I also knew many people of this kind, but I never acted in their way. I would only fight back when others treated me unfairly,' he said.

The skilled workers, both 'real' and 'false', reserved a special hatred for the factory security guards.

The community government provided security guard services for the factories that rented land from them. The factory in turn paid a reasonable service fee. This was to facilitate better control by the local authorities and police over both social order and industrial relations. According to a security guard who was employed by the community government, they would call first the factory owner and then the community official whenever there was an incident in the factory. The salary of a security guard was more or less the same as that of a skilled worker, but the guards said that their work was more relaxed than production work. Many of them had connections with the gangs.

However, the Sun factory employed its own security guard team rather than using the government service. In common with many other factories in Shenzhen in recent years, the new plant contracted out its security guard service to a police bureau-sponsored company for a short time after it opened. But the service was terminated in November 2004 and replaced by a team employed directly by the factory. Theft had been common in the factory, and the government-employed guards were said to be disloyal and not responsible enough to enforce regulations and protect company property. 'We just couldn't be bothered to make the effort' (*Women Buxiang Reshi Maiming*),' one government-employed security officer admitted.

The factory required all of its new security officers to present a retired soldier's certificate to show their military experience. They were also encouraged by the management to beat the workers if they deemed it necessary. If a guard fought with a worker, the company would provide proper medical treatment and hospital care for the guard while completely ignoring the worker.

The security guards frequently beat up workers before the strike in 2004, but thereafter they became more circumspect. 'Now workers know how to make complaints to the government our work is more difficult. Normally we will gloss over it by turning a blind eye (*Xishi Ningren, Yiyan Kai Yiyan Bide*) to misbehaviour,' one guard said.

Workers had to punch their time card whenever they entered and left the factory. One day, a skilled Si Chuan worker in the old plant who had used his own card to enter the factory punched a night shift worker's card to leave. The worker was stopped by a guard, possibly because his security supervisor was at the scene. The supervisor told the worker to hand over his own card. The worker did so, but then said: 'You want me to hand in the card, no problem. As soon as I hand it in, I know I will be sacked, and then disappear from this factory. But you should know what will happen to you tomorrow.' He then walked out of the gate. The supervisor called him back, but the worker started running away. The supervisor then chased the worker, caught him, and returned his card to him. Nevertheless, the supervisor was still brutally attacked by eight gangsters after he left work.

Xiao Liu told me about a young female clerk who did the record-keeping in the security kiosk at the entrance to the new plant. He would sometimes flirt with her when he passed the gate. One day, a security supervisor looking at him while he was doing so. Xiao Liu told the supervisor to apologise or else he would make trouble for him. The guard did as he was told. According to Xiao Liu, if you 'knew people' outside the factory (as he did), you could get away with many things, including 'stealing and robbing' (*Toutou Qiangqiang*), inside the factory. Moreover, he was unable to produce a temporary residence certificate during a police raid on his home, but as he had a local friend who knew somebody on the village Party Committee, he was let off.

Willis (1979: 196) suggested that the political discontent of shop floors was channelled into 'the symbolic sexual realm' of 'a transformed patriarchy . . . from the outside'. From a feminist perspective, Cockburn (1983) forcefully showed that men gained power over women by securing access to technology and skill in the printing industry in London. Recent studies of British service industries have further revealed how gendering, which is a constituent of and constructed by workplace power relations, was used by management to control workers (e.g. Leidner, 1993). This study explores the making and manipulation of masculinity in the global factories of contemporary China. Through the stories of Chen, Xiao Liu and many others, we can see how industrial masculinity, as a social process of gendering, has been constructed through the social processes of skilling and 'brothering' in the workplace and the wider community (Cockburn, 1983). This construction of industrial masculinity developed alongside the construction of industrial femininity, which we can see in the stories of Xiao Lin's Hu Nan workmate and Wang. However, industrial masculinity and femininity both showed their dual social functions. From Xiao Lin and Chen, we can see a sense of fairness and justice that might be valuable in labour protest, as Hodson (2001) pointed out, while sexism and violence are major drawbacks. Similarly, from the Hu Nan woman, we can see that women were sometimes more strategic and determined to claim rights and justice, although Wang seemed to be very docile in the workplace. Luo is a man, but industrial masculinity did not affect him due to his inferior market and production position. This further confirms that gendering of masculinity and femininity is a social process in the labour market and the production regime.

Concluding remarks

This chapter has illustrated community and shop floor culture in a migrant workers' community, Militant village, to explain how the social relations in the community influence the power relations in the workshop, and vice versa. As a background to the next chapter, the key argument is that the social relations in the community and production relations in the workplace are reinforced by, not separated from, each other. The culture of locality, gang, gender, generation and age worked together with labour market conditions to give rise to a group of workers in skilled and supervisory positions who were more confident, militant and violent than their colleagues.

This group of skilled and experienced workers has, in recent years, benefited from economic expansion and the corresponding shortage of skilled labour. The stratum of male workers with close gang connections was used to oppress and pacify subordinate groups of workers, and accounted for the general quiescence of workers in the Sun factory. Those who maintained looser attachments to the gangs and illegal activities (such as Xiao Lin and Chen), however, developed a sense of justice and pride through their struggle for a better life.

But for the majority of unskilled workers – most of them female, young or old – suffering from the boredom of the routine work, the inhumanity of harsh disciplinary rules and the despotism of localistic masculinity, working life was exhausting and frustrating. They attempted to regain control over the means of production (like Xiao Ying), entered the underground, informal economy and crime (like her younger brother), or merely tolerated the unfairness of the workplace. Their choices were largely dictated by the opportunities available, personal values and family economic conditions.

As many studies in European countries have shown (Thompson, 1963/1980; Hobsbawm, 1968; Katznelson and Zolberg, 1986; Berlanstein, 1992), comparatively privileged economic and social positions offered artisans a core role in workers' struggles in the early stage of industrialisation. However, in immigrant societies like the US, where the artisan tradition was less developed, place-of-origin-based gangsters and front-line supervisors took the pivotal roles in the labour market, community and production politics (Thrasher, 1927; Nelson, 1975;

Padilla, 1992). Perry (1993) pointed out that modern Chinese industrial society resembles that of the US in the nineteenth century. The scope and limits of the 'labour aristocracy', a term coined by Hobsbawm (1968: 272), in the context of China's global factories will be investigated in the next chapter.

4 Strikes and changing power relations in the workplace

Introduction

> Returning to the dispute about the strike's 'spontaneity', let us examine its implications more closely. . . . The dispute can be considered a 'quibble' only by implying that there is always some form of planning, whether by informal or formal leaders.
> (Gouldner, 1954: 91–92)

> A strike should have somebody acting as leader, but not anybody can be a leader. Usually it is only veteran workers who are able to be leaders. They have more interpersonal connections and respect, and they know more people. Also, what they say is more trustworthy so others are more likely to listen to them. And these leaders do not want to work any more, so they try to stir up some unrest before leaving.
> (A lacquering worker in Hui Zhou)

When I interviewed a twenty-year-old professional college graduate from Hu Bei province who worked on the shop floor in the Sun factory's new plant in Hui Zhou, his views on strike leadership were as illuminating as industrial sociologist Gouldner's ideas. I was reminded of the powerful relationship between the sociological account of industrial conflict and the day-to-day experience of industrial workers. Previous chapters have outlined how workers were divided by gender, place of origin, age, skill level and gangs. This chapter will explore the potential and limitations of multifaceted, non-class identities in the rise of workers' strikes and other forms of collective protest. By providing an account of the cause, process, consequence and impact of a strike in the Sun factory in 2004, this chapter focuses on the economic, cultural and organisational resources that underlie a workers' strike.

As we have seen, the 'unlimited supply of migrant workers' resulting from *Mingong Chao* (the tidal wave of migrant workers) since the early 1990s dramatically weakened the marketplace bargaining, workplace bargaining and associational power of workers (Wright, 2000). The most vulnerable workers in the market were scared of losing their comparatively highly paid jobs in the Sun factory and so chose to tolerate despotic management and even bullying from gangsters, while alienation at work forced those with less family pressure to quit and seek other life courses. Workplace conflict generally occurred along the lines of place of origin among the skilled workers. In short, in the terms of Hirschman (1970), the strategy of 'loyalty' or 'exit' overwhelmed that of 'voice' in the factory.

In this chapter, I will demonstrate how 'voice' and then 'exit' became the workers' new strategy as labour market conditions changed, facilitated by the locality-based gangster network in the community, industrial masculinity, and the sense of justice and fairness common among skilled workers. The chapter begins with a description of a significant strike in the Sun factory's Shenzhen plants and its influence on worker–management power relations in the workplace and the community. Then we will see how the strike experiences in Shenzhen were transferred to the factory's new plant in Hui Zhou and reshaped workplace relations there. On the way, the similarities in resistance and the differences in management strategy will be discussed.

The run-up to the strike in 2004

> I went to watch. It was a precious opportunity, the kind one has only once or twice in one's whole life.
>
> (A driver in the Sun factory describing the protest in 2004)

Workers in the Sun factory were pacified by a despotic gangster network based on skills, gender, place and seniority across the factory. One of the workers told me about the sole stoppage before the strike in 2004. The earlier stoppage, in 2001, illustrated the workers' misunderstanding of the law as well as their poor communications.

In the face of the high industrial accident rate in some departments, the factory bought industrial injury insurance for employees who had worked for more than three months in the painting, casting and aluminium processing departments. Although the insurance was solely paid by the employers, at that time it was bound up with social insurance and the factory deducted thirty-seven yuan from workers' salaries for their own contributions to the insurance. Workers, however, did not understand why their salaries were being docked and stopped work. The factory director and department manager explained the contribution ratio, benefits and legal requirements for social insurance, and the strikers soon resumed work. Social insurance, however, would become one of the main demands of the workers' collective action three years later.

Working conditions on the eve of the strike

In 2004, the employees worked seven days a week. The daily working schedule was as follows:

- Day Shift:
- Morning session: 7.30–11.00 a.m.

- Lunch break: 11.00–11.30 a.m.
- Afternoon session: 11.30 a.m.–4.30 p.m.
- Dinner break: 4.30–5.00 p.m.
- Evening session: 5.00–7.30 p.m.
- Night Shift:
- First session: 7.30 p.m.–12.00 a.m.
- Midnight break: 12.00–12.30 a.m.
- Second session: 12.30–7.30 a.m.

Night shift workers were allowed to take a rest within their workshop between 5 and 6 a.m., the exact duration depending on the department and on condition of not leaving the factory. The workers could leave the factory during lunch, dinner and midnight breaks.

In 2004, the municipal minimum wage was 480 yuan per month for a forty-hour working week. According to the law, weekday overtime pay was one and a half times the basic rate, and weekend overtime was twice the normal working rate (2.48 yuan per hour). But like workers in most private factories (A. Chan, 2001), those in the Sun factory were paid below the standard. An ordinary worker's basic monthly salary was 450 yuan, for six eight-hour days each week from Monday to Saturday. Overtime work beyond the forty-eight hours was paid at an hourly rate of 2.48 yuan. An ordinary worker usually received 700 to 800 yuan by working fourteen hours per day, seven days per week. One of the workers told me that he earned 970 yuan with 186 hours of overtime in one month, and 1,200–1,300 with more than 260 hours of overtime. This level was quite acceptable to most of the workers as overtime work was regular and paid more than in other factories.

I asked a middle-aged woman in March 2006: 'Was your salary enough for your family [in 2004]?'

She said: 'Yes, the cost of living was comparatively lower then. For example, the rent for a single room was only 80 yuan, and 120 yuan for a one-sitting-room and one-bedroom flat. Now it costs 150 for a single room, and 200 for a flat.'

On top of the basic salary and overtime pay, which were universal for all, there were extra subsidies based on job title, skill and environment to distinguish different posts. The environment allowance was universal for workers in the same department: for example, 45 yuan in metal, 70 in painting and plastics, 140 in aluminium processing and assembly, and 300 in the lacquering department. The skill subsidy depended on the worker's skill level at the supervisor's discretion. The line supervisor had a 400–500 yuan subsidy, and the workshop supervisor 700–800 yuan, but their overtime rate was the same as ordinary workers'. A skilled worker in the metal department, for example, received 45 yuan for environment allowance and 110 yuan for skill subsidy. The environment allowance in the lacquering department was the highest and more than double that in the second-place department (aluminium processing and assembly). This was justified by the fact that workers in the lacquering department were exposed to toxic chemicals.

The factory provided dormitories for all of the workers, and deducted fifty yuan per month from their salaries for rent and bills. However, more than 30 per cent of the workers, especially those on higher pay and with a partner working in the village, lived in privately rented rooms, so there were many vacancies in the dormitories. A skilled worker who lived outside the factory said that he had installed broadband at home, so he could surf the internet at night. By contrast, in the dormitory the gate was locked at night and the lights were switched off at 11 p.m.[1] But for lower-income and older workers, accommodation was chosen more by questions of convenience, living cost and security, rather than leisure. Working couples in the village tended to rent private rooms, and convenience for cooking was also a key consideration for them. Before the outsourced factory canteen closed at the end of 2004, workers could eat there at a reasonable price of two yuan per meal. But workers complained that the food was disgusting and many preferred to eat at food stalls and in restaurants, even though this was more expensive. Cooking at home provided a good alternative for those living outside the factory. As a result, only four or five beds of each eight-bed dormitory were occupied.

However, it was always difficult for workers to decide whether to live out or in. When a worker living in the dormitory complained of theft and expressed her intention to move out, one of her good friends, who already lived outside, discouraged her: 'Go and talk with your room-mates about installing a lock on the door. That would be a better choice. For people like me, more than 200 yuan of rent and bills is really a big burden.'

The incident that led to the strike

During my fieldwork, owners often complained that giant buyers like Wal-Mart kept requesting lower prices with the lure of a large order. In the face of keen market competition, it seemed that expansion and rationalisation were dual strategies of managements for their businesses to survive, which was the same strategy used by US enterprises in the late nineteenth century (Nelson, 1975). Like the Uniden factory (another supplier of Wal-Mart, discussed in Chapter 2), in 2004, along with a US$150-million new investment in Hui Zhou, a rationalisation programme was introduced in Shenzhen by the top management of the Sun factory. While expansion was difficult in the face of the widely reported 'shortage' of peasant workers (*Mingong Huang*), at least those with skills and experience, rationalisation touched off a new wave of labour protests. Workers in the Sun factory, like their counterparts in many other factories, exploited the opportunity to demand higher wages and better protection.

On the eve of the factory's dramatic expansion, Sun hired a management expert to initiate a reform to increase efficiency and rationalise production. Consequently, in April 2004, the factory began a new policy. During the half-hour lunch break from 11 to 11.30 a.m., workers were requested to punch their time cards out and back in. (Most of the workers had their lunch outside the factory.) This move indicated the management's awareness of a regulation loophole and abuse. As workers previously did not need to punch their cards at either lunch or dinner breaks, it was very common for skilled workers, especially those with gang connections, not to return to work until the evening session. The new policy brought trouble for even honest workers, though. A long queue formed for the punch clock. Those who worked on the upper floors of the factory might have to wait ten minutes or more before they got the chance to punch out on the ground floor. As a result, their break time was drastically reduced

The strike

First day

The strike began in April in the lacquering department, which was situated on the fifth floor. Workers complained that they no longer had enough time to eat their lunch. However, the location of the department and the long wait to punch out were not the sole reasons why workers from this department led the strike. With the highest environment subsidy, the lacquering department attracted the most gangsters and their cohorts. Consequently, it had the most 'people who don't need to work' and 'false' skilled workers. The primary targets of the reform – workers who did not return immediately to the factory after lunch – were mainly from this department.

All workers in the department staged a hunger strike at lunchtime, sitting in the workshop and refusing to eat or work. The management sent instant noodles, but the workers still refused to eat. Taiwanese managers then came to negotiate with the strikers. The workers demanded a salary increase from 450 to 480 yuan, and an increase in the overtime rate from 2.48 to 3.50 yuan per hour. The management agreed with these wage demands, and the workers returned to work. Nonetheless, the strike spread to the whole factory the next day.

Second day

A notice was posted up by the factory the next morning, saying that the workers' salary would be increased to 480 yuan. However, overtime pay would be 2.90 yuan per hour rather than the promised 3.5. Workers in the lacquering department were furious. In response, they planned a factory-wide strike. Later that morning, notices calling for a strike were pasted up in every department. Nevertheless, most of the workers stayed at work.

In order to attract public attention and state intervention, between 100 and 200 workers from the lacquering department walked out of the factory to block a national highway (*Guodao*) near the village. As there were two junctions from the village to the highway, the workers split into two groups and each went to one junction. Their move aroused the attention of both the management and the police. One group was stopped and escorted back to the factory by their managers; the second, which had walked onto the highway, was driven off by the police. The police also arrested seven of those who rushed into the front line, even though they were not representatives or leaders of the workers. As the police found it impossible to identify the ringleaders, they simply detained those who appeared to be most violent and radical. The seven workers were separated and detained in the town and district-level police stations. As the dispute developed, the police were eventually forced to release them without charge: after one week for those detained in the town station and two weeks for those in the district station. No retaliation was directed towards these workers after they were freed and they returned to work in the factory.

The detention of the workers annoyed and further radicalised their colleagues. A group of young men from the lacquering department ran to several departments, where they turned off or even broke the general electricity switches. The older, more sophisticated skilled workers and gangsters in the department were active behind the scenes to incite their younger subordinates, whose anger grew into fury as a result. Those who tried to stop them were severely attacked by the group. Soon, almost all of the workers walked out of the factory. No formal assembly meeting was held among workers, but thousands of them stood outside the old plant, in which the administrative office was located, while others wandered around the village or simply went home.

The residential district government (*Jiedao Ban*) and police officers arrived outside the factory as soon as workers started to gather there. The mayor tried to persuade the crowd: 'Any matter can be solved step by step. Let the government handle your dispute.' But he failed to convince the workers. At noon, the factory requested the workers elect their representatives. There was no formal election, but ten male workers stepped forward to volunteer. Among them were four Si Chuan provincials, and five workers from the lacquering department. Most of the ten were line-supervisor-level staff. According to other workers I interviewed, these men were 'ready to quit the factory' and wanted to 'play up' (*Gaoyigao*) before they did so.

Negotiations were held in the new plant in the afternoon. Workers moved to the plaza out of the canteen in the new plant to wait for the result. However, at the end of the meeting, the ten representatives were taken out of the factory in a police van which then drove off. The other workers presumed they had been dismissed and forced to leave the factory immediately, but a rumour circulated that they had each received a compensation payment of 30,000 yuan. One of the representatives from Si Chuan was said to have been physically punished and coerced to leave as a result of his resistance to this arrangement. Uncertainty and suspicion were rife among the mass of workers, and another rumour spread that the representatives had been killed by gangsters hired by the factory.

The night shift workers followed their day counterparts. In the evening, some of the workers were annoyed enough to rush into the administrative office, break the computers, and drive the Taiwanese general manager and local factory head to the entrance of the plant, where thousands of workers had gathered. A witness recalled the scene:

There were two to three thousand workers at the factory entrance, and also a certain number within the factory complex, who requested the Taiwanese

Lao [the general manager] to come out and explain. The Taiwanese *Lao* finally came out at nine o'clock in the evening. As soon as he appeared, those standing at the entrance pushed inwards, while those inside crowded out. All were screaming a 'wow wow' sound. Someone shouted: 'Kill him! Kill him!' The factory director, who was accompanying the Taiwanese *Lao*, said: 'Don't act this way, it can't sort out anything.' The workers did not stop screaming. The Taiwanese *Lao* who was surrounded by the crowd was then beaten by somebody. Four or five security guards promptly dragged the Taiwanese *Lao* and the director into the factory, and closed the gate of the factory. By then, most of the workers had come out of the factory. Some angry workers managed to climb over the high iron gate, making the 'wow wow wow' sound. Others flung cigarette butts, water bottles and rubbish at the Taiwanese *Lao*. The Taiwanese *Lao* did not lose his temper. On the contrary, he said: 'Don't throw this stuff, stop it. Wages can be raised.' One of the workers cursed at him: 'You Taiwanese guys do not treat us [mainland Chinese] as human.' The Taiwanese responded: 'We are all the same.' Workers shouted: 'Raise the wages according to the law!' He said: 'I agree. I promise to raise salaries, from 450 to 480 yuan. The overtime rate will also be raised to 3.50 yuan per hour, 1.5 times the normal rate. It will be double time on Saturdays and Sundays. If you have other demands, you can raise them, and let's talk.' The workers continued dialogue with him.

Around 100 workers stayed on overnight outside the entrance to block the factory and stop it sending out goods.

Third day

The next morning, a notice was posted by the factory stating that the wage would rise to the minimum legal standard. It was also said that a collective agreement had been signed between the management and the workers' representatives, with copies now kept by the factory, the representatives and the LSSB. But the dispute remained unresolved. One group put a big card behind the punch clock, informing workers to sign a petition to the city government for 'the return of people' (*Yao Ren*): that is, the release of those who had been arrested and the return of the ten disappeared representatives. The notice was not removed by management. One worker said: 'The security guards did not restrain activity in those few days. With several thousand workers involved, how could they restrain us? Even when the police came, they dared not restrain us either.'

Two to three thousand workers then again walked from the factory to the national highway later that morning. Some of the workers began to raise funds for a long-term struggle. They claimed the money would be used to buy cameras and loud-hailers to record events and make public announcements. This time all the workers walked on the same route to the highway. They were not stopped until they had walked for ten minutes along the highway to another industrial village where hundreds of riot police and guards from various security companies affiliated to the police bureau stood by. LSSB officials on the scene persuaded the workers to return to their factory and promised that they would meet them there later: 'As long as you go back, we can talk about any conditions on the table.' The workers then walked back to the factory.

When they arrived, their Taiwanese managers all fled to another Taiwanese factory next door. So no negotiation took place. The workers wanted to leave again soon after they realised they had been deceived, but the gate of the factory had been locked. However, some militant workers threatened the security guards and managed to leave. Riot police were positioned outside the factory, but as there was no further violence, they withdrew in the afternoon. Almost all of the day shift workers left the factory at 3 p.m.

Then the night shift workers continued the strike. They arrived at the factory and punched their time cards, but they did no work and soon left. Fury and discontent spread among the workers. In the evening, a bigger mobilisation began. In every corner of the factory grounds and the village, skilled workers and supervisors gathered in groups to discuss the next day's action. With the money that had been raised, organisers paid a company to make two big banners. Others spontaneously prepared their own slogan boards for the demonstration.

Fourth day

In the early morning, a message spread widely among the ordinary workers. 'In dormitories, private buildings and on street corners, people were asking others to "go to the city government",' one worker recalled. Later, the two banners were hung out, bearing the slogans 'Return Our Ten Workers' Representatives' and 'The Sun Factory Violated the Labour Law by Not Raising Wages!' No department superintendent joined in, but gangsters, supervisors and skilled workers all took leading roles. The organisers with loud-hailers, who directed the strikers into specific positions around the banners, were recognised by the ordinary workers as their line supervisors.

At 8 a.m., between 4,000 and 5,000 workers departed from the village and headed towards the highway. Some acted as pickets, stopping vehicles and buses en route. They suggested that the drivers should use other roads. When some drivers ignored these suggestions, their windscreens were broken by furious workers. In spite of the turbulence, though, the protest was better organised, planned and coordinated than the previous day's had been. The highway, connecting the province's two most prosperous cities, Shenzhen and Guang Zhou, and passing through another big manufacturing city, Dong Guan, is one of the busiest in the country. As the workers had marched onto this key road on three consecutive days, the police were well prepared to block them again at the highway entrance. However, rather than confronting the police at the first junction, the workers adopted an alternative strategy. As soon as the crowd arrived at the junction, a leader announced through a loud-hailer: 'Listen, we don't walk onto the main road.' The workers began to flood onto the pavement instead. First, the police used the bodies of policemen and security guards to block all the junctions to the main highway. Ten to twenty men stood across each entrance. Then, hundreds of police officers and security guards tried to stop the workers from moving forward on the pavement. Workers who found themselves surrounded by police and security guards resisted by throwing bricks, stones and even clumps of grass at the officers. In one of these battles, two guards were struck on the head. More security guards were dispatched from other towns to provide support.

The strikers had at least three loud-hailers, as well as several cameras and fundraising boxes. Younger ordinary workers held up the banners, rather than the gangsters and supervisors, who discreetly gave directions at critical moments. Not long after the workers arrived at the highway, policemen grew angry with the workers who were holding the banners and shouted: 'Put them down! Put them down!' The workers backed down and the banners were lowered and taken away. While ordinary workers held the loud-hailers and led the slogan chanting, some middle-aged 'brothers' made the 'wow wow' sound to raise morale. On the fundraising boxes was written: 'For our common interests, please put in your money.' They were soon full. The cameras photographed workers being beaten by police, but not vice versa.

Some reporters walked along with the marchers and interviewed workers. One outspoken man told a reporter: 'Our factory doesn't pay wages according to the law. We elected ten representatives, but we don't know where they have gone now. They were probably killed.' However, no significant reports appeared in the media. The workers believed that this was due to government pressure.

More and more workers from other factories joined the march, to show support or just for fun. One worker said: 'We had so many people. They were unable to stop us at all.' At 1 p.m., five hours after they had left the village, the protesters, whose number had reached 7,000 to 8,000, arrived at the immigration control station. This had been built in 1979 to separate China's first SEZ from other parts of the country. Non-SEZ residents needed a pass from the police to pass through the station and into the SEZ. The district government building was beside the control station, while the city government was several hours' walk away. The workers' intention was to go through the station and head to the city government. This, however, clearly would not be tolerated by the police. More than ten ambulances and over thirty water cannons stood in front of the station.

Police officers and workers confronted each other. The police used the water cannons to drive back the workers. But as soon as the cannons were turned off, the workers lobbed stones and bricks at the police. The missiles were like 'a hail of bullets raining down' (*Qianglin-Danyu*), one worker said. The policemen protected themselves with their shields. Xiao Lin, Xiao Liu, Chen, Qi and many of their fellow skilled and experienced workers were in the front rank at this point. A supervisor in his factory uniform stood in the centre of the workers, calling for them to push forward (*Xiangqian Chong*) through a loud-hailer. Police tried but failed to move in as the stones rained down on them. Coincidentally, the road was being resurfaced, so there were plenty of stones, bricks and lumps of cement lying around for the workers to turn into missiles.

Later, though, the police hit upon a new plan to drive back the workers. Qi, whose feet were stabbed in the battle, told me:

> Some policemen fell down. It seemed like a battlefield in a war, terrible. At the beginning, the police did not have a good strategy, but later they sent plainclothes men to mix with the protesters. They caught people within the crowd and hit them fiercely. Some of us lost shoes when running away. They used the stones to hit our feet. When we in the front fell down, those behind us screamed, and others were afraid and retreated.

Eight workers were arrested on the highway, and more than twenty at the control station. However, they were all soon released. Thirty workers were taken to hospital. Their medical expenses were all paid by the police. Qi and more than ten other workers remained in the district hospital for two weeks. According to Qi, the head of the district police bureau came to visit them and gave all of them – workers, policemen and security guards – 100 yuan each.

I asked Qi: 'Will you walk at the front and fight with policemen and guards again if there is another protest in the future?'

'Certainly not! I will sit down somewhere to watch [others fight],' he said.

One and a half hours after the confrontation at the control station, when the workers returned to the village, vehicles still could not move at all. Although no media reported the events of the day (which disappointed the workers), the traffic jam and eyewitness accounts of the violent battle meant that residents and other workers in the district were well aware of what had happened. For those participating in the protest, the overriding sensation was that it had been 'fun'. 'It was fantastic. Everybody came together for fun. Wow, all of us felt great!' Xiao Lin said. The workers were especially thrilled when they heard a rumour that the mayor had gone to the control station to take command of the police in person.

Fifth day

The next afternoon, workers were instructed to attend a meeting in the canteen. District LSSB officials, the police, the general manager and the factory director were all present. The general manager apologised to the workers with tears running down his face. He reassured them that both lunch and dinner times would be extended to one hour, and promised that the factory's policies would fully comply with the law. This brought down the curtain on the strike, although the ten disappeared representatives never returned. The factory was closed for two more days to recover from the chaos, and then everyone returned to work after a company notice was posted confirming the salary increase in line with the law. Workers heard that the manager who had introduced the lunchtime punching-out measure had been dismissed.

Workers on the strike

There were no obvious signs of departmental superintendents being directly involved in the organisation of the strike. Yet, according to the workers, they must have lent at least tacit (*Moren*) support, because no successful strike could have been organised without it. The superintendents knew all about the workers' discontent and about their plans to act, and of course they had very close patron–client relationships with their subordinate supervisors. The role of workshop supervisors was ambiguous. They certainly attended the demonstration and the various planning meetings, but they did not seem to take an overt leading role. The line supervisors, then, were the front-line organisers and leaders of the strike, with the support of a range of skilled and experienced workers. And those with close gangster connections, especially from the lacquering department and the provinces of Si Chuan and Gui Zhou, were the most active ringleaders. The most militant and violent group comprised male workers in their early twenties, who enjoyed the support of their supervisors. Ordinary workers, although they widely participated in the strike, were generally enthusiastic followers rather than leaders. However, there was a small group of slightly older workers (in their early thirties) who acted behind the scenes to influence the whole process. Men working in other factories or not working at all also appeared on the demonstration. Many of them claimed to be there 'on behalf of our wives' – female factory workers who had remained at home. Their husbands were normally unemployed and many were involved in gang and other illegal activities in the village. On the other hand, many Sun workers did not turn up for the highway protest. In addition to the female workers mentioned above, men in weaker production and market positions and older unskilled workers tended to stay away.

The male skilled workers I met in hospital after the demonstration were thrilled about my research topic and talked extensively about their strike experiences. However, one female worker in the plastics department told me that she had stayed on the production line throughout the protest, even though she supported the strike's aims. Aged thirty-two, she complained that her work in the factory was 'too tiring and too hard', but she had no plans to leave. She had worked nowhere but the Sun factory since leaving home in 2003.

Similarly, neither Luo (the middle-aged man who was bullied at work by his supervisor) nor Wang (the injured worker who suffered a subsequent mental collapse) joined the protest. Nevertheless their views on the strike provided an insight into the world of the factory's ordinary workers.

Author:	Did you join the protest?
Wang:	In July 2002 my wrist was broken, and three surgeons operated [on it]. At the time of strike, I was staying at home on sick leave. It was inconvenient for me to join.
Luo:	I stayed at home and did not go.
Author:	Why not?
Luo:	Too many people . . . hmm. . . . Well, if you went, they would sack you. You could see those leaders were all sacked, and some

	others were beaten. For people of my age it is not easy to find a job, so I should think of my wife and children, who depend on me.
Author:	Wang, if you had not been injured, would you have joined the protest? Or did you fear being sacked, too?
Wang:	Why would I fear that? Could they sack so many people?
Author:	How long did the strike last?
Wang and Luo:	Around a week.
Author:	So did neither of you go to work for the whole week?
Luo:	Every day we went to the factory to punch our time cards, and then came out. You could go wherever you liked. If you didn't want to go anywhere, staying in the factory was also fine. I usually stayed at home and slept.
Author:	When the strike began, you were working on the shop floor, right? Can you tell me how the workers in your workshops stopped working?
Wang:	Somebody turned off the light, so nobody could work any more.
Author:	And why did you return to work?
Luo:	The factory posted a notice, saying wages would be increased. Then we went back to work.
Author:	Were you informed by somebody, for instance those who led the strike, that you should return to work?
Luo:	No. I followed the others. Workmates would talk.
Author:	In your experience, how is a strike initiated?
Luo:	It should have some leading people. For example, if we want to lead a strike, then a few of us should gather together to discuss, and issue a statement, saying the wage is too low, and then ask others to sign up, and call for more to strike. In this way, a strike is organised. If a worker runs out saying: 'No more work today, let's strike,' others would follow. Ordinary people would listen to the others. In our department, if the plastics department upstairs began to strike, we would follow.
Author:	Did you know which department started the 2004 strike?
Luo:	I did not. But in our department, the worker who first asked others to stop working was sacked.

Luo seemed more informed than Wang about the strike, despite his hesitation to join the protest. The interview was conducted in the company of Xiao Lin, who offered his opinion of workers like Wang and Luo after they left:

There are many people like them, very timid. When others strive for a wage increase, they can share in the success without any cost. Wang said that she did not go to protest as she was injured, but that was an excuse. I was in hospital at the time, but I still came out to join. I was curious, you know, and it was fun. Actually, many youngsters showed up at the protest. It was very exciting to rush ahead with the police. Some of them did not really come for the money, but to enjoy themselves and let off steam.

Xiao Lin's point was confirmed by the experiences of many other interviewees. Workers joined the protest for a variety of reasons, but curiosity, prolonged discontent and a sense of unfairness seemed to be more important factors than the wage demand. A driver whose monthly income was over 3,000 yuan said that he joined the protest because he would probably have only one or two chances to do something like that during his lifetime. His wage structure was different from that of the production workers, so he never thought he was fighting for an increase in his income.

Chen, the technician in the metal department, attributed his attendance primarily to his discontent towards his departmental superintendent:

> Having worked here for such a long time, I deserved a higher wage. The salaries of friends and relatives of the Hu Bei superintendent were always adjusted promptly and frequently, two times in a year! These guys worked less than me, but their salaries were higher than mine; that was why I felt uncomfortable. Even if I was arrested, I would not regret [joining the protest and fighting with the police], although I have got two children at home.

The knock-on effect of the strike

As Hyman (1989: 135) put it: 'Consciousness of the efficacy of strike action can also be affected by other groups of workers.' The success of the Sun factory workers' wage struggle had a knock-on effect on the struggle over working conditions in the village throughout the next month. Struggles to demand wage adjustment according to the law broke out in almost all of the eight big factories (those with more than 1,000 workers) in the village. But it was not only workers who learned from the Sun factory; government and management also drew lessons from the strike and contained the subsequent workers' unrest swiftly. As soon as there was a sign of a strike, the management informed the government, then the main gate of the factory would be locked and the grounds surrounded by riot police. Without the need for any negotiation, the other factory owners promptly increased wages in line with those paid in the Sun factory.

Development of industrial relations after the strike

Although Marx imagined that proletarian factory workers would play the leading role in the class struggle, empirical studies after the 1960s generally agreed on the vanguard role of skilled and semi-skilled workers in workplace struggles (Gould, 1995). In China, Perry's (1993) study of strikes in 1920s Shang Hai also revealed the leading role of the artisans and skilled workers before the intervention of communist intellectuals. The artisan tradition in Shang Hai, however, was also related to place of origin, gender and gang. As the proletarianisation thesis argued, the radicalisation of artisans and skilled workers was a response to the erosion of their autonomy in the production process (Freidson, 1984; Tilly, 1984).[2] Once the management introduced rationalisation reform to weaken the control of the technical workers and front-line supervisors in workplaces, the rudeness, violence, militancy and confidence forged in their social and industrial lives and used to pacify other groups of workers turned against the management in the general interest of workers (Nelson, 1975). It was at such a critical moment that workers of different ages, genders, places of origin and skill levels acted together to voice their collective interests. This moment, however, is a historical 'happening', to borrow a term from Thompson (1963/1980: 10), referring to working-class formation, with various political, economic and cultural factors acting together. For the Sun factory, this moment came in 2004.

During this moment, workers were united on the basis of law to request the implementation of the minimum wage rate. However, the wage rate or immediate economic interest was not the sole aspiration of the workers. For example, the workers' vociferous appeal for the return of their representatives was not only a strategy to attract public attention but a sign of mature consciousness. Although the workers' wage rate was increased, their aspiration to establish control over their work remained unresolved, and their discontent rose even after the pay rise. As a consequence, the strike ended, but the struggle between management and workers over the control of production continued.

New control mechanism

The factory's first attempt at rationalisation through better attendance control encountered dramatic resistance, but its effort to lower the production cost, increase efficiency and take power from the technical and supervisory workers never ceased. The implementation of the minimum wage rate and later contribution of social insurance undoubtedly increased production costs. But the factory then introduced a series of new strategies to lower costs.

First, part of the production process was relocated to the new factory in Hui Zhou, where both market and legal wages were lower than in Shenzhen, and outsourced to small factories in the village, where labour law was not well enforced. According to a worker in the painting department, his daily wage on Sunday was fifty-eight yuan, while a similar worker in a small outsourcing factory earned only twenty-seven yuan. Workers' working hours, therefore, were constrained and working days were reduced from seven to six per week to avoid the double pay on Sunday (and comply with the one rest day per week requirement of the Labour Law). As a result, although workers benefited from shorter hours, their total income did not increase much.

Second, an internal contracting system was set up, in which the department superintendents or managers were required to meet a certain output figure after a lump-sum payment to their department. While this system drew resistance from workers, piece-rate payment was extended to departments in which time-rate had been operating.

Third, 'false' skilled workers were dismissed or demoted.

Fourth, the boundary between Taiwanese management and mainland Chinese supervisory teams was broken down by promoting four mainland department superintendents to assistant general managers, and sending Taiwanese staff to be commissioners under mainland superintendents in some departments.

Fifth, the power to recruit workers was removed from the internal department superintendents and personnel officers, by outsourcing to an external job agency.

Sixth, the factory tried to increase output targets to push up the intensification of work, and strictly enforced the fines system.

All of the above strategies counterbalanced the concessions gained during the strike and sparked struggles and resistance from the workers. The management–labour power relationship in the factory was, therefore, dramatically reshaped.

Workers' rising discontent

Workers' most prominent discontent after the strike concentrated on the intensification of work and strict enforcement of the fines system. The responses of Luo and Wang to my query about their perceptions of management concessions surprised me.

Author: To what extent did this factory change after the big strike compared with when you began to work here?

Wang: Not much.

Author: But the wage was increased, wasn't it?

Luo: Yes, the wage rate was increased, but there was no more overtime on Sunday, so our total monthly salaries are almost the same. You know, there are four Sundays each month. Hourly rate on Sunday was 6.7 yuan, working ten hours in one day. In this way we lost 260 yuan per month. The increase in wage rate was offset by the loss.

Author: But you can now rest on Sunday.

Luo: Yes, but our work is more intensive, too. The piece-rate, say ten cents before, has been reduced to seven cents now. And so the target per day was increased accordingly. It is more tiring to finish the target if we want to avoid a deduction from wages. In my workshop, more than 200 yuan was still deducted from one boy although he had worked very hard.

Luo and Wang were among the most quiescent and passive stratum of workers, so I had assumed they would be satisfied by the new regime, but their responses showed that was not the case.

Catnapping had been fairly common for night shift workers. In Qi's workshop a line supervisor who snoozed at night was fined after the strike. 'The factory does not treat us as human,' Qi complained with fury. He also felt angry that more than 200 working hours in one month were deducted from the wages of one of his new workmates. 'I told him to complain to the labour bureau. It is illegal!' he said, stressing the injustice of the penalty.

Based on the experience of the strike, asking for implementation of the Labour Law seemed to be an effective tool to force the LSSB to pressure the management. Fines and wage deductions drove many workers to complain to the LSSB. Guo, a twenty-three-year-old worker in the metal department, was one of them. However, he found complaining about this issue did no good. An official told him straight: 'Fines are also quite common for those of us who work for the government. It's not just a problem for you guys in the factory.' When the file of complaints started bulging, the LSSB officials occasionally visited the factory to investigate. Usually they would fine the factory anything between several thousand and several tens of thousand yuan. But whatever fine was issued, the factory did not change its practice. Guo and his mates found that it was hard to push the issue forward. The complaints were usually in the form of an individual or small group of workers' query to the LSSB in person or by phone. Making complaints in this way did not consolidate shop floor solidarity, especially when workers' interests were divided. (New starters tended to be penalised much more than the experienced workers.)

As the fines system failed to attract much attention from the LSSB, the workers sought other legal means to make trouble for management. After the strike, the wage was adjusted to comply with the law, but a basic working week of at least sixty hours was far beyond the legal limit of forty hours per week plus up to thirty-six overtime hours per month. However, it was obviously in the financial interests of the workers to work as much as possible, so their long hours did not become a basis for struggle. As Qi mentioned, in 2001, workers had staged a stoppage because of deductions from their wages to pay for social insurance. Four years later, generally, workers in Shenzhen were still not enthusiastic about paying for social insurance, as it seemed to them that the money was being taken straight out of their pockets for little benefit. In the Sun factory, however, social insurance became a rallying point in a well-organised collective complaint.

The complaint about social insurance

According to the law, migrant workers are entitled to social insurance covering retirement, injury and medical benefits. In Shenzhen, the injury and medical parts of the insurance were paid in full by the employers. As far as the pension was concerned, employers and employees contributed 8 per cent and 5 per cent of salary, respectively, to a fund run by the municipal social insurance bureau. Two per cent of that 13 per cent was pooled into a shared fund, while the remaining 11 per cent was held in a personal fund. There was no mechanism to allow part of the retirement fund to be transferred back to their home counties when peasant workers returned to their villages, constrained by the household registration system (*Hukou*). As peasant workers were only temporarily settled in one city and usually moved between homes and different cities frequently, this policy seriously discouraged workers from making contributions and provided an excuse for their employers to avoid doing so, too. Accordingly, the law stated that the personal fund could be returned to workers when they quit their jobs.

Local governments compete with each other over the participation rate of migrant workers in social insurance. Shenzhen was always proud of itself as the first city to introduce social insurance for migrant workers (as early as 1992) and boasted the highest participation rate in China. To keep the participation rate and absolute number increasing, all levels of government set targets every year for their subordinate authorities. At the bottom of the state hierarchy, the residential district (*Jiedao*) social insurance station, with the help of the community government, would push the factories to buy insurance for their employees. As a response to the state pressure, the factories would buy insurance for parts of their workforces so that they could get a certificate from the social insurance bureau. In 2004, therefore, some workers in the Sun factory had already joined the social insurance scheme, while others did not do so until May 2005.

Again, discontent first arose in the lacquering department. In the face of escalating disciplinary control on the shop floor, a group of workers was said to be planning to quit the factory. One day in May 2005, they went to the LSSB and the social insurance bureau and filed a complaint about the factory's failure to pay social insurance. The workers threatened to 'drop from on high' (see below) if the officials did not take their case seriously. As the complaint was made in a collective form and the legal basis was sound, the two bureaux responded promptly and the management was forced to post a notice during the day to inform workers that the factory would buy social insurance for all workers from that month onwards.

This comprehensive result left workers in the lacquering department little leeway to demand any more. The triumph and the issue of social insurance were then discussed in every corner of the factory. In the metal department, some workers expressed their feeling of 'unfairness' during a teatime chat among night shift workers. Some of them had worked in the factory for many years, but they had been told the social insurance could not be backdated. However, one of them mentioned that the workers in an electronics factory, where his girlfriend was working, had successfully demanded that their factory contribute to social insurance for the previous two years. The good news propelled the workers in the metal department to copy their lacquering department counterparts.

A handwritten sheet was posted on the wall of their department, informing others that they would go to the LSSB and social insurance bureau the next day to demand the previous two years' social insurance. The next morning, fifty workers from the metal department went to the two bureaux to file their case. They did not inform workers in other departments what they were doing. I asked Guo why they did not talk with workers in the lacquering department, for instance, and he replied simply that he did not know any workers there. Moreover, the notice had been torn down soon after it was seen by the commissioner. As a result, the members of the fifty-strong delegation were all from the night shift. In the offices of the bureaux, they were asked to write down their names and were informed that officials would soon hold talks with the management. Fifteen days later, the factory agreed to pay insurance fees for the previous two years into the social insurance fund.

A list of the representatives' names in both complaints was sent to the factory. Guo said that he and his fellow signatories had not expected this. 'People in both LSSB and the social insurance bureau do not really help the workers,' he groaned. After they returned to work, the signatories were denounced by their manager. The factory did not dismiss them, but most of them resigned in December 2005. In fact, the majority had been planning to quit for some time. Obviously they had the most to gain from backdated social insurance payments, because they could reclaim them as soon as they left.

Guo was one of the few representatives still in the factory in March 2006, when I conducted interviews there. Nevertheless, after working in the factory for six years, and having risen from an ordinary worker to a technician, he also planned to quit soon. He had come from the south-western province of Yun Nan after graduating from junior secondary school, and Sun was the only factory he had worked in so far. He hoped it would be the last, too, as he wanted to go home and farm. His opinion of *Dagong* was that it was 'meaningless'.

Department-based strikes

Two months after the metal department workers' complaint about social insurance, a strike – or, in strict terms, a collective absence from work – occurred in the same department.

The factory was closed on 28 and 29 (Thursday and Friday) July 2005 as a result of the electricity supply failing. Unusually, the factory decided to make up for these two lost days on the last Saturday and Sunday of August. In other words, workers were asked to work at weekend but would not be entitled to double pay. Workers were informed by their departmental superintendents of the decision just one day before the weekend. The workers were highly discontented, especially as they had had to do overtime work on five consecutive weekends. While the workers grumbled to each other, one of their line supervisors suggested that they should not go to work, before adding: 'It's up to you.' In the end, none of the workers went to work over the weekend. In the workers' understanding, the factory's action violated the Labour Law, but if their supervisors had asked them to work, they would have done so.

The factory finally dismissed the workshop supervisor from Hu Bei as well as five line supervisors, two from Si Chuan, and one each from Gui Zhou, Hu Bei and Jiang Xi. The factory then appointed a Hu Bei man as the new shop supervisor, and three more workers from Hu Bei, one from Si Chuan and one from Jiang Xi as line supervisors. On this occasion, the departmental superintendent from Hu Bei promoted many *Laoxiang* as supervisors, which meant the workshop became dominated by Hu Bei provincials. The dismissed staff were sacked on the grounds of making mistakes and so were denied service severance compensation. All six then filed a lawsuit against the factory for compensation, but they lost the case.

This was only one of many department-based strikes that happened after the 2004 strike. Around the same time as the metal workers' refusal to work, a stoppage occurred in the aluminium processing department to demand a higher environmental subsidy. The strike was led by a group of veteran workers who had each worked in the factory for more than five years. Workers sat beside the production line but refused to work. The factory then directed the departmental superintendent to negotiate with the workers, who returned to work an hour later, after obtaining a promise from the superintendent that their environmental subsidy would be raised by sixty yuan per month.

Next, a similar wildcat action took place in the casting department. Then, in August 2005, the painting department went on strike. All workers had to pay thirty-five yuan for an annual health check organised by the factory. The painting department workers believed that the company should pay for the check, especially in their department, where the working environment was among the worst in the factory. After the mediation of administration officers, the factory declared that the charging policy would be abolished for the whole factory.

Drop from on high

The dismissal of the six supervisors in the metal department was part of a deliberate assault on the stratum of skilled and supervisory staff. From July 2005 onwards, there were many cases in almost every department of veteran workers being fired without compensation or being forced to quit. According to the law, the factory should have paid severance compensation equivalent to one month's salary for each year's service if workers were fired before the end of their contract without reasonable grounds. As already noted, workers who did not properly perform their duties had generally worked in the factory for many years and had gangster connections. Therefore, dismissal was just one of the management's strategies to cope with the slacking and fraud of some 'skilled' workers. In some cases, the factory attempted to transfer them from simple and light skilled posts to physically heavier and more routine tasks, in the hope that workers would resign. While stricter enforcement of the fine and wage deduction system affected mainly the ordinary workers, the dismissal or transfer policy specifically targeted workers in skilled positions. But there was stubborn resistance from those affected. In the face of this escalating pressure, the attraction of work in the factory withered, so many skilled workers prepared to quit. First, though, they bargained with the management, on the grounds that changing the nature of work was equivalent to an act of unreasonable dismissal in cases where employees did not accept the change, and thus demanded service severance compensation. The factory countered that it had the right to move workers, and rejected the compensation claims.

While some workers chose the legal route to claim compensation, others utilised a more radical strategy – threatening to 'drop from on high' off the factory building. Individual workers in China frequently threaten suicide in this way over unpaid wages, in an attempt to catch the attention of the media and force officials to take their wage claims seriously. The first case involved seven workers from the lacquering and painting departments, who climbed onto the roof of the factory and then called the newspapers and the police. Reporters, policemen, ambulancemen and LSSB officers all arrived at the factory, and the management agreed to pay some compensation. From July to September 2005, there were at least four similar cases involving groups of workers from the lacquering, painting, aluminium processing and casting departments. In one of the these cases, the workers chose the day on which the auditors from a key client came to perform an audit in order to exert extra pressure on the management. However, when the strategy became an epidemic among the workers, both the management and the state refused to tolerate it any longer.

One day in September, a group of workers from the aluminium processing department who were on top of the building were told by the management that any condition could be negotiated if they agreed to come down. But once on the ground they were arrested by the police and detained for fifteen days on the charge of 'disturbing the social order'.

A wave of resignations

From October 2005, the newspapers began to report a social insurance reform. Under the new system, only employees' own contributions could be put into a personal fund after 1 January 2006. The policy, if applied in Shenzhen, would mean that workers could claim back only 5 per cent of their salary (rather than the 11 per cent they were entitled to under the current system) when they quit their job. However, as an SEZ, Shenzhen could override this national measure if it so desired. In neighbouring cities like Guang Zhou and Dong Guan, there was a wave of resignations in order to claim the higher proportion of social insurance before the new policy came into force. Influenced by this, workers in Shenzhen also began to quit. The Shenzhen city government then announced that it would not introduce the national policy in the foreseeable future. Workers remained unconvinced, though, and even more started to hand in their resignations in Shenzhen, where the number of workers entitled to social insurance was greater than in any other city. According to the official figure at the end of September 2006, the migrant workers of Shenzhen who enjoyed retirement, injury and medical insurance accounted for more than 30 per cent of the overall national figure (*Shenzhen Shangbao*, 20 October 2006). Furthermore, the proportion of the personal fund in the total contribution in Shenzhen at that time was higher than in any other city. In Guang Zhou, for example, only 8 per cent of the salary was put into the personal fund, 3 per cent less than in Shenzhen. So, if the new policy were implemented in Shenzhen, the cost to the city's workers would be higher than in other cities. Consequently, their response was more dramatic.

The uncertainty about social insurance further shook the delicate balance of labour relations in the Sun factory. On 26 October alone, 300 workers tendered their resignation. The norm in the region was that resignations were valid only after the personnel department had formally approved them, although the law stipulated that workers had the right to leave by giving advance notice of one month. Workers who left without permission from a factory, having given advance notice or not, would have their wage retained. First, the management played for time by claiming that the personnel managers were on leave and no one in the factory had the authority to grant approval; they also said they were unable to approve so many resignations at the same time. This created an atmosphere of suspicion and nervousness among the workers. By the end of November, resignation applications were as high as 3,000. The factory then recognised that it was powerless to stop the outflow and began to recruit an abundance of workers through a job agency. It also announced three dates when leaving certificates for workers would be granted. A long queue formed in the factory on the three days as thousands of workers waited for the certificates that would allow them to claim their personal social insurance funds. Qi was one of those who quit in this wave of resignations, but he returned to the factory just two months later.

Author: Why did so many workers quit the factory?

Qi: For some veteran workers, they could take back 7,000 to 8,000 yuan [from the social insurance fund]. Moreover, they could get another job as soon as they left this factory. If you wanted to find a job in smaller factories in the village, it was not hard at all. Some of us also wanted to go back home for New Year. It was ideal to go back home early and start job hunting after the New Year.

Author: Were there many people just like you, returning to work here after trying other factories?

Qi: Yes, many workers did that. Hundreds, I think.

Qi earned 1,500 to 1,600 yuan per month before leaving the factory in December – higher than the average 1,200 to 1,300 because he had spent seven years in the same department and so was very experienced. But he still sought a better life: 'I had been at the Sun factory since 1999, so I wanted to try a new job, a better one. I also felt that working hours in the Sun factory were too long.' After he left, he went to a big printing factory in the surrounding area, where he was responsible for paper cutting and earned 1,200 yuan per month. He quit after just one month, as he found he was more tired as well as worse paid there. Then he returned to his home village, where he found the only other inhabitants were schoolchildren and pensioners. Finally, he went back to the Sun factory. In one sense he was lucky, as it was factory policy not to re-employ anyone who had quit for at least six months after their resignation, but exceptions could be made for skilled and experienced workers. However, before Qi quit his job, he was entitled to 120 yuan of skill and 70 yuan of environment subsidies; once he returned as a new worker there was no subsidy (although his superintendent promised that he would get a 100-yuan skill subsidy if a proposed internal contracting system was not implemented – see below).

Worry over losing a significant amount of their social insurance fund money was the main reason why so many workers quit. Although the city government repeatedly promised that its policy would not change, workers felt much happier putting the money in their own pockets. But for some workers, including Qi, their resignations were not all about the money. Although his wages were now lower, he did not regret his decision to quit. 'I wouldn't have been satisfied if I hadn't tried to work in other plants,' he said.

Many unskilled workers quit on account of false rumours that were rife at the time. A twenty-eight-year-old woman who had worked in the plastics department told me that she resigned because two-thirds of the employees in her workshop had done the same, and because she had seen the Shenzhen mayor on TV saying that the social insurance could not be refunded after 1 January 2006, and the new policy would continue for ten years. She was therefore surprised that workers could continue to apply for the refund after that date. I explained that she had misunderstood what the mayor had said. But she still insisted that her interpretation was correct.

Luo and Wang, on the other hand, chose to stay at work amid the tide of resignations.

Author: How many workers in your department quit from the factory last year?
Luo: Two-fifths.
Wang: Around half.
Author: Why did so many resign even though your wage rate was increased.
Wang: To get back the social insurance.
Author: How about you? Why did you not follow them and resign?
Luo: It doesn't matter if you have social insurance or not. Having a job is good for me. So I did not leave.

Qi was different from Luo and Wang because of his age, skill level and market position. He could easily get a new job, which explained his confidence. Luo and Wang's pessimistic adjustment to the workplace norms of 'not much change [in working conditions]' and 'workers in protests were all sacked' can only be understood in the context of their working and life experiences. Family pressure, inferior economic status, bottom position in production, and experience of being bullied by gangsters all helped in the construction of a negative world-view and seriously diminished their self-confidence. To put it bluntly, as soon as Luo's family economic pressure was removed, nothing was stopping him from participating in the protest, but he still chose to stay at home during the strike.

Resistance to internal contracting

On the surface, the threat of social insurance reform accounted for the huge wave of quitting, but in fact the workers' determination to leave was a response to the factory's repeated efforts to undermine the autonomy of the skilled workers and supervisors and intensify the work process of the ordinary workers.[3] The plan to introduce an internal contracting system was one example of this.

From late 2005, a rumour about internal contracting spread among the workers. In fact, a similar but more radical plan had already been implemented in the production of the company's moulds, which was now outsourced to a small factory. The mould department therefore became a joint venture of the Sun factory and this local partner. The original mainland department superintendent then became a subcontractor of the small factory. Under this system, the Sun factory granted the contractor a lump sum fee to cover workers' wages and her or his own profit, while assets were still provided by Sun. The contractor, in turn, guaranteed the delivery timing and quality of the output as stipulated in the contract. Under this system, the common interests of superintendents, supervisors, skilled workers and gangsters would be eroded, putting the department superintendents into conflict with their subordinates. The first department to implement this system was the warehouse, where the number of workers was small. But the plan was to extend the system to all departments from 1 April 2006.

Tension on the shop floor escalated as the date approached. Departmental superintendents started to keep a close eye on production efficiency. Supervisors were under pressure to exercise stricter control, and workers were told to work faster. More importantly, deception by supervisors and skilled workers was seriously constrained. According to Chen, in the metal department: 'If you listened carefully in the middle of the night in the old days, the sound of the machines was in rhythm, one by one, not noisy at all, which indicated that not many machines were in operation. Now it is very different. All the machines are running.' Chen usually woke up at 3 a.m. to take a look at the breakage reports, but if there had been few breakdowns, he would go back to sleep. At 5 a.m., he would get up and fix all the machines that needed to be repaired. Then he would go home at 6 a.m. Obviously, as more machines started to operate simultaneously, there were more breakdowns and more demand for repairs, meaning more work for the technicians.

Guo also recalled the old days:

> If a machine broke down at 3 a.m. and the workers' total output was less than the requested target, then the line supervisor would report that the incident had happened at 1 a.m. and the machine was fixed at 6 a.m. They [the line supervisors] wanted to have fun too. Nobody wanted to work hard. Less output was the business of the factory, not theirs.

But then the line supervisors became self-censoring as their line output would be linked with the profits and interests of their boss and patron, the departmental superintendent. As a result, irrespective of whether their relation with the superintendent was good or bad, all of the workers faced pressure. The proposed new initiative persuaded many workers in skilled positions to resign *en masse*.

When Chen resigned, his superintendent tried to retain him with a promise of raising his skill subsidy to 200 yuan, because the department's newly employed technicians' salary was higher than his, even though their skill level was not. The superintendent added that he could increase Chen's salary even further as it would be up to his discretion after the internal contracting was introduced. But Chen refused: 'I had worked there for four years and he had not increased my salary so far, even though it was the factory's money. So I could not trust him to increase my salary with his own money!'

Some departments also reported further reduction of the piece-rate to prepare for the implementation of internal contracting. However, in the end, the contracting system was not introduced. Wang and Luo described the situation.

Author: When did the piece-rate reduction happen?
Luo: Last month [March 2006]. It was because the factory planned to introduce a system of contracting from this month. But now no one mentions it. We don't know whether this policy will be implemented or not.
Author: Wang, what about your department? Did you hear of the contracting policy?
Wang: I heard of it before, but no one talks about it any more.

Before April, workers, especially skilled workers and supervisors, began to discuss the new system and its possible effects. Many of them predicted that it would spark more strikes if it were implemented. Others said that it would be impossible to put into effect. A workshop supervisor, for example, said in a casual talk with his *Laoxiang* and previous workmates while I was in the workshop:

> To achieve success, there should be multi-level subcontracts where the factory contracts to the departmental superintendent, and the superintendent contracts to the workshop supervisor, and then the line supervisors. Otherwise, it won't work, because if only the departmental superintendents have interests, they won't get support from the supervisors.

Failure to gain the support of the supervisors and skilled workers was an underlying reason for the failure of the plan. But the direct cause of its abandonment was a strike in the assembly department. There were two superintendents in the department, one in the new plant and one in the old. The previous superintendent in the old plant had been promoted to assistant general manager in 2005. A conflict of interest arose among the three men, according to the workers. The factory's proposal was to make the assistant general manager a contractor so that production in the two plants could be better coordinated. But a few days before the contract was due to come into force, there was a day-long strike in the old plant. After this strike, the plan for the internal contract was formally withdrawn from the table for the whole factory. The departmental superintendent in the old plant was removed, with the superintendent in the new plant being put in charge of both plants.

As described above, workers in the most labour-intensive departments, including assembly, were paid by time-rate. As an alternative to the internal contract system, the factory planned to introduce a piece-rate system in the assembly department from September 2006. An experiment was first conducted on a production line in the old plant before being extended to the whole department. In mid-August 2006, I interviewed two workers in the department, a woman and a man, and asked what they thought of the new system. The woman seemed to know little about the new system. She said she had heard piece-rates would be implemented from September, but she had no personal preference as both systems had 'merits and drawbacks'. By contrast, the young man, although he had worked in the factory for only six months, had firm opinions on the new system:

Worker: Workers won't agree with it. It is piece-rate. For example, if you've done 300 pieces today, you only get paid after the 300 pieces have been delivered to the customer, and the quality has been proved OK. There is huge pressure.

Author: Did the factory discuss things with you? For example, how and when the piece-rate policy would begin?

Worker: Not at all.

Author: So will you talk with your supervisors if you disagree with the piece-rate system?

Worker: No. Disagreement will lead to a strike. If the piece-rate is put into effect, I will stop work.

He claimed the management in the Sun factory was less strict than in any other factory he had worked in: for example, workers were allowed to talk when working. Striking was always a popular topic in the workers' chat during or after work. I asked him if he knew about the big strike in the factory in 2004. He replied: 'You are joking. Everybody in this village knows about that. People were always talking about it.'

After learning that the contracting system would not be implemented, Chen expressed great regret at his decision to quit: 'If I knew there was no contracting, I definitely would not have left. Even though the salary was not increased, it was a good job, because the management was very lax, we had fun at work every day.' I suggested that he should talk with his superintendent, as he might be happy to re-employ Chen. But he said: 'He begged me to stay on when I resigned, but now I should beg him? No way. I don't beg.' He was offered a job in a metal factory with a salary of 1,800 yuan, 300 more than his previous job at Sun, but he did not accept the offer as the post required him to commute between the three plants of the factory. 'It would be more exhausting,' he said. Finally, he went back home to visit his family in April. Regarding the future, he said his brother, who was working in Zhe Jiang province, had asked him to work there too. He would try, but thought he would probably come back to Shenzhen eventually: 'It is not hard at all to get a job if you have skill. The only thing that matters is if the job is tiring or not.'

Outsourcing recruitment

In response to the huge wave of resignations, the factory held a recruitment campaign through a private job agency. There were banners stating, 'The Sun factory is recruiting a great deal of ordinary workers and skilled workers' outside the walls of the factory, beside the main road of the village and around the agency for a year. Job agencies, both local-government-run and private, have proliferated in recent years, as a result of the shortage of migrant workers. The traditional system of posting a notice outside the factory was no longer sufficient to attract enough applicants. The delay of the Sun factory in using a job agency might be explained by its comparatively good working conditions. However, outsourcing recruitment also indicated a determination in the company to introduce modern and scientific management by removing, or at least weakening, the power of the local supervisors to control personnel and build up their own status in the workplace.

A special counter was set up for the Sun factory in the job centre and staff used a loud-hailer to encourage applicants. When I visited the centre in March 2006 and approached the counter, the first thing they asked was: 'Where are you from?' I replied: 'Guang Dong. Is that important?' The staff said that the factory would not employ workers from BJ county in Gui Zhou or NY county in Si Chuan, which were both notorious for gang activity in the village. Workers said that the factory tried to exclude anyone from either province soon after the strike. But without employing people from these two provinces, they could not find enough workers. So then just the two counties were excluded.

The applicant was asked to fill in a form, which was scanned by a member of the agency staff, who paid special attention to work experience. She or he was then given a brief interview by two factory staff. The staff then handed out two more forms to be filled in by the candidate. Candidates were next asked some simple questions, and then, if they were deemed satisfactory, were told to go to the entrance of the factory at 9 a.m. the next day. They were not guaranteed a job at this point, and could be refused employment at the factory gate. The day I was at the job agency a total of sixty-seven workers passed the interview process, roughly half men and half women.

The next morning, some of the applicants arrived at the factory as early as 7 a.m. Some were visiting it for the first time. A group of three young women, after talking to workers about conditions in the factory and seeing the obsolete old plant, called the job agency and asked for the return of their 300-yuan introduction fees, as they felt the work would be too hard for them. The agency replied that the fees were non-refundable, but the women could apply to other factories. Another applicant, from Guang Dong, said that she knew she would be taken on, as a friend who 'worked inside' had asked her to apply. At 9.15 a.m. a list of sixty-seven names was posted up, meaning no one had been turned down. However, one middle-aged man grumbled to a security guard that he could not find his name. The security guard checked the internal record and excluded the possibility of a typing error. The worker then argued strongly that his place must have been taken by someone who knew 'somebody inside'.

After a half-hour briefing on factory regulations, the new workers were divided into male and female groups, each of which was led by a supervisor on a tour of the factory. Work duty was assigned after this. The workers discussed which department's work was heavier. I talked with some of them *en route* from the old plant to the new plant. Many of them seemed to have a good understanding of the structure and work culture in the factory through friends who were already working there. In the afternoon, they were sent to a health check in a town hospital, where they were each given a health certificate. The Guang Dong woman, who was assigned to the plastics department, told me some days later that only about forty workers turned up to work the following day. So more than twenty workers either did not turn up at all or decided to quit after the orientation day.

The same exercise was repeated throughout the month. However, although such a large-scale recruitment exercise was under way, the total number of workers still declined, due to the high resignation rates of both old and new workers and the dismissal of unskilled old workers at the end of their contracts. The factory also moved some machines and equipment to the new factory in Hui Zhou, where the basic salary was much lower.

State policy and wages

After the outbreak of the strike in the Sun factory and other serious labour disputes in the region, new policies were adopted by the local government to stabilise labour relations. At residential district (*Jiedao*) level, a government document, focusing on the Sun factory strike, showed how its measures effectively combated labour unrest.

On the one hand, propaganda was distributed among workers under the slogan 'When protecting rights, don't forget obligations; protecting rights must follow the law' (*Weiquan Buwang Yiwu, Weiquan Bixu XunFa*). Fifteen thousand booklets on labour laws and regulations were distributed among workers. A 'labour dispute administrative compliance guideline' and a notice for an 'unpaid wages hotline' were posted in all communities, industrial zones and enterprises with more than 200 workers. The guideline suggested that unauthorised assembly, demonstrations, rallies and strikes were illegal. Workers were encouraged to make complaints through representatives, and were advised not to bypass the lower level of administration (*Yueji Shangfang*).

On the other hand, systematic monitoring was inaugurated in factories with unstable labour relations. An 'engagement mechanism for labour-dispute-prone enterprises' was established to persuade factories to comply with the law. Following a thorough and in-depth investigation, all of the 2,000 factories in the town were categorised into one of four groups: red, yellow, blue and green. The most volatile factories were subjected to special monitoring. The fifty-two-strong official team in the town labour station was retrained in labour laws and state policy. Each official was responsible for monitoring a certain number of factories. As a result, 2,286 complaints were filed by workers to the station from January to July 2005. Compared with the first seven months of 2004, the number of serious labour dispute cases was reduced by 65 per cent, and enterprises that seriously violated the law declined by 86 per cent. The new measures accounted for the prompt and proper handling of Sun workers' complaints against the factory.

At the city level, among others, the minimum wage rate was increased by an unprecedented rate. The minimum monthly wage was increased from 480 yuan to 580 yuan on 1 July 2004, and to 690 yuan one year later.

Management used different strategies to deal with the rise in the minimum wage. Some medium-sized factories charged more for accommodation and catering fees. Small factories, of which there were many in the village, flouted the law. The Sun factory and some other big factories in the village simply adjusted their wage levels in line with the new rate. In August 2006, when workers received their wages for July, some ordinary workers found that their pay had never been so high – as much as 2,000 yuan. Summer was the factory's peak season, and as there were still not enough experienced staff, workers had been asked to work on Sundays. Many had only one rest day in the whole month. The work schedule was similar to that of early 2004, but the workers' salaries were almost double the levels before the strike.

Establishment of a nominal trade union

One day, when I had lunch in a restaurant with Xiao Lin, Chen and Guo, we talked about the fines in the factory. Guo mentioned the trade union. After the social insurance complaint in 2005, workers in the lacquering department had signed a petition demanding a trade union in the factory. But the three workers all agreed that without the support of the management, it was difficult for a union to function successfully. Chen added that it was necessary to form a 'real' trade union in the factory to defend the workers' rights: 'Without a labour union to represent workers, it is very hard to do things (*Hennan Gao*). After you make trouble for the factory, the factory will make more trouble for you.' Guo emphasised the workers' lack of understanding of the labour ordinances: 'We have absolutely no idea of how a trade union can be formed according to the law, and what it should be. We went to ask for information from the labour bureau, but it was useless. They did not help the workers.'

None of them had any idea of the development of trade unionism after the lacquering workers' campaign. But further investigation showed that a trade union had been formally established in the factory in 2005. However, it was totally management controlled, involving no elections and no union activity. In fact, most workers did not even know of its existence. Limited information about the trade union came from a line supervisor who had worked in the factory for ten years, a worker who was responsible for driving the Taiwanese manager, and a security guard who had worked in the factory for seven years. They told me that the formation of the trade union was a response to pressure from the workers. The security guard said: 'The factory had no choice but to follow the demand of workers. They were afraid of a workers' strike.'

Legacy of the 2004 strike

The Sun factory dispute was just one of a wave of strikes from 2004 to 2005. During my stay in the city from September 2005 to August 2006, striking was still an effective way of expressing grievances in workers' collective memories. The wave of strikes dramatically reshaped the workplace relationship and exerted significant pressure on the local state regulation strategy. The locality- and gender-based 'despotic' labour regime (Lee, 1998) was challenged by the workers during the strike, and rank-and-file workers rose to be key players in industrial relations through their collective action.

Although one of the main priorities of the Party state was to maintain proper social order and its legitimacy to rule, its leverage had been handicapped by local state officials, who preferred to maintain a favourable investment environment to implement the Labour Law and regulations (Lee, 2007a). As this case shows, workers' actions forced the local authorities to make concessions over improving labour protection, for example by raising the minimum wage rate and through better monitoring of illegal labour conduct.

Pressure on the management was twofold, coming from workers disrupting production and the new legal requirements imposed by the state. Both factors led to increased wages and production costs. As competition in the global market over price was intense, new business and management strategies – for example, production relocation, outsourcing, proposed internal contracting and new recruitment practices – were adopted to sustain profitability.

In the face of the new state policy and management strategy, workers also changed their struggle strategies. They became more vocal and tactical after the strike. Their post-strike protests were very flexible, creative and brisk, from a series of individual resignations and publicity-generating actions to waves of collective administrative complaints and well-planned, short strikes. As Edwards and Scullion (1982) suggested, quitting is a form of industrial conflict if we put it in the context of unresolved workers' grievances. To be sure, workers' discontent was not created during the strike, but embedded in a coercive day-to-day labour process. However, without a 'culture of solidarity' consolidated in a strike (Fantasia, 1988), that discontent was not well articulated as a collective form. As soon as it was voiced, though, it encouraged further action in their workplace and beyond.

In the following section, I shall explain how the 'culture of solidarity' was transferred to the new plant of the Sun factory in the city of Hui Zhou.

The new subsidiary plant: the endemic effect of strikes

> Striking has become endemic. The epidemic also affected the new plant in Hui Zhou. Workers take strikes very casually. A little incident can lead to a strike. As soon as the old plant strikes, the new plant [in Hui Zhou] follows.
>
> (Dong, a supervisor in the Hui Zhou plant)

Dong, aged thirty-three from Si Chuan, was a workshop supervisor in the metal department in Hui Zhou. Previously, he had been a line supervisor in the old plant. He was among the 300 skilled workers and supervisors who were transferred from Shenzhen to the new plant in 2004. They were all promoted to higher positions or paid an extra subsidy as a reward for relocating to the more remote area. In Shenzhen, Dong's basic wage and subsidy was 1,200 yuan, plus about 500 yuan overtime, making a total monthly income of around 1,700 yuan. After he was promoted to workshop supervisor in Hui Zhou, his subsidy was increased by 400 yuan to make his basic wage 1,600. But as his overtime pay, which was based on the minimum wage rate, was only 400 yuan or less in the new factory, his total salary was just 2,000 yuan.

Portrait of the new factory

The new factory grounds were fenced within an area of three square kilometres. The factory bought – or rather rented for a period of thirty years – the land from the local village.[4] The village, with rows of newly developed multi-storey houses, lies beside the factory. The nearest town, with 20,000 residents, is two miles away. Between the village and the town are agricultural fields, except for the factory complex. Hui Zhou is adjacent to Shenzhen, but the average price of industrial land there was 50 to 60 yuan per square metre, compared with 300 yuan in Shenzhen. The city government granted a three-year local tax exemption for all new investors, while in Shenzhen the policy was a two-year exemption followed by a 50 per cent discount for three years.[5] In early 2006, the minimum wage rate in Hui Zhou was 410 yuan, compared to 580 yuan in Shenzhen. The lower rent, tax and minimum wage persuaded many companies in Shenzhen to relocate all or part of their production to Hui Zhou.

A main road divided the industrial estate, leaving the administration building and workers' dormitories on one side, and the production buildings on the other. An estate of superior accommodation was under construction for Taiwanese staff in March 2006. In total, the developed area accounted for only one-third of the fenced territory.

The new plant was much lighter, cleaner, tidier and fresher than the Shenzhen plants. While the old and new plants in Shenzhen were four and five storeys high, respectively, the production lines in Hui Zhou were all situated in six–seven-metre-high single-storey buildings with energy-saving glass ceilings, except for the front part of the main workshop hall, which had two storeys. The upper floor, from where one could see the ground floor, was housed administrative and R&D departmental offices. As in the Shenzhen plants, the names and photographs of supervisory staff, from departmental managers to line supervisors, were posted up on the shop floor walls. But unlike Shenzhen, other wall decorations promoted teamwork and industrial safety, such as a poster which reminded workers: 'Paying no attention to safety is like killing a hen for its eggs!' and a painting of a group of smiling young workers bearing the slogan: 'The most enthusiastic team services our customers with the most sincerity.'

The work schedule and the requirement to register in and out were the same as in Shenzhen (although workers in Hui Zhou swiped an electronic card rather than punching a card), but disciplinary control was much stricter. Workers lined up for collective gymnastic exercises on the ground floor before 8 a.m., walked into the workshops applauding and handed their passes into their supervisors at the entrance. Later, they queued up and applauded again to take back their passes when they finished work. The Taiwanese managers described the applause as a method 'to encourage with love'. Night shift workers were not required to do the gymnastics, but the other procedures were enforced.

It was largely compulsory to live and eat at the factory, with deductions of 30 yuan for accommodation and 190 yuan for catering per month. Twelve workers, normally from the same department, shared a dormitory room. Prior approval from the workshop supervisors was necessary if workers wanted to live outside the factory, while workers in Shenzhen only needed to inform the factory before moving out of the dormitory.

Unlike their counterparts in Shenzhen, who were allowed to sit, staff in the assembly and processing departments at Hui Zhou stood while working. (There were some fixed benches available for non-working time on the shop floors.) In the metal department, chairs were provided only once workers complained about the difficulty of operating the machines after standing for a long time.

Technology and the assembly line

The machines were all new and imported from Taiwan or Japan. By contrast, most of the machines in Shenzhen were virtually obsolete, although the factory had begun to replace some of them with the same models as in Hui Zhou. For instance, in the metal department of the Hui Zhou plant, the machines ran faster and were fitted with an autonomic switch and a protective transparent cover to avoid crunching fingers. In Shenzhen's metal department, by contrast, the accident rate was extremely high; the factory was at the top of the industrial injury blacklist announced by the municipal social insurance bureau.

In the assembly department, a Taylorist production line was introduced. In Shenzhen, workers sat in a row, facing each other's backs, with boxes on one side to fill with finished and semi-finished products. In Hui Zhou, workers stood face to face with a belt moving the parts between them. In other words, while workers in Shenzhen could control their working pace, their counterparts in Hui Zhou were embedded into the pace of the moving belt.

The most radical difference was in the plastics department. In Shenzhen, workers, who sat beside the machines, opened a barrier in the machine at the end of a compression process to take out a plastic product with a clip and then put it into a box. When full, the box was moved to another location for further processing. In the new plant, the whole workshop was integrated into an autonomic line, and robotic arms took the plastic parts from the machines and placed them onto a moving belt. Workers sat on both sides of the belt to process the plastic pieces simultaneously. The workshop supervisor said the new technique allowed the department to reduce its labour force by a third.

Recruitment and the labour force

Despite the automation, however, the new factory could not recruit sufficient workers. In the plastics department, for example, workers were unable to process all of the products moved by the robotic arms, so boxes of plastic pieces were put aside to await processing.

In the same way as at the Shenzhen plant, a recruitment banner hung outside the factory: 'The Sun factory is recruiting long-term female ordinary [low-skill] workers (*Changqi Zhaopin Nu Pu Gong*)'. The difference between the two banners was that the one in Shenzhen asked for male and female ordinary workers *and* skilled workers, but the new factory specifically wanted female ordinary workers.

There was a total of 4,000 workers in the new factory in March 2006. The gender and age composition of those workers was different from Shenzhen. There was a much higher proportion of women and younger workers, with the majority between twenty and twenty-five years old. The small number who were older than thirty were either supervisors and skilled workers transferred from Shenzhen, or newly recruited male skilled and female ordinary workers. In the plastics and assembly departments, almost all of the workers were female, while all of the supervisors were men. Among 200 day shift workers in the plastics department, there were only 15 male workers – 11 in one workshop and 4 in the other.

The Shenzhen plant recruited workers through a local job agency, but the new plant hired through labour service departments (*Laowu Bumen*) and mid-level professional schools outside Guang Dong province.[6] While the practice had been prohibited in Shenzhen, the new plant also still recruited workers directly from those who had read an advertisement and walked in off the street. *Guanxi* (personal relationship) was still an important channel of admission into both the Shenzhen and Hui Zhou factories. However, this was officially frowned upon in Shen Zhen and entailed the corruption of supervisory staff, whereas in the new plant current workers were positively encouraged to introduce friends and relations. In Shenzhen, the factory was reluctant to hire workers from Si Chuan, but this discrimination did not exist in the new plant. As a result, the number of Si Chuan workers had declined in the Shenzhen plants, but the province supplied the largest number of workers in the new factory.

In sum, the old plant faced a shortage of skilled and experienced workers but had a surplus supply of unskilled workers, while the Hui Zhou plant was understaffed throughout, even with respect to unskilled ordinary workers. The automation, Taylorisation and rationalisation were all responses to this shortage of labour and rising labour costs.

New workers' opinions of the old factory

In the eyes of the new factory workers, the old factory in Shenzhen was a paradise which had higher wages, shorter working hours, higher status, more opportunities for fun and more open-minded people.

After learning that I had visited the old plant, a group of nine women and one man who worked on the same line in Hui Zhou called me over for a chat. They had worked in the factory for between three days and six months, and said that all of the old workers had already left. Three of them were especially outspoken:

- A: female; thirty years old; joined the factory three months previously from an electronics factory in Hui Zhou.
- B: female; twenty-five years old; joined the factory half a year previously from a factory in Shenzhen.
- C: female; twenty-seven years old; joined the factory two months previously from an electronics factory in Hui Zhou.

They understood the situation in the Shenzhen plants very well, being aware of the fact that the basic salary was 300 yuan higher than theirs and that workers could take leave on Sundays.

A: If our salary was as high as the old plants, we would not want to work on Sunday too.

B: [joking] Let's go to work in the old plants.

C: The old plants would not want people like us. There everybody is an official.

Author: Did you go back home for the New Year [festival]?

A: No. Very few workers went back home from this factory. We got only nine days of leave.

Author: Why didn't you resign?

A: Many people submitted application letters, but they [the managers] did not approve them. They told us that the manager had gone home for the New Year already, so no one could grant permission.

Author: Did you give up so easily?

A: We had no choice.

Author: Actually, you don't need their approval to resign. It is your right to resign if you inform the factory one month in advance. In Shenzhen, many workers go to the labour bureau to file a complaint if they cannot resign successfully.

B: Right. When I worked in Shenzhen, the labour bureau officials would come to our factory as soon as someone called them to tell them that there was a strike. Here it is so different: no one cares about us when we strike.

Author: When your old plant first began to strike, no one cared about them either. But then they blocked the highway, turned the strike into a very big issue, and then the officials came. Afterwards, complaining was very effective.

A: Oh, really?

C: But we do not have a highway here. It is a remote village.

B: Shenzhen is different. There is the Labour Law and everything is standardised there. The law here is different.

Author: No. The Labour Law is a national law, applicable everywhere. But the minimum wage rate is different from place to place.

A and B: Really? Is that true?

Author: Of course. The law was announced by the nation (*Guojia*).

C: I hope you can talk with people in the old plant for us. Our wage is too low.

Author: I only knew workers in the old plant, so it's hard for me to help you, although I wish I could. How are wages in this factory compared with others in the city?

A: How can I put it? There are factories with higher wages, but there are also some lower than us.

Strike and conflict

The first factory-wide strike in Hui Zhou took place in December 2004. It was started by workers in the aluminium department. In interviews I found that the younger workers in the department (those in their early twenties or younger) did not understand the process of the strike too well. It was left to twenty-six-year-old Bing, a male worker from Jiang Xi province, to tell me about the cause, process and result of the strike in detail. He talked with me in the workshop during lunchtime, when his supervisors were away. Before joining the factory, he had worked in three other factories.

There were two canteens in the factory, one for managers and the other for workers. The workers' canteen, their only eating place, was contracted out by the factory to a local businessman. In December 2004, workers repeatedly wrote signed petitions to the owner to complain about the poor quality of the food and demanded improvements. One day, several workers from the aluminium processing department complained again to the owner during breakfast. Later, when they were queuing for lunch, seeing that the food was as bad as ever, they threw their metal food coupons and left the canteen. No one was injured, but the scene caused some disturbance.

To prevent a similar incident, the next day ten security guards were stationed inside the canteen. Like the supervisory staff, the security guards had been transferred from Shenzhen. The canteen always had a long queue, and some workers from the assembly department pushed forwards. The guards grabbed three and punched two of them, knocking them down. The workers then rioted, chasing the guards to a small hill near the factory. Work stopped in the afternoon throughout the factory.

Performing a similar (but more violent) role to that of the lacquering workers in Shenzhen, around thirty young workers from the aluminium department ran through the factory and broke equipment in various departments. 'The stuff in the administration department was also smashed by us,' Bing told me with satisfaction. In the plastics department, some workers kept working at first, but they were forced to walk out after the aluminium workers smashed their equipment.

There were more than ten workers from Shenzhen in the aluminium processing department, and they told their workmates all about the strike in the old plants. During the Hui Zhou strike, however, it was the locally recruited workers, with backgrounds similar to Bing's, rather than the veteran workers from Shenzhen, who broke machinery.

In the evening, the factory announced that the security guards had been fired. Workers resumed work the next morning, but they remained dissatisfied with the quality of the food. In Shenzhen, the factory immediately terminated the canteen service to avoid a similar event.

Just like the highway protest in Shenzhen, the first strike in Hui Zhou became a hot topic among workers, so even new employees knew about it. After this factory-wide dispute, workers staged many department-based strikes, one of them in the plastics department in March 2006.

In the Hui Zhou plant, workers' wages were paid according to the law. But as the local minimum wage rate was comparatively low, workers' total income was highly dependent on the double pay of overtime work at the weekend. Workers were generally unhappy about their low pay, especially when they compared it with their counterparts in the old plants. Lan, aged twenty-eight, had come over to Hui Zhou from the Shenzhen factory. She was not transferred by the factory, but resigned during the quitting wave prompted by the social insurance issue in December 2005. Like many others, though, she soon regretted resigning, especially when she was not allowed to return to the old factory. So she travelled to Hui Zhou and applied for a post in the new factory. In the old plant she had earned 1,200 to 1,300 yuan per month for a six-day working week. Now she was working seven days a week and earning only 900 to 1,000 yuan. Unsurprisingly, workmates grumbled a lot to each other about the unfairness of the pay structure in Hui Zhou: longer working hours but lower income. This general discontent about wages, alongside the catering quality concerns, was the context for the plastics workers' strike.

The strike began on a Friday. As there had been no work on the previous two Sundays, workers were nervous about the coming Sunday. With no news from the management, workers in two plastics workshops walked out to the open space outside their workshops. They said that they did not stay within the workshops because 'it was easier to be persuaded to [go back to] work' in there. They asked the general manager to come to talk with them, but he did not appear. Instead, the Taiwanese departmental manager negotiated with them. The manager asked the assembled 200 workers what they were demanding. A woman who had worked in the factory since its establishment spoke up: 'Our wage gets lower and lower. Now there is no overtime work on Sunday, so our wages cannot be more than 800 yuan. Furthermore, 220 yuan is deducted for dormitory and food, but the food was disgusting. What is "to encourage with love"? Are all of these love?' The manager immediately dismissed her. She replied: 'That's OK. I don't want to work any longer.' She left the factory in the evening.

No other workers spoke; they just remained silent outside the workshops. The next day they did the same thing. The management was worried that the strike would spread to other departments, so a notice was posted stating that there was not enough work in the plastics department, so the department had been closed for one day. However, on the Sunday morning, the workers gathered in the same place. Managers and supervisors arrived to persuade them to return to work, but they were ignored. At 10 a.m., the factory posted another notice, this time stating that there would be work every Sunday in the plastics department, and even when there was insufficient work for them to do, workers would rest only in shifts. The workers then returned to work.

When I talked with a workshop supervisor in the department about the cause of the strike, he provided an explanation which seemed to have been deliberately withheld by the ordinary workers. On the first day of the strike, one of the two workshop supervisors and my interviewee's predecessor quit the factory. According to the new supervisor, the workers' action was in support of their outgoing supervisor. The previous supervisor, from Guang Xi, had been transferred from Shenzhen, where he had held the same position since 2004. His fixed wage and subsidy increased from 1,400 to 1,600 yuan in reward for the transfer. But as his overtime pay was much lower than it had been in Shenzhen, his total monthly income remained at around 2,000 yuan. The promise to increase his wage had never been realised, and that prompted him to quit. The whole team of skilled workers and line supervisors in the new plastics department had been brought over by him from Shenzhen. The new supervisor hinted that his predecessor had always intended to stage a strike before he quit. According to the law, an employee who resigned was not entitled to any severance compensation, but the strike forced the factory to negotiate a secret deal with the unhappy supervisor. He finally left the factory on the Saturday, and the management fully expected the workers to resume work the next day. It was only when the workers continued the strike on the Sunday morning that the factory was forced to offer the Sunday work guarantee.

The old supervisor was held in high esteem by his subordinates. 'He did not denounce workers. Whenever he saw something unacceptable, he would condemn the line supervisors rather than the workers,' a skilled worker told me. The workers were more ambivalent about their new supervisor, who complained about the problems of managing such a united group of employees.

This strike was followed by one in the lacquering department, where all of the workers were male. The follow-up strike was initiated by a group of veteran workers from Hu Nan province who had worked in the department since the first day of the factory. All of those on the day shift joined the strike, which lasted for a Monday morning. The factory's vice-general manager, who was responsible for the operation of the new plant, came to meet them. The workers demanded a wage increase, but the vice-general manager firmly rejected the request by saying: 'It is impossible, as wage adjustment is not a question of only your department. If we increase your wage, then workers in other departments will raise the same demand, and the factory is not able to bear that.' He then tried to persuade the workers to return to work. Most of them did so, but eleven veteran workers continued to strike. They were all dismissed and left the factory at 4 p.m.

Management and work culture

With the introduction of a modern production system and stricter discipline, the new factory exercised stricter control over the workers. However, the work culture remained loose. Gangsters and place of origin functioned much less as bases for both subordination and resistance in the new plant. A shortage of labour and propensity to strike were two essential factors accounting for the maintenance of a higher degree of control among workers.

One day at 4.15 p.m., when I walked into the workshop of the lacquering department, some workers were sitting on the ground at the entrance, while others were working inside. The scene was very similar to what I had witnessed in the same department in the old plant when I visited one afternoon in November 2005.

I talked with a twenty-two-year-old woman worker from Hai Nan in the assembly department. There were very few workers from Hai Nan in the factory, but her unusual place of origin background did not make her quiescent. While I talked with her, her middle-aged male line supervisor was standing on the opposite side of the assembly line.

I asked the worker: 'Are you afraid to talk with me with him standing there?'

She replied: 'Why should I be? What can he do to us? The worst [thing for him] is [for us] to quit. They find it hard to hire people now.'

I then asked about her attitude towards striking.

'If you come to work here and lead a strike, we will follow,' she answered straightforwardly.

In the production technology department, which was responsible for developing models for new products, skilled workers enjoyed even more freedom and autonomy. The departmental superintendent was currently on leave, and the factory had appointed the most senior craftsman as acting head. While he himself was working very hard, two of the younger workers were playing with toys.

During a casual talk with workers in the metal department, we discussed the proposed internal contract system. A twenty-year-old worker said: 'It is not my business, contracting or not. If my wage is lowered as a result of the contract, I will leave. I very much hope it gives rise to another strike.'

From Shenzhen to Hui Zhou: spaces of capital and labour

After thirty years of industrialisation, by which time Shenzhen had become one of the country's most metropolitan cities, migrant workers there had developed the highest level of consciousness of their rights and interests. The Sun factory's relocation of part of its production from Shenzhen to Hui Zhou was driven by the same dynamics as the industrial relocation from the West to Asian tiger economies in the 1970s, and from the Asian tigers to China since the 1980s. As Harvey (2001) illuminated, space is central to our understanding of the history and struggle of capital and labour. Globalisation is a persistent social process of capital searching for less organised labour, lower legal and law enforcement standards, and cheaper land and environment to satisfy the needs of its accumulation. Certainly Hui Zhou provided much cheaper land, labour and taxes for global capital due to a lower level of economic development and the local state's desire to compete for investment.

However, as workers enjoyed some freedom of movement, there was a trend for them to travel from a place with poor working conditions to another with better ones. The flow of capital in search of lower costs in the history of capitalism has been accompanied by a continually changing pattern of labour migration for better working and living conditions (Cohen, 1987). Both workers and management in the PRD explained the shortage of labour in terms of workers in the region moving to the YRD, where a higher wage could be earned. This also explained why the Hui Zhou plant found it more difficult to recruit and keep ordinary workers than the Shenzhen plant, although skilled and experienced workers were greatly desired by both due to the high turnover rate. As a result, a more active recruitment strategy was employed in Hui Zhou to bring in workers directly from their schools and home counties. Despite the fact that the supply of migrant workers seemed to be unlimited in the early 1990s (Lee, 1998), rapid economic growth had rapidly pushed up the demand, but not necessarily the wages, for labour, as Lewis's (1954) classic study predicted.[7] To a large extent, the level of wages was a result of class struggle in specific social spaces, as Friedman (1977) suggested.

Comparing the Hui Zhou and Shenzhen plants, it was easy to find a contradiction. While physical infrastructure was more advanced and modern in Hui Zhou, its labour practices were more alienating and inhuman. As the Hui Zhou plant was an ideal site for social audits from client TNCs, and OHS was one of the key elements in labour inspections, it was obvious that the slogans 'Paying no attention to safety is like killing a hen for its eggs!' and 'The most enthusiastic team services our customers with the most sincerity' were posted not only for workers, but for inspectors and auditors. But the automatic assembly belt and robotic arms were undoubtedly installed to exert more control over the workers. With these new technologies, workers had to perform more routine and boring tasks at a faster pace (and while standing in some departments). The large drill ground was not provided for workers' leisure and physical exercise, but to impose military-style discipline on them. In Shenzhen, informal control relying on locality networks was much more prevalent than in Hui Zhou, where the Taiwanese management exercised more direct control through formal regulations. In the history of Western industry, Taylorism was regarded as a technical precondition for Fordism. In contemporary China, however, technical Taylorism has been exploited to reinforce a coercive labour regime, as we have seen at the Sun factory.

To rebel against the despotic regime, workers in Hui Zhou needed time and experience to forge a strategy and consciousness in line with those of their Shenzhen counterparts. Apparently, experience transferred from Shenzhen through interpersonal networks of skilled and supervisory workers played an important role in the development of workers' protest in Hui Zhou. There were close similarities between strike and struggle strategies in the two plants, although organising scale and impact were still small in Hui Zhou compared to Shenzhen.

Concluding remarks

In this chapter, I have provided an account of the condition, organisation and social functions of migrant workers' protests and their relationship with the geographical movement of both capital and labour in contemporary China by describing the case of the Sun factory.

Wang and Luo in Shenzhen and the twenty-year-old lacquering worker whom I quoted at the beginning of this chapter, as well as the invitation from the Hai Nan girl in Hui Zhou for me to lead a strike, all confirmed an industrial sociological notion: the necessity of leadership in a strike. In the modern Western world, union shop stewards generally took the leading role in wildcat strikes (Gouldner, 1954; Hyman, 1989). In contemporary China, this function had been borne by the locality-, community- and gang-based informal network of skilled and supervisory workers. Their privileged position was clear through their power on the shop floor, in the labour market and in the community. First, top Taiwanese management needed the assistance of supervisory staff to transform 'labour power' into 'labour', in the words of Marx (1967: 177), while supervisory staff needed the cooperation of skilled workers to make production more efficient. Second, the growing shortage of labour and the resignation option have encouraged the aspirations, confidence and militancy of skilled workers, and to a lesser extent even ordinary workers in Hui Zhou, in line with Western studies of industrial action (e.g. Franzosi, 1995; Kelly, 2002). Third, gangsters' activism in Militant village resulted in a higher level of militancy among workers, and that militancy was then transferred to Hui Zhou. This contradicts the casual observation that migrant workers' actions were 'more individual' (Lee, 2002a: 217), 'spontaneous', 'random' and 'sporadic' (Lee, 2002b: 62–63).

While leadership played an essential role, specific issues affecting workers' general interests and lasting discontent embedded in the labour process both contributed to the strike. As soon as workers' general grievances are articulated as a common demand at a critical moment, a 'culture of solidarity' with a sense of injustice emerges among those workers (Fantasia, 1988). In this case, 'pay wages according to the law' and 'guarantee Sunday work' were the common demands, while the new attendance policy and worries about declining income were the critical issues that triggered the strike. In other words, a strike always has its own rationale (Hyman, 1989): ordinary workers are not passively mobilised by organisers, but rather are active creators and constructors of 'cultures of solidarity' during the strike, as Fantasia (1988: 20) has suggested. Honig (1986) and Hershatter (1986) argued that a strike is not an ideal scenario in which to study class-consciousness, because workers' participation might be forced by gangsters or motivated by traditional loyalty, for example, rather than prompted by modern class-consciousness. But as this case shows, even though workers were initially forced by gangsters to stop working, they were well aware that it was in their own interests to do so. In Shenzhen, the organisers used banners and loud-hailers to call others to join the demonstration, and all of the participants joined in voluntarily. Some workers did not participate, but this was more because of their comparatively weak 'marketplace bargaining power' and 'workplace bargaining power' (in Wright's (2000) terms), than through lack of consciousness. In Hui Zhou, the hidden self-interest of the outgoing workshop supervisor was compatible with the general workers' interests in a guarantee of Sunday work. In the words of the young worker from Xi An: 'If our wage could not be raised, neither could theirs [the supervisors'] and vice versa.' Workers well understood that their interests were the same, although the wage structure and standards were different.

While Olson's influential *The Logic of Collective Action* (1971) assumed a rational process of individual-based interest maximisation behind a collective action, recently Kelly (2002) argued that the mobilisation theory of Tilly (1978) and McAdam (1988) was more powerful in explaining industrial militancy in both short and historical terms. Tilly (1978) contested that collective action was a balanced consideration of interest, organisation, mobilisation and opportunity. McAdam (1988) added that a sense of injustice gave rise to workers' collective action. This study confirmed that the sense of 'injustice' and confidence that developed from industrial masculinity was a prominent factor in the workers' enthusiasm for the protest. In the words of Xiao Lin, workers attended the rally for 'fun' or to 'let off steam', while Chen acknowledged that the unfair treatment of the departmental superintendents drove him to protest and resign. However, Qi said that he would 'sit down somewhere to watch' if there was another conflict with the police. Experience could reconstruct the balance between workers' emotional 'justice' and their rational self-interest. Attention should also be paid to the fact that in all of the strikes and complaints documented in this chapter, there was always a very clear material demand articulated by the workers. Therefore, we should put the workers' language of 'justice' into a broader material context of collective interest.

By studying the collective actions of unorganised workers, in the Western sense, I have attempted to present rank-and-file workers as key participants in industrial relations in China. All of their actions bypassed official trade unions, but they still exerted significant pressure on management and the state. While the local state responded to the workers' activism by enhancing the wage standard and ensuring better enforcement of the Labour Law, the management adopted new strategies, including new regulations and relocation of production to reduce costs. However, the workers' struggle strategy also changed over time due to a new legal, social, economic and political context. Significantly, workers in the new plant were able to raise confidence and consciousness through their collective experiences, which were transferable through interpersonal networks.

This case also showed that although place of origin and its attached gangsters were usually exploited by management to divide and pacify workers, they could function in the interests of workers when their structural power was increased. The strike was a significant turning point of the changing power relations in the workplace, community and society. The dynamics for this transformation came from the enhancement of migrant workers' 'marketplace and workplace bargaining power' due to the further development of global capitalism in China. Their wage standard, for example, was significantly increased after the strike. There were two reasons for this: first, the shortage of labour (workers' 'marketplace bargaining power'); second, the wave of strikes (workers' 'workplace bargaining power'). The high turnover rate and the consistency of resistance in the workplace are new forms of workers' struggle that reshape the class power balance.

However, workers' associational power in China is still fundamentally weak. The trade union which was formed in this case did not play its primary role. Without a representative body in the workplace to channel the interests of workers, it was understandable that they adopted other forms of protest – from quitting and signing petitions to stoppages, strikes and demonstrations – to express their grievances. This has made workplace relationships highly unstable (C. Chan, 2009).

In the following chapters, I will continue to explore the potential and limitations of class solidarity and class organisation in contemporary China's global factory, with reference to state power, civil society and workers' collective experience.

5 Workplace conflict, legal institution and labour regime

Introduction

> Historical institutionalism and historical materialism can cross-fertilize. The former approach provided an analytic framework for the repertoires of action between collective actors . . . while the latter laid the foundations for an analysis of power and conflict. Both work fruitfully in tandem, and analysis would be incomplete in the absence of either perspective.
>
> Steinberg (2003: 487–88)

In Chapters 3 and 4, we saw that the wage was always one of the main concerns during strikes, but wage demands were always within the limits of workers' legal rights (Lee, 2007a). In July 2005 and 2006, the Shenzhen government significantly increased the minimum wage rate. As the workers did not ask for this increase during the strike, though, it is reasonable to assume that it was introduced in response to the shortage of labour rather than to placate the strikers. In July 2007, however, contrary to the workers' expectations, the municipal authorities did not increase the minimum wage as they had done in the previous two years. This pay freeze triggered a new round of strikes in the region. These first forced the factories to raise their wages to above the legal minimum, and then the city government to increase the minimum wage in October 2007. This confirmed the significance of state regulation and legality in the 'politics of production' in China (Burawoy, 1985; Lee, 2007a), but contradicted Lee's (2007a) proposal that migrant workers' actions were based on their legal rights as citizens.

As an extension to Burawoy's theory of the 'politics of production' or 'labour regime', Steinberg (2003) pointed out that the labour regime is in fact embedded in legal institutions. According to him, 'free labour' (which Burawoy took for granted from Marx's analysis of the capitalist labour process) is not an inherent feature of capitalist production. In fact, it is a result of class conflict that is reflected in the historical development of legal institutions.

Building on Chapter 4, where I suggested bringing the role of 'unorganised' workers into the analysis of industrial relations, this chapter continues to explore the dialectic and dynamic relationship between legal institutions and workplace relations. While Steinberg (2003) brought in the legal institutional context for the labour regime, taking the example of the rise of 'free labour', I attempt to provide a material account of the transformation of the legal context, referring to the minimum wage rate, one of the most significant issues for the local state, management and workers in China. On the one hand, legal institutions frame the workplace relationship; on the other, workplace struggle reconstructs the legal framework. Workers' struggle and legal institutions have worked together to reshape China's labour regime (Lee, 1999), which I call 'contested despotism' in this stage.

Legal institution of the minimum wage in Shenzhen

As the first SEZ, the municipality of Shenzhen has been a pioneer of labour legislation reform. A legal minimum wage was introduced by the city government as early as 1993 and extended nationwide in the 1994 Labour Law. The power to set the minimum standard is delegated to local authorities according to cost of living and economic development conditions. According to a State Council regulation, the minimum wage can be adjusted on a biennial basis. In Guang Dong province, the provincial government decides the rates for its subordinate municipalities. However, as an SEZ, Shenzhen enjoyed a certain level of legislative autonomy and its minimum wage policy was set by the Shenzhen Employees' Wage Payment Ordinance. Under this ordinance, the minimum rate was decided by the SZMLSSB after consultation with the municipal State Property Management Committee (*Guo Zi Wei*), the SZMFTU and the city's general chamber of commerce, and was then sent to the city government for final approval.[1] Until 2005, the city government announced a new minimum rate for inside the SEZ and another for outside the SEZ every April, with the new rates to come into effect on May Day.

Before 1 May 2004, the minimum wage of Shenzhen was always the highest in the country (600 yuan inside the SEZ and 465 yuan outside in 2003–2004). However, then the 'difficulty of worker recruitment' (*Zhaogong Nan*) and 'shortage of peasant workers' (*Mingong Huan*) became serious concerns throughout the country. Consequently, minimum wages started to increase in many areas, especially in the YRD. The rate in Shang Hai reached 635 yuan, while Nan Jing, Su Zhou, Hang Zhou and Ning Bo (all in the YRD) set their rates at 620 yuan. In late 2004, Guang Dong province categorised its affiliate cities, except for Shenzhen, into seven grades and announced a new minimum for each grade. The rate for the first grade, which included only the city of Guang Zhou, was 684 yuan. The second grade (including Fo Shan, Dong Guan, Zhu Hai and Zhong Shan) was 574 yuan. And the third grade (including Shenzhen's eastern neighbour Hui Zhou) was 494 yuan. All of Shenzhen's main competitors in both the YRD and the PRD had a higher minimum wage than the outside SEZ rate for Shenzhen. This exerted great pressure on the city authorities to increase the legal minimum in 2005 (*Southern Metropolitan Daily*, 3 March 2005).

Huang Zhao Ji, the vice-head of the SZMLSSB, spoke at a press conference: 'The difficulty of hiring labour (*Yonggong Jin*) has become an important factor in constraining the economic development of Shenzhen. . . . We believe adjustment of the minimum wage can play a role in easing the labour shortage problem' (*Southern Metropolitan Daily*, 3 March 2005). As a result, for the first time in its history, the SZMLSSB held a large-scale conference to debate the issue (*Lunzheng Hui*), with the participation of representatives from the SZMFTU, the chamber of commerce, various enterprises, workers, government departments and academic experts. In addition, 10,000 questionnaires were distributed among workers and enterprise owners to collect their opinions. Because of this wide consulta- tion exercise, the effective date of the new minimum wage was delayed until 1 July 2005.

Table 5.1 shows the minimum wage rate in Shenzhen from 2000. As can be seen, the rate increased very modestly until 1 July 2005, at which point the inside rate increased from 610 to 690 yuan while the outside rate increased from 480 to 580. Although Guang Dong province did not change the minimum wage until September 2006, the Shenzhen government launched an even larger-scale consultation in that year. The policy-making process reflected the difficulty for the local state of balancing the interests of labour and capital, or, in the terminology of Lee (2007a), legitimacy and accumulation. The official press statement which announced the new rate in 2006 stated:

> In order to set the 2006 minimum wage reasonably, we did our job in two ways: first, we had to understand the people's opinions comprehensively, so we collected suggestions widely through a questionnaire survey, listening to people's suggestions in the media, and holding twelve seminars and a large- scale conference to debate minimum wage adjustment proposals; second . . . we had to consider that Guang Dong province and some main cities in the country planned to increase their minimum wages remarkably, we had to guarantee a balance of supply and demand of the labour market, and we had to facilitate a harmonious and stable development of labour relations in our city.
>
> (SZMLSSB, 2006)

Table 5.1 The legal minimum wage rate in Shenzhen

Year	Inside SEZ (yuan)		Outside SEZ (yuan)	
	Monthly rate	*Hourly rate*	*Monthly rate*	*Hourly rate*
2000–2001	547	3.14	419	2.41
2001–2002	574	3.30	440	2.53
2002–2003	594	3.41	460	2.64
2003–2004	600	3.45	465	2.67
2004–2005	610	3.51	480	2.76
2005–2006	690	3.97	580	3.33
2006– 30.09.2007	810	4.66	700	4.02

Source: Shenzhen Municipal Statistics Bureau, various years

According to Huang Zhao Ji at the press conference held on 30 May 2006 to announce the new rates, in Shenzhen enterprises accounted for slightly more than 50 per cent of GDP, labourers slightly more than 30 per cent, and the state about 15 per cent. This meant the gap between enterprises and labourers was the largest in the country (*Xinhua Net*, 31 May 2006). Notably, 'harmonious and stable labour relations' and labour–capital interest imbalance were both highlighted in the press conference. This hinted that the significant increase in the minimum wage was in response to both a labour shortage and the unstable workplace relations which have been discussed in previous chapters.

On 17 April 2006, the SZMLSSB invited the members of the municipal People's Congress and Political Consultative Conference, delegates from industrial associations and representatives from both the workers and local enterprises to attend a consultation conference (*Ting Zheng Hui*) where two proposals for the minimum wage were presented. One was 800 yuan for inside the SEZ and 700 yuan for outside; the other was 850 yuan for inside and 750 yuan for outside. These two packages were proposed after wide consultation with the workers and enterprises before the meeting. To gauge the workers' opinions, the SZMLSSB had sent out 20,000 questionnaires. Most of those attending the meeting supported the lower package (*Xinkuai Bao*, 18 April 2006). Interestingly, this included most of the workers' representatives, who were primarily middle-level managers or personnel officers. The enterprises' representatives generally insisted on no more than 800 yuan inside the SEZ. Some People's Congress members and scholars suggested a middle way between the two packages (*Nanfang Ribao*, 18 April 2006). The SZMFTU was not reported to be present at the meeting, and the city Party was not supposed to participate in such consultations. Ordinary workers' interests were not reflected at the conference. Although it was an informal consultation, and the final decision rested with the city government, the opinions expressed at the conference did have an impact. The government finally tended towards the lower package, although the inside rate was slightly increased from 800 to 810 yuan. Nevertheless, this was still the largest absolute increase in the legal rate since it had been introduced in 1993, and was second only to the 1999 increase in percentage terms. However, in both 2005 and 2006, the inside SEZ rate was lower than that for Shang Hai.

All of this suggested that the trade unions did not actively represent the interests of workers, and the workers' representatives who attended the conference were in fact manipulated by the management. As a result, not even the middle-way proposal suggested by People's Congress members and academics could garner enough support to be passed.

From minimum wage to reasonable wage

Minimum wage and strike

On 30 May 2006, the Shenzhen municipal government announced that the legal minimum wage would rise from 580 to 700 yuan in July – a remarkable 20.7 per cent increase. In July, Xiao Lin suggested that I should extend my stay in Shenzhen because: 'If [the factories] do not increase the wage, [the workers] will certainly strike.' Workers were well aware of the new rate and the date that it should be introduced from the media and discussions with each other.

Some small and medium-sized factories in the city raised workers' fees for accommodation and food to offset the wage rise. Workers informed me that they accepted this as it was 'legal'. But all factories with over 1,000 workers in the Militant community increased wages according to the new legal minumum without increasing fees. No significant strike occurred in the community or the surrounding towns, contrary to Xiao Lin's expectations.

Interestingly, though, private landlords did increase their rents after the workers' pay was raised. One worker complained in August 2006:

> Today my landlord came to see me. He said that the rent is to increase from 200 to 250 yuan and added: 'Your pay has risen, so why shouldn't I raise the rent?' Ten years ago, when my older brother worked in Dong Guan, 300 yuan could rent a big flat with three bedrooms. Today we can rent only a small room. Living in Shenzhen is more and more expensive. The wage rise doesn't mean the *Dagong* people will be much better off.

Although there are no reliable statistics of the strike rate in the city, I observed that workplaces throughout 2006 were relatively peaceful compared with the previous two years. I did not find any significant strike activities when I revisited the village in December 2006. In March 2007, the Guang Dong provincial government announced that the minimum wage rates in the province would not be increased that year. On 27 June, the spokesperson for the SZMLSSB said: 'Shenzhen will continue to adjust the minimum wage, but adjustment doesn't necessarily mean rise: remaining unchanged and reducing are also kinds of adjustment' (*Shenzhen News*, 28 June 2007). Finally, the city government did not announce any minimum wage rise from July 2007, going against the policy of the previous two years. When I paid another visit in August 2007, a new round of strikes was taking place to demand a 'reasonable wage' that was much higher than the legal minimum. This put pressure on the city government to increase the minimum wage from October 2007.

In the following section, I will examine one of these strikes. It occurred in a German-invested company that I call the Moon factory, and offers a good example of the changing relations between local state legal institutions and workplace conflict on the issue of wages.

Factory background and working conditions

Like the Sun factory, the Moon factory operated two production sites in the Bao An district of Shenzhen. But unlike Sun – whose two plants were within the same community, just a five-minute walk from each other and under the same management team, with workers living in one group of dormitories – the two

Moon plants were situated in different towns, a one-hour bus journey apart and under different management teams. However, supervisory staff could be dispatched to either plant as and when needed. The main plant of the Moon factory, where the strike began, was just twenty minutes on foot from the Sun factory. In fact, it was adjacent to one of the places where workers from the Sun factory had fought with police during the 2004 strike – at a junction of the highway. Many Moon workers, as well as hundreds from other factories, had joined that march, too.

The German-owned business produced mobile phone chargers and other components for the global market. Since being set up in 1993, it had expanded into the two large plants in Shenzhen and another in Beijing. Each of the Shenzhen plants employed about 8,000 workers, with almost identical working conditions and management strategies in the two factories. As in the Sun factory, the wage level was higher than that in most smaller factories in the area. Moon also made contributions to social insurance for all of its workers from the day they joined, and each worker was given a contract. The minimum hourly wage rate was observed, although workers generally worked more hours than the legal maximum. The factories operated in two shifts. The day shift was from 7 a.m. to 7 p.m., with a one-hour lunch break from 11.30 a.m. to 12.30 p.m. The night shift was from 7 p.m. to 6.45 a.m., with a forty-five-minute break from 11 to 11.45 p.m. Ordinary workers usually worked six days per week and their monthly income was between 1,000 and 1,400 yuan. However, unlike the Sun factory, 90 per cent of the ordinary workers were women aged between eighteen and thirty, as there were fewer positions with heavy manual and technical demands. Most of the production workers were from He Nan and Guang Xi provinces, while the skilled workers were generally from Guang Dong.

In both plants, segregation on the basis of skill and gender was very apparent. Ordinary manual workers were called *Yuangong* (employees), while managers, supervisors, engineers, technicians and office clerks were called *Zhiyuan* (staff). Most of the *Yuangong* lived in the eight blocks of factory-provided dormitories, where eight or twelve workers shared a room. Inside each room, two electric fans, a bathroom, toilet and hot-water heater were provided. Thirty yuan was deducted monthly from wages as rent. Until 2006, the factory gave a fifty-yuan subsidy to those production workers living outside. Skilled workers, supervisors and managers received higher subsidies: the subsidy for line supervisors, for example, was 200 yuan. As a result, most of the skilled workers and supervisors lived outside the factory. Unfamiliar people not wearing a factory uniform were asked to show their factory ID cards by security guards before being granted entry into the factory or the dormitories. As in the Militant community, there were lots of small restaurants and corner shops that supplied food and goods at affordable prices. But by contrast, the factory was situated within a well-planned and developed industrial zone where there were no local peasant-owned private houses. So those living outside had to walk around fifteen minutes to reach their homes in a nearby area. Nevertheless, workers claimed: 'It is more convenient to live outside, especially when friends come round.'

Workers could eat meals in the factory canteen or outside. The factory ID cards had a digital function to record the number of meals workers took. Breakfast was one yuan while lunch and dinner were both two yuan. During hot days, workers generally preferred to eat out. Some just stood beside the food stalls to eat traditional bread and dessert while others sat in fast-food restaurants to eat a three-yuan dish. Many women workers did not seem to have much appetite and preferred to eat just a snack for lunch. However, the factory prohibited the workers from bringing snacks into the factory. So they had no choice but to stand outside the factory entrance to finish eating cake, fruit or tofu before returning to work. Some brave women concealed their snacks in umbrellas in order to bring them into the factory. One told me: 'I did not want to eat lunch, but I will be hungry this afternoon. I prefer a snack, although I am very worried about being found out by the supervisor.'

In July 2005, when the minimum wage rate in Shenzhen was raised to 580 yuan, the factory adjusted its salary accordingly. Yet the *Zhiyuan*, whose salary was much more than the legal minimum, did not receive a pay rise. A department-based one-day strike by the machinery repair technicians then occurred in the engineering department and forced the factory to increase their salary by 100 yuan. As in the Sun factory, most of the technicians were middle-aged men who enjoyed lots of privileges that ordinary workers did not.

Labour intensification, rationalisation and grievances

After two years of pay rises, from late 2006 the factory attempted to lower production costs by increasing the work intensity of *Yuangong* and restricting the overtime of *Zhiyuan*. First, the work quotas assigned to each production line were increased steadily. Time is a key aspect of discipline control in industrial capitalism (Thompson, 1967). As usual, this control was used in parallel with a coercive piece-rate policy in the Moon factory. If workers in the line did not finish their quotas, their lunch break the following day would be shortened so they could perform the unfinished tasks. This created conflict between efficient experienced workers and inexperienced employees, as well as between the front-line supervisors, who announced the new quotas and forced their subordinates to work faster, and the ordinary workers. But none of the interviewed workers thought the policy violated the law. Staff from the engineering department recorded the paces of different lines and units and suggested new quotas. Some workers not on conveyor belts reported that they cooperated with workmates to lower their work pace collectively, but assembly line workers always tried to work as fast as possible to avoid unpaid work in their lunch break the next day. As a result, 'too exhausted' rather than 'low pay' became the most common cause for discontent in the factory. In fact, many workers stayed on because 'the wages are good'.

Nevertheless, many others quit after a few months of the new regime. To tackle the high turnover rate, the factory restricted the right of workers to resign. As we have seen, according to the law, workers can resign from a job if they give one month's advance notice. But the management granted only two 'permissions' for resignation in each production line each month. As a result, workers had to queue up to quit. For those quitting without proper 'permission' – which the workers called 'leave by oneself' (*Zi Li*) or 'immediate leave' (*Ji Li*) – the factory kept part of their last wage packet and they were banned from rejoining the company for six months. Some workers wrote letters of complaint to the LSSB about this issue, but LSSB officials simply talked the matter over with the management, without any contact with the workers. There was no improvement in the situation after the meeting.

One of the workers who was forced into *Zi Li* said: 'In this factory, those on work cannot eat, and those off work cannot sleep, only drink water and cannot eat food. Fifty-five kilos [of body weight] when entering the factory is soon reduced to forty-five. It is really exhausting, especially on the night shift.' Many others like her were also forced into *Zi Li* as they could not physically tolerate the working conditions. But there was one exception. Xiao Lan, a twenty-three-year-old woman from Guang Xi, displayed great boldness and knowledge of her rights when quitting the factory in late 2006:

> I had a row with our shop floor supervisors first. Then I walked to the administration department to see the director. I asked him on what grounds the factory was not allowing me to resign. The Labour Law protects the right of workers to leave a job. The director said, 'You can resign . . . everyone can resign. . . . Who said you cannot resign? . . . Go back to work first. I will see.' I then went back to work for several days, but there was still no news on my resignation. Then I left the workshops after the normal working time. The supervisor asked me to stay on. . . . I objected. . . . I said that the Labour Law said that overtime work is voluntary. My workmates all looked at me very surprised. . . . He then let me go. . . . The next day I went to see the director again . . . and finally they let me go without deducting any money.

Workers like Xiao Lan are rare. Most of the workers at Moon did not know that restricting their right to resign was illegal. Others did know but were not (yet) brave enough to speak out like Xiao Lan did.

The second strategy for lowering costs targeted the *Zhiyuan*. In late 2006, the factory announced a policy to restrict their overtime hours. This was finally implemented in March 2007. From July 2007, the maximum overtime hours of *Zhiyuan* were set at seventy-two per month. They did not receive any extra pay if they worked more hours than that. The impact on front-line supervisors was that they had to take care of more lines when other supervisors were on leave. For the technicians, a smaller number was on duty during every shift. As in the Sun factory, as repair technicians needed to work only when a machine broke down, some of them simply left the factory after punching in their time cards and asked others to punch out for them. To tackle this, a new punching machine was installed at the main entrance of the factory in August 2007 especially for *Zhiyuan*, with CCTV and security guards observing everyone arrived and left.

While high production targets and resignation issues were the two major grievances of *Yuangong*, and new restrictions on overtime and attendance were the main concerns of *Zhiyuan*, the problem of working in high temperatures applied to both parties. The electricity supply was often suspended in the city, and when it was, the factory operated its own generators, but these only powered the basic machinery. With no air-conditioning, workers had to work in extremely high temperatures and sometimes amid toxic fumes as ventilation facilities were not operated either. Some workers quit because they could not bear the hot working environment. In the summer of 2006, a petition to the top management was signed by some workers who asked for 'comfortable working conditions' (see Box 5.1).

**Box 5.1   Petition to the top management about
working conditions in the Moon Factory**

Dear factory leaders,

Hello. We are staff of your company. We now feel that we should explain something about the conditions in our factory to the company's leaders.

We have to work three to four days every week in a workshop without air-conditioning. As many staff work in a workshop and the machines in operation emit a great deal of heat, the workshop becomes very hot when we are working, but we have to work as usual. Such a production environment is extremely detrimental to our health. So we hope that the factory can provide us with a better working environment.

The thing is that the supply shortage of the electricity company in XX causes a rotational power cut to industrial zones. Our factory is one of those subjected to a rotational power cut. A power cut will influence production to some extent. In order not to halt production, the factory uses a generator. As the resource and capacity of the generator are not sufficient, the factory does not turn on the air-conditioning during the power cut. Also, no fans are installed in the workshops with lots of workers and high-temperature machinery, such as tin soldering and bearing machines.

We work in such an environment, and the factory does not reduce the production output or provide any facility to reduce the workshop temperature for workers. Many workmates resigned . . . because they could not bear such an environment. Staying in such a tedious and stuffy environment is very detrimental to us. The consequences can be imagined. . . .

Moreover, the leaving of workers will affect production. Therefore, for the sake of our company, us and our common interests, we hope the factory can provide us, the workers, with a comfortable working environment and satisfy our small request without affecting production efficiency.

[Signatures]

Yet no significant improvement was achieved by this campaign. The long-term discontent over work intensification, difficulty resigning, high temperatures and so on mounted and precipitated an across-factories strike in August 2007. However, the immediate causes of the strike related to the minimum wage policy of the city government. As mentioned above, the city had significantly raised the minimum wage rate in July 2005 and 2006, so workers generally expected a similar pay rise in July 2007, but the government decided not to implement one. A strike began two days after the workers had received their July pay slips.

Organisation and development of the strike

In-depth and follow-up interviews with workers showed that the strike was well planned at least from June by machinery repair workers with the assistance of supervisory staff. In order to maximise the chance of getting approval for their resignations, workers often stated something like 'mother is sick at home' on their applications. But from June 2007, all of such applications were returned to workers by their line supervisors, who told the workers that their supervisors had asked them to write such reasons as 'there is no air-conditioning in the workshop', 'working conditions are too harsh' and 'work is too hard and wages too low'. Workers believed that this was a sign that the middle-level supervisory staff wanted to pressurise the top management into improving conditions.

Workers received their pay slips for July on a Thursday in August. The slips indicated that their salary had not been raised. Furthermore, technicians and supervisors found their income had been severely reduced due to the overtime restriction. For example, one of the technicians, whose salary had always been well over 2,000 yuan, received only 1,400 yuan. The following evening, when the managers (who worked only during the day) had left the factory, a public letter was posted on the noticeboard of every workshop (see Box 5.2).

The letter was issued in the names of all Moon factory workers and entitled 'Voices from the staff and employees (*Zhiyuangong Xinsheng*)'. It began by pointing out that the management had attempted to lower salaries from the end of 2006, and now their income had been reduced by 50 per cent from the same period the previous year, while the work quota and living costs had doubled. 'We have reasonable demands,' the letter began. It ended by stating that the workers wanted the company to answer the points that had been raised in writing and that they would not accept an oral reply from anybody, including the company CEO. Not a single word about a strike was written in this letter, but rumours began to circulate among the ordinary workers that the technicians were about to go on strike. The letter was then torn down by somebody.

Nothing significant happened over the weekend until the night shift technicians stopped work on the Sunday night. However, up to that moment, ordinary workers could not imagine what part they might play in what was essentially a dispute between the *Zhiyuan* and the company.

On Monday morning, soon after the first group of ordinary workers walked to their workshops at 7.45 a.m. as usual and prepared to begin work, the electricity

---

Box 5.2   Public letter posted in the workshops before a strike in the Moon Factory

1   To adjust our current wage standard. We . . . well know the market wage standard now, and thus demand our wage to be adjusted to . . . *Yuangong*, 1,500 yuan or more; second-level *Zhiyuan*, 2,000 yuan or more; third-level *Zhiyuan*, 2,500 yuan or more; fourth-level *Zhiyuan*, 3,000 yuan or more; the above figures should exclude any subsidy.[2]

2   To raise the accommodation and food subsidy for those living outside. (Now rent and prices have risen to more than double last year, but our subsidy is still the standard of the end of the last century.)

3   To improve the welfare conditions, provide reasonable allowances for posts that are prone to high temperatures, toxic substances, outdoor work, and occupational diseases as well as providing regular occupational disease and body checks.

4   To provide night shift subsidy and snack allowance for those working on the night shift.

5   The company should buy unemployment, maternity, hospital and all of the other insurances stipulated by the Labour Law.

6   To solve the hygiene problem of drinking water.

7   To improve the fairness of the overtime work (. . . when normal working time has been exhausted, not only is the work target not reduced during overtime work, but it also adds up to two persons' work being performed by one person, in the name of controlling overtime).

8   The trade union should function appropriately and its core members should include grass-roots staff and employees (*Zhiyuangong*).

---

supply suddenly stopped. There was one electricity control room in each building. Somebody had run into the control rooms and turned off the power. Supervisors told the workers that a strike was ongoing and asked them to leave the workshop. In a wire department workshop (workers called it the wire factory – *Xian Chang*), where the strike began, the gate was locked from the outside before the workers could walk out. The workers shouted from inside and somebody broke the lock on the outside. When another group of workers arrived at 8 a.m., the workers from this workshop had run down to the ground floor. The newly installed punch clocks for *Zhiyuan* were found to be broken, and thousands of workers were standing around the main entrance of the factory.

The factory had a small annexe located outside its main complex. The main gate of the annexe had been locked. Some of the workers attempted to climb over the gate to escape but they were unsuccessful. Thousands of workers from the main factory then rallied to the scene, shouting: 'Open the gate!' The security guards did as they were told and the hundreds of workers inside joined the protest. From the very beginning, male technicians from the engineering department directed the mass of workers. 'A technician waved his work uniform [to attract attention] and several other technicians around him shouted: "Go! Go!" The workers then followed them,' one striker recalled.

After workers from the annexe had joined in the others, the technicians led the crowd to a local crossroads. The ordinary workers did not know where they were going until they arrived. The crossroads was not busy, and few cars passed through. Several policemen just stood by peacefully among the workers. Some even chatted with them in a friendly way. 'One policeman told us that it was useless to stay there and we should go to the national highway (*Guodao*),' one worker said. Half an hour later, the group did exactly that and occupied half of the main road. Hundreds of official forces soon appeared, including patrol police, military police, transport police and local government security guards, followed by LSSB officers, the residential district government (*Jiedao Ban*), the Party secretary-general and the factory managers. The secretary-general, an LSSB representative and a top manager, speaking through loud-hailers, tried to persuade strikers to return to the factory for negotiations. Government officials told them that it was illegal to obstruct the highway and that anything could be discussed in the factory, while the manager asked the workers to elect representatives for the negotiations. Some workers responded: 'We are all representatives!' and 'We have no representatives!' A manager then asked several young men standing in the front rank if they would act as representatives. Most of them flatly refused, but some followed the manager for a while as he walked back to the factory. But then they also turned around and rejoined the crowd. The technicians who had led the workers kept silent. Other workers told each other that in a strike some years before, the workers' delegates had all been sacked after the strike. By now, no one was willing to be a representative.

Then more police arrived and began to drive back the workers. Some young workers in the front rank, most of them women, resisted and there were some scuffles with the police. I talked with Ling Ling, a nineteen-year-old from Guang Xi, who had been at the front. She was very petite but had a strong sense of justice.

Author: Were you scared when you were in conflict with the police?

Ling: Not at all. It was their mistake, not ours! You know, it was very peaceful at the beginning. Some of them [the police] joked with us. But suddenly they pushed us forward roughly.

Author: Some workers were arrested. Did you think you might be?

Ling: I did not think so at the time. I was just angry. I could not think of anything. . . . But I would not have regretted it, even if I had been arrested.

After several protesters had been arrested, the rest of the workers retreated to the pavement and shouted: 'Release the people! Release the people! (*Fangren!*)' Some of them were released there and then, but others were detained for about a week. Once the police had taken control of the crossroads, the workers gathered at a nearby petrol station and then dispersed peacefully.

In the afternoon, the management called all of the *Zhiyuan* to a meeting. Most of the technicians and supervisors attended. However, as soon as the factory asked them to sign their names, almost all of the technicians and some of the supervisors left. So the meeting took place largely between department heads and managers. No formal notice was posted, but rumours soon circulated that the meeting had decided to increase the basic salaries of *Zhiyuan* by 300 to 500 yuan, depending on position, and of *Yuangong* by just 30 yuan. The supervisory staff were mostly satisfied with this offer and went back to work that night. But not one ordinary worker followed. Workers punched their time cards in and out as usual and then immediately left the factory.

On Tuesday, the strike continued. A notice was posted by the factory to announce the aforementioned salary package and some other concessions formally. A fifty-yuan subsidy was granted to those living outside, including all workers. Night shift workers were granted a one-yuan allowance per day. The managers and supervisors tried their best to persuade the workers to return to work, with some going into the dormitories. Many workers also had calls from their supervisors asking them to return to work or to provide information about who had already returned.

But the ordinary workers were beginning to sense that the management had 'betrayed' them. Some of them pasted up slogans on the dormitory walls: 'Strike to the last moment!' Others passed around handwritten flyers expressing their support for the strike and encouraging others to remain committed to the cause. Text messages also circulated among the workers calling for the continuation of the strike. One of the workers recalled that when she punched out her time card, her shop supervisor and departmental head stood by the machine:

> They asked me to work. I refused. They said that I could just sign my name. I thought that it was no problem if I only signed a name. I went into the workshop to sign my name. But afterwards, they did not allow me to leave and soon the gate closed. There were not enough workers to run a single line. Around ten workers just sat there for several hours with the lights on. After several hours, we were allowed to leave and we got pay for the full day of eleven hours. I felt very upset. I thought I had destroyed the solidarity of my workmates. So I did not go back to work on Wednesday. I just slept in bed unhappily.

During Tuesday evening, while the managers 'persuaded' workers like this one to return to work, a well-typed pamphlet circulated among the ordinary workers (see Box 5.3). Some copies were thrown out of dormitory windows to be collected from the ground; others were distributed by workers outside the factory. The pamphlet began by denouncing the *Zhiyuan* and calling for unity among the *Yuangong*.

Encouraged by all of this, most of the ordinary workers continued to strike on the Wednesday, although the management persisted with its tactic of 'persuading' (or deceiving) staff back to work.

A significant incident occurred at noon on Thursday. The company posted a new statement announcing that those who resigned in three days would be paid

Box 5.3 Pamphlet circulated during a strike in the Moon Factory

All *Yuangong* brothers and sisters,

We must be united. We don't need to worry about those shameful *Zhiyuan* and shouldn't believe their lies. They have achieved their own goals. We don't want to waste the time of both sides as well. We have very clear demands: if any of the following items cannot be accepted by the factory, we will definitely not walk half a step into the workshop. Our demands are:

1   Basic salary 810 yuan.[3] Pay during holidays should also not be lower than the basic salary.
2   No deduction of fees for living in dormitories; living outside should gain the appropriate subsidy.
3   Night shift should have a night snack allowance of 150 yuan paid on a monthly basis.
4   Give those workers in toxic and detrimental conditions an appropriate subsidy and subsidise staff who work outdoors, according to the Labour Law (150 yuan).
5   The drinking water of *Yuangong* should meet hygiene standards.

If you want to be a piece of meat on a cutting board or a shameful Han traitor, then you can sell your body before we receive our wage demand! We believe absolutely none of us is this kind of person. Fellow countrymen, it is our most vulnerable moment as those *Zhiyuan* have achieved their aims and forgotten the interests of us *Yuangong*. *Yuangong* brothers and sisters from the whole factory, for the sake of our own interests, let's unite together. Chairman Mao said: 'Our revolution has not been successful yet, struggle should continue, [we] should wait, insist! Insist . . . and insist.

From all *Yuangong*

all of their compensation and wages immediately, and others should return to work. Workers who returned to work within three days would receive an extra allowance: fifty yuan for the first day; thirty for the second; and ten for the third. Otherwise, they would be considered 'absent' and to have 'left by themselves', implying that they would not be paid as usual.

This was good news for the workers who were on the long waiting list to quit or were preparing to resign. And the strike persuaded others to leave, too. Three thousand were said to have queued up in the administrative department to apply to leave. However, this divisive management strategy fatally shook the confidence of those workers who wanted to stay on, in particular those suffering family economic pressure. When the supervisors phoned again to ask the workers to return to the factory, they did not resist any longer. They were convinced that they now had only two options: resign or return to work.

Although the management had clearly outmanoeuvred the strikers, some concessions were made. The company immediately provided distilled water in both dormitories and workshops, and it promised to install air-conditioners in workshops and to set up a common room with a TV set on each floor of the dormitories. Further promises were made to hold regular meetings with supervisors and to listen to suggestions from ordinary workers.

Strike in a sister factory

One of the significant features of this strike compared with the 2004 strike was that it happened almost simultaneously at two factories in different towns. Technicians and, to a lesser extent, supervisors could be dispatched to either of the plants from time to time. Therefore, the machine repair technicians in these factories knew each other well.

The strike in the suburban sister factory was less organised and started later than the one in the main factory, but it developed in a very similar way. All workers there knew that the strike had originated in the main factory. And while workers in the main factory had some previous strike experience, those in the sister plant told me that there had never previously been any significant stoppages in their workplace. No public letter was posted on the Friday evening. The strike began on the Monday afternoon. The factory gate was locked by security guards after the workers stopped work, but the workers shouted at the guards to reopen the gate, and they did so. Hundreds of workers (staff levels were much lower than in the main factory) gathered at a local crossroads but were soon driven off by police. They then attempted to occupy the same national highway that had been targeted by the main factory. 'They were more radical but more dispersed and less organised,' one witness to both protests told me. However, the management eventually made exactly the same concessions on wages, subsidies, welfare, working conditions and regular meetings with supervisors as it had at the main factory.

More than two years before this strike (on 13 January 2005), a worker from this factory had posted a notice on an internet forum dedicated to discussion of the Labour Law and labour rights (see Box 5.4). The message shows that the Moon workers' struggle for a legal wage and social insurance dated back almost as far as the similar struggles at Uniden and the Sun factory. Interviews conducted in August 2007 indicated that the factory had been persuaded to buy pension insurance for the workers. The question of the workers' welfare committees will be discussed at length in Chapter 6, where the difficulty of resisting management pressure will also be highlighted. The 2005 internet posting also proves that the well-organised strike of 2007, in which the leaders' identities remained cleverly concealed, was the result of several years' experience.

Box 5.4   Letter posted on an internet forum expressing workers' grievances

We are staff of XX factory in XX town, Bao An district. We are extremely unhappy with the behaviour of the factory. But as a weak community (*Ruo Shi Qunti*), unable to antagonise the factory at all, we can only seek your help here.

As a supplier to Nokia, monthly export of Nokia mobile phone chargers from a single factory in XX (with factories in XXX town and Beijing as well) is over four million. However, the Labour Law is not fully enforced in the factory; the factory has never bought pension and medical insurance. Moreover, no wage increase was initiated by the factory although living costs rose. Two strikes were started because of this and these finally forced the factory to raise wages. But by another means, the factory increased the basic wage (according to Shenzhen city minimum wage), but cancelled the seniority allowance (staff who had finished a full year's work had been entitled to twenty-six yuan monthly subsidy before); bought social insurance for employees (supervisory level or above), but cancelled the original five per cent of monthly provident fund. Furthermore, the organisers of these two strikes were all dismissed with different excuses.

In 2004, the factory established a staff welfare committee under some pressure or for some interest considerations, but even committee members, a low position, are controlled by the factory. For example, the committee director is a relative of a production department head. Two days ago, several committee members planned to make a complaint to the labour bureau upon a request from the workers, demanding that the factory buy pension and medical insurance. They got signed support from more than 200 workers. However, these basic demands were still not accepted by the management. Several welfare committee members who were organisers were sacked overnight. Many people were affected. All of the supporters were warned or dismissed.

We beg for help from experienced people. I thank you here first!!!

After the strike

The factory recruited new workers partly by extending its maximum age restriction from thirty to forty. Hundreds of young workers queued up outside the entrance to the factory in the mornings after the strike to apply for a job. But stress caused by the work quotas remained the main problem for workers. The newly recruited workers were less experienced, so it was more difficult for their lines to complete the assigned work targets. Many of the ordinary workers said that they would quit the factory before the Chinese New Year.

Those who left the factory applied for new jobs. Some other factories set up recruitment booths around the factory and even pointed out that their conditions were better than those in the Moon factory. But some workers swore never to enter a factory again. Ling Ling and one of her friends, also from Guang Xi, became waitresses in a hotel during the second week of the strike. Their monthly salary for a ten-hour working day was 900 yuan, much lower than they had earned in the factory. But they were happy with their new jobs because they were less stressful. 'We will never go back to a factory,' they told me.

A common source of discontent remained after the strike: 'Too exhausting . . . the work target keeps on rising. If you can finish 1,000, they increase it to 1,200,' one worker said. None of them thought there was any possibility of collective bargaining with the management on the quotas. Moreover, they believed that the quotas were set by their supervisors. I reminded them that the supervisors might only be implementing a policy laid down by the top management. But almost all of them insisted that the supervisors forced them to work hard. One of the workers said:

> Those line supervisors are all very selfish . . . only interested in their own promotion. . . . They keep increasing our work tasks. Even slowing down a bit would arouse a serious denouncement from them. . . . They just walk around from here to there. . . . What kind of contribution do they make? It is too unfair on us.

The female production workers' perception of the machinery repair workers, who were generally believed to be the leaders of the strike, was much better. The mechanics had nothing to do when the machines were working. As described in Chapter 3, they would talk or flirt with the women on the production lines from time to time. And when the workers whose machines needed fixing came to the production line, whether to have fun with the women or to assist in their work, the supervisors would condemn neither the repairers nor the female workers. However, the production workers still felt that the repairers looked down on them.

Despite these divisions, after Xiao Lan told others the story of her successful resignation, a worker from He Nan was inspired to do something more. She said that she would be leaving soon, so she might do something good for the other workers, such as write a letter of complaint about the 'unbearable' work quota.

The issue of the trade union was repeatedly mentioned by active workers, first in an internet letter, then in the public letter posted on the first day of the August strike. I asked the production workers if they knew there had been a trade union in the factory before the strike. Some did, others did not. Contrary to my expectations, Ling Ling, the woman who had fought with the police, said:

Ling: I did not know.
Author: Did you see the notice posted on Friday?
Ling: Yes, I saw it.
Author: Were you aware that the notice talked about a trade union (*Gonghui*)?

Ling: Yes. But . . . I was thinking . . . it meant the workers (Gong*ren*) should gather together to have a meeting (*Kai*hui).

Ling Ling had left home to *Dagong* two years earlier, but she did not have any idea of what a trade union was. Apparently, she was not aware that it is an organisation. Rather, she thought *Gonghui* (trade union) was just a meeting of workers. Her ignorance was due to the absence of any associational tradition in rural China. After the strike, all of the workers had a better understanding of what a trade union is, but none of them felt they were capable of running one: 'We are just little *Yuangong*. We are not powerful enough to do things like that. No one will listen to [us].'

As in the Sun factory strike in 2004, the knock-on effect of this strike was obvious. Encouraged by the Moon workers' success, workers in many large factories nearby staged strikes or planned to do so. Management made concessions after just hours of stoppage or even before a strike formally began.

I accompanied Xiao Lan one day when she visited her old friends in the factory. Although she had left six months before, she still went back to see them in the dormitory from time to time. She had to borrow a factory uniform from a friend in order to gain access. But as a man, of course I could not do that. In the Sun factory, skilled machinery repair workers had taken me into every corner of the factory and workshops. Here in the Moon factory, all of my contacts were ordinary production workers, none of whom had the power to let me in. So our interviews were usually conducted in restaurants. I talked with them in groups with Xiao Lan and other friends we had in common. Despite having received some material gain after the strike, the ordinary workers' perception of being 'betrayed' by the *Zhiyuan* was still very apparent. Most of them did not think it had been a successful strike. They always compared the 300-yuan-plus salary rise of the *Zhiyuan* with their paltry 30-yuan increase. Some even said they would not join any strike organised by the technicians again.

On 1 January 2008, when I revisited the workers, some of those who had quit during the strike had returned to work at the factory. One of them told me that she had been hired as a warehouse clerk, but she had no confidence in her ability to do the work. She had reapplied to Moon because of its relatively high salaries. On the other hand, another worker enjoyed her job as a clerk. However, she said that she never saved any of her 1,500–1,600-yuan monthly income because the cost of living was now so high. Her rent, for example, had risen to 500 yuan for a two-room flat.

Those staying at the factory had to work even harder as the factory could not employ enough workers after thousands quit during the strike and the work quota kept rising. Workers in a semi-finished product department told me that New Year's Day was their first rest day after the strike as the factory could not hire enough workers. Their counterparts in the finished product department were luckier, but even they enjoyed just a few rest days two months after the strike. Work targets also continued to rise. One of the workers told me that when she joined the factory in November 2006, the quota for one of the products was 500 per day. It was increased to 530 before the strike, and 550 in October. The latter target had never been reached. Moreover, the workforce was cut and some production lines were combined. For example, in one of the workshops, there were two lines with thirty-nine workers each before the strike. After it, eight people were cut from each line and the remaining sixty-two workers joined together to form a single line. But the previous work targets for the two lines were combined to produce a new quota for the longer line, despite the number of workers having been reduced. The tasks of machinery repair workers also increased due to restrictions on overtime work. In parallel with work intensification, workers' salaries were considerably increased again from October 2007 as a result of the minimum wage rate adjustment. By then, the average monthly income of an ordinary worker was between 1,800 and 2,000 yuan.

Formulation of a new legal minimum wage

During the strike, some rumours circulated among the workers that the LSSB did not want the factory to increase the wage on a large scale as workers in other factories would raise similar demands. There was no evidence to support this rumour. It was most likely a strategy from the management to sidetrack the workers. However, another rumour circulating among workers was proved to be true three months later. Many workers told me that the city government would increase the minimum wage soon. From 1 October, the inside SEZ minimum wage was increased to 850 yuan and the outside wage to 750 yuan. Again, the inside rate was more than in Shang Hai, which was 840 yuan at the time, and so became the highest in the country. It was announced that the rates would be effective until 30 June 2008. To formulate this minimum standard, as in the past two years, the government had launched a web-based survey of 13,801 people in about 1,000 enterprises and a paper survey of 17,000 people in 1,100 enterprises. The surveys collected 30,974 valid questionnaires. References were also extended to the minimum wages in competitive cites like Bei Jing, Shang Hai, Tian Jin, Jiang Su, Hang Zhou and Guang Zhou. But unlike the previous two years, alongside the municipal State Property Management Committee, the SZMFTU and general chamber of commerce, which were all guaranteed consultation rights in the formulation of a new minimum wage, LSSB officials from the districts of Bao An and Long Gang were also invited to the seminar to offer opinions on the new wage package (*Jing Bao*, 8 October 2007). It should be noted that Bao An and Long Gang were the two most industrially intensive and strike-prone administrative districts in the city.

Concluding remarks

Inspired by Steinberg's (2003: 486) approach to cross-fertilise 'historical institutionalism and historical materialism' in the study of the 'politics of production', this chapter has connected the two social processes of wage politics in Shenzhen – the formation of a legal minimum wage by the municipal government and the development of a cross-factory workers' strike demanding a reasonable wage. Here the politics of wages was used to explore the changing politics of production in China. Wages, rather than other interest bases, were the focus because the wage remained an essential, although not exclusive, component in workers' struggles. Day-to-day discontent was embedded in work intensification, discipline, OHS and the working environment. The articulation of these grievances in collective action, however, always rested on the issue of wages. No strike happened only because of air-conditioning or the work quota, for example, although these were both long-term complaints of workers that caused many to quit. Moreover, increasing the work target was in fact a management response to maintain surplus value in a competitive global market amid the rising local wage standard. We saw that alongside a shortage in the labour market, industrial conflicts and state regulations worked together to push up the wage rate. The relationship between the labour market, industrial conflict and legal institution is discussed below.

Based on her fieldwork in the 1990s and early 2000s, Lee (2007a: 24) argued that 'given the large labor supply, the prevalence of unskilled and low-waged jobs, and the non-existence of independent unions, Chinese workers can hardly be described as having much marketplace, workplace, or associational bargaining power'. However, my empirical data from 2004 has repeatedly challenged Lee's notion. Skilled workers, in particular, were not in 'unlimited supply' when the economy was in the process of rapid growth (Lewis, 1954). In this chapter, we have seen rising market bargaining power evidenced by workers' confidence to quit, especially after a strike, their capacity to gain new jobs, and the pressure on the local state to increase the minimum wage for the good of the local economy. Workers' market power also had the potential to strengthen their confidence in the exercise of workplace and associational power. Workplace bargaining power was uneven, as the supervisors and technicians had more power than the ordinary workers. This was not only because they were more scarce in the labour market, but because their position in production and powerful influence in the workers' community, as shown in Chapter 3, provided them with more organisational resources. On the second day of the strike in the Moon factory, ordinary workers tried to organise themselves, but their organisational resources were significantly weaker than those of the supervisory and skilled workers. The former could only encourage workmates to continue to strike by distributing pamphlets in their dormitories and on the street and by sending text messages. They did not have influence on the shop floor, whereas the supervisors and technicians did.

This uneven distribution was also seen in associational bargaining power. The workplace trade union did not have any function during the strike and so there was no evidence of associational power. We could conclude that workers' associational power was fundamentally weak due to the management's manipulation of the workplace trade union. However, the hidden organisers of the strike and drafters of the Friday-night public letter, who demanded rank-and-file representatives in the trade union committee, clearly had more consciousness than the ordinary workers on the question of association. Even Ling Ling, a woman who was well prepared to stand up for her rights, did not have any idea what a trade union was before the strike. Moreover, in the case of the Sun factory, I described the role of informal networks in the organisation of the strike. By contrast, in the Moon factory, there was a more mature network acting behind the scenes to plan and push forward the strike, as was evidenced by the perfectly timed and well-presented public letters posted in all departments on the Friday evening, and the almost simultaneous striking in the two factories. This built on previous struggle experiences in 2004 and 2005.

Although the factor of the labour market should be highlighted, the wage is not only a reflection of the labour market in an orthodox economic sense, but an effect of class struggle in a political sense (Friedman, 1977). Here I mentioned the role of workers' subjectivity and state legal institutions in the politics of wages in particular, and the pattern of workplace relations in general.

There are three reasons to highlight workers' collective subjectivity. First, as has been shown in this chapter, the formulation of a new minimum wage took workers' actions as well as the shortage of labour into account. The implication is that legal institutions always constrain but are also actively reconstructed by the pattern of workplace struggle. The cyclical relationship is: workplace struggle to legal institution reform to a new pattern of workplace struggle to a new round of institution reform. Second, as far as the labour shortage was concerned, the key challenge for the management was the high turnover rate or wave of quitting. After the strike, for many consecutive days, hundreds of workers queued up at the factory entrance in a bid to join the factory. But often new workers did not stay for long. In the face of this high turnover rate, factories had to compete with each other to recruit *and keep* workers, and the wage was an essential element in this. Quitting was an individual decision which was constrained by factors such as family economic pressure and the availability of other job opportunities, but sometimes it was expressed collectively. Individual workers quitting a factory was already a problem for the management. It explained the illegal policy of the management to restrict the workers' right to resign and the local state's ignorance of this behaviour. But a bigger problem for management was when workers resigned from the factory collectively, in their thousands. The factory allowed workers to do so because of fear of the continuation of the strike. Third, the Moon factory case showed that workers, especially those in supervisory and skilled positions, were able to strive for a wage standard higher than the legal minimum by their collective action. This form of protest might have been more common without the prompt response from the state to enhance the legal standard.

Lee concluded that 'decentralization, cellular activism, and legalism' were characteristics of protests by all social groups, including migrant workers (Lee, 2007a: 236). This conclusion was not confirmed by my study. It reminded me of the importance of the historical dimension in workers' struggle. Legalism was just an institutional tool workers used to protest for their interests in a specific historical context. As soon as the law was enforced, and their interests could not be reflected within the law, workers might ask for more than the law, as in the 2007 strike. It seems clear that their struggle is interest-based, rather than rights-based, as Lee suggested.

The regulatory role of the state in workplace relations was illuminated by Burawoy (1979; 1985) in his prominent concept of the 'politics of production' or 'labour regime'. He categorised two kinds of labour regime in capitalist industry – 'market despotism' and 'hegemony' – depending on the extent of state intervention, as well as a 'bureaucratic despotic regime' in socialist states. As ownership and management have restructured to come to terms with global capitalism, the Chinese state's administrative hierarchy has not been involved in the internal management of enterprises, at least not in the private sector, so the concept of 'bureaucratic despotism' is invalid in post-socialist China. Burawoy (1985: 12) describes market despotism as 'the state is separated from and does not directly shape the form of factory regime', while in hegemony 'the state shapes the factory apparatuses by stipulating, for example, mechanisms for conduct and resolution of struggle at the point of production'. The Chinese state is now increasingly active in intervening in workplace relations. The minimum wage policy is just one example of this. As Steinberg's (2003) supplementary to Burawoy revealed, a labour regime is in fact embedded in a changing context of legal institutions.

Along with the 1994 Labour Law, which provided significant leeway for workers' struggle, in 2007 three significant laws were legislated, namely the Employment Promotion Law, the Labour Contract Law and the Labour Dispute Mediation and Arbitration Law. The second strengthens workers' individual and collective rights, while the last allows more active intervention in the resolution of labour conflicts by either workplace or judicial mechanisms. Does this mean the labour regime in China is on the way to hegemony? 'Effort bargaining' (defined by Burawoy (1979: 161) as 'the monetary reward for labor expended or the reward for effort') took place in the form of industrial conflict and local state regulation of the minimum wage. However, without an effective workplace trade union and a shop steward culture, coercion is still the dominant form of management of ordinary workers. Therefore, 'despotism' rather than 'hegemony' is the more appropriate term to describe the labour regime in China. To solve this dilemma, Lee (1998) conceptualised the foreign-owned factory as 'localistic despotism'. However, in the case of the Sun factory, I argued that the resource of 'locality' was not always in the hands of the management in a changing context of labour market and workers' struggle. In this chapter, we continued to see that 'locality' as a base of control was far from obvious in the workplace. Female ordinary workers complained of being 'betrayed' by the supervisory and skilled workers on the basis of production position, not place of origin. Therefore, I prefer to portray the workplace relations in post-socialist China's integration into the global economy as a changing labour regime. Because despotism still prevails while the state's intervention and workers' collective action increasingly press management, I refer to the factory regime at this stage as 'contested despotism', which might give way to a new power balance in the future, developing R. C. Edwards' (1980) notion of 'contested terrain'.

Burawoy (1979: 179) suggested two 'motor[s] of change' – 'class struggle' and 'capitalist competition' – in the transition of a labour regime in advanced capitalism. As I emphasised in the discussion of workers' market bargaining power, the expansion of global capitalism into China, driven by the deepening of advanced capitalist competition since the mid-1970s, is one of the main factors contributing to the transformation of workplace relations in recent years. Both management and the local state competed for workers. Shenzhen formulated its minimum wage with reference to other industrial cities. Neighbourhood factories set up recruitment booths to promote their claims of better working conditions shortly after the Moon factory strike. Therefore, 'capitalist competition' remains a valid factor to explain the transformation of the labour regime in globalising China. However, Burawoy's concept of 'class struggle' is not fully satisfactory in explaining the social and political process of labour regime transition in post-socialist China. When describing 'class struggle', Burawoy (1979: 179) adopted a narrow definition of 'between the organized representatives of capital and labor – namely management and Union'. In China, the official trade union, especially in the workplace and at the local level, so far has not represented workers in a comparable way to its Western counterparts. At the central level, the ACFTU did have a positive role in the formulation of the Labour Contract Law (K. Wang, 2008), and even in Shenzhen trade unions were starting to defend workers' rights and interests more actively (CLB, 2008). However, as Clarke and Pringle (2007) pointed out, these advances resulted from internal political pressure from the Party state in response to rising worker activism.

As Burawoy (1979: 178, 179) rightly put it: 'Struggles on the shop floor are largely shaped by conflicts between different levels, and among different factions, of management. . . . In the normal everyday life of the shop floor, workers are not organized as a class.' In the Sun factory, we saw that locality-based conflict was dominant; while in the Moon factory, divisions were based on production positions – *Zhiyuan* versus *Yuangong*. However, as far as industrial conflict was concerned, demands were ambiguously targeted on the interest concession from capital. It is arbitrary to argue that all workplace conflict has a class nature, but even under Burawoy's definition, the workers' struggle in China has an element of 'class struggle'. He distinguished three levels of 'class struggle': economic, political and ideological. For him, economic and political struggles are designed to 'reshape or maintain the distribution of economic rewards . . . and the relations in production', respectively, while ideological struggles 'take us beyond capitalism' (Burawoy, 1979: 177, 179). There was no evidence of ideological struggle in this study, and political struggle was not very potent, but Chinese workers' struggle exerted a profound impact on the policies of local authorities, the reform of the official trade union and the labour legislation of the central government, which in turn reshaped 'the distribution of economic rewards' that was Burawoy's (1979: 179) perception of 'economic class struggle'.

To underline the specificity of class struggle in post-socialist China, I call it 'class struggle without class organisation'. The limitation of this form of class struggle is that it is effective on the economic aspect of effort bargaining on the issue of the wage, but less effective on the political struggle of 'the relations in production' (Burawoy, 1979: 179). Certainly, there was significant confrontation from the supervisory and technical staff over the rationalisation that was designed to erode their autonomy and control power. But it was a defensive resistance which could only slow down, not halt, the reform. A proactive strategy to gain more control or autonomy over production was absent, not to mention an internal labour market and internal state that post-war US workers achieved through trade unions' participation in collective bargaining (Burawoy, 1979). In fact, this end is scarcely achievable without effective workplace representation. It explains why a 'contested despotic' labour regime was not advanced to 'hegemony', although a legal framework for this transition was available.

In the next chapter, I will explain why effective workplace representation could not be installed in China through a study of international civil society's efforts to facilitate workplace democratic organisations.

6 International civil society, Chinese trade unionism and workplace representation

Attention is not only given to formal unionism: labour activism through organisations not usually classified as 'industrial' – especially non-governmental organisations (NGOs) – is also examined, as well as the (dis)organised responses of workers outside any formally constituted body.

Hutchison and Brown (2001: 2)

Introduction

Western labour scholars have underlined a significant role of class organisation in the formation of class-consciousness and class solidarity (Hobsbawm, 1984; Katznelson and Zolberg, 1986; Clarke *et al.*, 1995). In China, as we saw in previous chapters, the question of workplace trade unionism has always been a central concern during major workers' strikes. In Chapter 2, we saw that a 'temporary trade union' was formed during the strike by Yong Feng workers in 1994 but declared 'illegal'; and workers more ambiguously listed the establishment of a trade union as a key demand in the Uniden strike in 2004. Like their counterparts in Uniden, some skilled workers in the Sun factory recognised the significance of a trade union (see Chapter 4). However, in both factories, the trade union established after the strike remained management-controlled. Worker activists took part in the union election in Uniden and won, but they could not resist the pressure from the management and soon resigned. Strikers in the Moon factory asked for rank-and-file representatives to be included in the existing union committee in an effort to reform the trade union (see Chapter 5). However, their demand was not properly addressed by the management. Management manipulation of the workplace trade union has remained a key barrier to the implementation of collective consultation and has given rise to wildcat strikes as a more effective channel to improve workers' wages and conditions (Clarke *et al.*, 2004; Clarke and Pringle, 2007), as we have seen in previous chapters. This turmoil in workplace relations has forced the ACFTU to launch unionisation campaigns in foreign- and privately owned enterprises since 2006.

On the other hand, the absence of freedom of association (FOA), one of the three core labour rights in International Labour Organisation (ILO) conventions, is a major drawback of Chinese trade unionism and is criticised by international trade unions and NGOs. The new social movement unionism thesis has suggested that collaboration of different social forces at the global level, in particular trade unions, NGOs and progressive political parties, is essential for social change in the age of globalisation (e.g. Waterman, 1999; 2001; Munck, 2002). Waterman (2001: 153), for instance, called for trade unions to go 'beyond internationalism' to 'global solidarity' by integration with new social movements, including the women's, peace, ethnic, ecological and consumer movements that have emerged in industrialised countries since the 1960s. He argued forcefully for 'the necessity for the existing labour organizations, national and international, to convert themselves into a global social movement around work' (Waterman, 2001: 206). Empirical studies of new labour organising strategies have also reminded us of the specific role of NGOs in Asian NICs (Hutchison and Brown, 2001). Within this trend, corporate social responsibility (CSR) was highlighted by academics, policy-makers and trade unionists as a new alternative to guarantee the basic rights of workers in the developing world. However, the implementation and monitoring of CSR practice has remained problematic (Pearson and Seyfang, 2001; Whitehouse, 2003), especially in China, where FOA is absent (D. O. Chang *et al.*, 2004).

This chapter explores the complexity of the implementation of workers' representative mechanisms and their dynamic relationship with the state, trade unions and civil society.

Codes of conduct and FOA in China

Pressed by consumer campaigns in the USA and Europe, TNCs in the West introduced corporate codes of conduct for their suppliers in developing countries from the early 1990s. Some of the social movement organisations have recently adopted a more cooperative way of engaging in CSR campaigns. For example, a number of MSIs have been formed by leading retail corporations, trade unions, campaign groups and NGOs as benchmarks in Western countries to promote CSR, such as the Fair Wear Foundation (FWF) in the Netherlands, the Ethical Trading Initiative (ETI) in the UK, the Social Accountability Initiative (SAI) and the Fair Labor Association (FLA) in the US (Pearson and Seyfang, 2001). The practice of CSR was launched in China in the mid-1990s (Pun, 2005a). As Pearson and Seyfang's (2001) study showed, sixteen of the main twenty codes of conduct in the world include a clause for FOA. As a result, in order to demonstrate their compliance with the code, some suppliers set up trade unions in their factories. However, as Pun's (2005a; 2005b) study revealed, the trade unions specially set up for CSR social audits in the PRD barely functioned at all, although those in the YRD did perform some useful functions. The director of a factory commented on its trade union (in which all committee members were management staff and the chair was a representative from the city-level industry-trade union federation and a Party member) in this way:

> We see many good sides to having a trade union. We won't worry about letting workers be organized. If the workers have their own organization, they

could organize leisure and welfare activities according to their liking. It is good for boosting productivity if the workers are happy working in my company. They can work faster, you know.

(Pun, 2005b: 28)

As we can see, the trade unions that were formed to satisfy CSR social audits were typical state socialist trade unions whose main activities in the workplace were to encourage labour discipline and productivity by organising production campaigns and social events (Clarke, 2005), while many others did not have any functions at all. This kind of trade union is not a 'real' trade union in the Western sense, so international trade unions and labour rights organisations were not satisfied that FOA had been implemented. To push the implementation of FOA forward, some TNCs and MSIs initiated pilot projects in China, as well as in other developing countries, to look for sustainable models of democratic workers' representative mechanisms in the workplace.

In one ground-breaking pilot project beginning in 2000, Hong Kong-based independent organisations were invited to provide training for workers in two shoe factories supplying a leading sportswear company, the first in Shenzhen, followed by another in Fu Jian province. In both factories, a democratic ballot was held to elect the union committee. However, the pro-labour Hong Kong NGO staff's involvement in the training of the ACFTU rank and- file aroused the attention of both the official trade union and the management. In the Fu Jian case, the local ACFTU branch banned the participation of the Hong Kong trainers from the very beginning, while in the Shenzhen factory the project was stopped by a new factory management in 2002, suggesting that the Hong Kong trainers were not allowed to work with the trade unions. Trade union committees existed in both factories.[1] In late August 2007 I was in the region when workers in the Shenzhen factory went on strike to protest against the company's plans to relocate production to another city and downsize the workforce without proper compensation. Some activist workers sought help from an independent NGO in the district and complained that their trade union was 'pro-management'.

The ACFTU's stance made TNCs, MSIs and their NGO working partners change their strategies in 'implementing' FOA in China. A Hong Kong labour NGO trainer in the shoe factory pilot project shared his experience with me:[2]

Our first experience [in the pilot project of trade union training] was very successful; we invested a lot. You know, we even rented a flat near a factory so that the trainers could have good contact with the trade union officers. The factory is big, there are 4,000 workers, and all of the trade union officers, except the president who was appointed by the management, were elected in a well-planned election that we monitored. Members were very enthusiastic, especially the vice-president. Unfortunately, the success story was discovered by the international media, which alerted the ACFTU, and we were forced to terminate the project. In one of the factories, soon after we [the trainers] withdrew, the vice-president left the job to join a social audit company. . . .

She used what she had learned from our training to pursue her own career interests. . . . To avoid political trouble, we began to think that the alternative committee model was more sustainable and practical.

As the trainer said, after the intervention of the ACFTU in the project, practitioners compromised with a new strategy to address the issue of FOA in China by facilitating the establishment of a workers' committee, welfare committee or OHS committee. This new model was being applied generally when I began my fieldwork in 2005. Many TNC brands and almost all of the main MSIs in the West were proposing committee pilot projects in China.

The next section examines this new development through the case of the Star factory, where I worked as an NGO trainer. On the one hand, I will see if there are any significant differences between the new model and a workplace trade union. On the other, I will explore the structural barriers and possibilities embedded in the dynamic social relations of the production regime, labour market, society and the state.

Background of the factory and welfare committee

The Star factory in Shenzhen was owned by a Taiwanese industrialist. It was established in the early 1990s in a tiny, walled industrial estate. The estate was owned by a collectively owned local villagers' company under the community government.[3] In line with common practice, the community government sent in a local Party Committee member to act as a so-called 'Chinese side' director and monitor the factory. In reality, this 'director' did not have any specific duties in the factory, except for communicating between the management and the local government.

The only member of staff from Taiwan in the factory was the GM, but the owner came to visit from time to time. The management was highly paternalistic. The GM intervened in every detail of the administration and management, although a director was in charge of routine production. The factory was split into various divisions. Within each division, a head coordinated a number of group leaders, who in turn supervised the work of ordinary workers.

Inside the factory grounds, there were three production and two dormitory buildings. Until 2001, the production buildings were viewed as one industrial plant by the workers, and the working conditions in the three buildings were identical. From 2001 onwards, the three plants were formed into two plants, A and B, and the employment conditions in these plants varied considerably. The wage standard in plant A was increased to satisfy a social audit from the buyer TNCs, while plant B was kept hidden from audit and the wage remained unchanged. As the nature of work in the two plants was basically the same, workers in plant B felt unfairly treated and staged a short strike to protest. The strike was unsuccessful, but the issue of equality between the two plants remained a basis for solidarity among workers in plant B as well as a source of conflict between workers in the two plants.

The factory was persuaded by one of its buyers to participate in a pilot project of management and workers' training intended to result in the establishment of an elected workers' welfare committee. A Hong Kong-based pro-labour NGO was invited to provide the training by a Western MSI, but the buyer who brought the factory into the project did not actively participate in the training process.

Before the training began, the only grievance channel was a suggestion box. The GM responded to some of the complaints in his regular meetings with the director, divisional heads and group leaders, but replies to workers who filed complaints were not guaranteed. Some workers also made complaints to the LSSB from time to time, and the LSSB officials would visit the factory to investigate. The owner of the factory told me of one case from September 2005:

> They came after a worker phoned them to complain that we did not abide by the law. I told the investigators: 'Of course, some factories are better than ours, but at the same time there are also many factories that are worse than us. If you can point out one factory that fully obeys the law, we will follow [it]. Please go back and tell your head [that] if the Labour Law is strictly enforced, all of the factories in the region will shut down.

The training project lasted from 2004 to 2006. At the beginning of the project, there were 700 workers in the factory, but the number was reduced to 500 at the end of 2004 as the factory relocated part of its production to an inland province. The first year of the project was to facilitate the formation of a welfare committee, while the second year was for training the committee members.

During the project, a series of talks and workshops was held for all of the workers as well as the management staff, covering the themes of globalisation, ILO fundamental labour standards, the consumer movement and CSR, labour laws, OHS, management–worker communication and so on. A survey of workers' generic concerns and grievances was conducted and found that the wage was the first priority of most workers. Afterwards, an organising group for the welfare committee was formed by representatives of both the management and the workers. The workers in the group were recommended by other workers or volunteered during a group discussion in the training session with facilitation from NGO trainers. The organising group was assigned to discuss the form, composition and function of a workers' representative body and facilitate its birth. In the name of the organising group, a factory-wide direct election of welfare committee members was held. The group agreed that management staff, including group leaders and divisional heads, would be excluded from candidacy as committee members. In China, the Trade Union Law stipulates that all employees are members of trade unions, and this in practice has led to the management staff's dominance of trade union committee positions, especially the union chair (Clarke *et al.*, 2004; Cooke, 2005; A. Chan, 2006b). The exclusion clause was suggested by the trainers to eliminate this abuse and made the committee more like a workplace representative body in the West. Workers were divided into twelve constituencies according to work groups and divisions. All ordinary workers were allowed to nominate themselves or other colleagues as candidates. One representative was elected from each constituency by secret ballot that was overseen by the trainers.

The second year involved consciousness-building, skills training and personal follow-up of the committee members. The trainers provided twelve sessions of training on topics such as minute-taking skills, teamwork and internal communication, internal division of work, complaint-handling procedures and collective bargaining. After the formal training ended, the committee was supposed to function as a representative mechanism to channel workers' grievances to the management, and trainers continued to provide advice and support for its work.

This chapter is mainly concerned with the operation of the committee, rather than the preceding training process. Over a period of seven months, the training team, including myself, paid ten visits to the factory and maintained close but informal contacts with the workers. The following section outlines how the committee operated and the impediments it faced when attempting to channel workers' grievances.

Operation of the welfare committee

After the training, the trainers and core committee members held a working meeting with the manager. In the meeting, the GM agreed to the committee members' request to allow trainers to support them continually. He promised a monthly regular meeting with the committee members and a regular time slot for the members to hold their own meetings. But he insisted that working proposals of the committee must receive approval from either himself or the director. Hong, the chair, Deng, the vice-chair, and Ma, a committee member, were the most active and outspoken committee members at the meeting.

Two weeks after the end of the training programme, the committee held its first meeting, with the trainers invited to attend. In the meeting, the members reflected that some workers had showed discontent about the committee as its members had enjoyed much paid time off work for training and meetings, but so far had not addressed any workers' concerns, especially the problem of low wages. As soon as the question of wages was raised, a prolonged conflict between members from plants A and B was manifested. A member from plant A mentioned that the better working conditions in her plant were justified as the 'quality' of workers was higher than in plant B. Her opinion sparked fury among members from plant B. One of them said: 'Let's race with each other, and see whose skill is better.'

To consolidate support from rank-and-file workers, and to understand the full extent of the conflict between workers in the two plants, members agreed to conduct a factory-wide survey about wages. Three days after the questionnaire was finalised, Hong presented it to the GM, who took it but never returned it to her. Hong and another member, who were told by the committee to make copies of the questionnaire, then felt pressure from both sides: the GM and the committee members. They told the trainers that they wanted to resign. The trainers suggested discussing the issue at the next meeting. However, throughout the next month, workers, including committee members, were required to work overtime in the time slots scheduled for meetings, on the premise that there was a tight deadline to meet. One month later, the GM told Hong that the questionnaire could not be distributed.

The operation of the committee was at a dead end until the trainers held an informal meeting with the members. Many members criticised Hong for allowing the GM to read the questionnaire. They also said: 'Without you [the trainers], they [the factory management] will ignore us. [The GM] will not keep his promises at all.' When the members discussed the workers' main grievances in different divisions, there was more conflict. Hong said that the GM had promised to pay a transportation subsidy for workers in her division but had never fulfilled his promise. Deng argued that working conditions in Hong's division were already very good, so there was no point in demanding transport fees.

The trainers urged the GM to convene a meeting with the committee. This cheered up the members. One week before the scheduled meeting, the members held a pre-meeting to work out a consensus and formulate an agenda for presentation to the GM. This was the first time members held a meeting without the trainers' presence. As the GM was not in the factory, members obtained consent from their group leaders to hold the meeting during working hours. The meeting seemed to be very effective. Members had been advised by trainers to collect workers' grievances in their divisions and report them to the meeting. They did a very competent job, listing concrete points that concerned workers. For instance, the workers living outside the compound wanted to take drinking water from the factory home with them. Other workers wanted improvements in the canteen's food quality and did not want to clean the floors of their workshops after overtime work. Most importantly, they demanded a reduction in working hours. One of the members prepared good minutes of all of these points and planned to raise them during the meeting with the GM.

However, the GM came back to the factory and denounced the members, especially Hong, for failing to ask his permission to hold the pre-meeting. Then he met privately with Hong and rejected most of the points raised in the minutes. Unsurprisingly, the morale of the members fell. Some even suggested dissolving the committee. In the face of this crisis, the trainers intervened and mediated between the two parties during the scheduled meeting with the GM: on the one hand, they advised committee members to try to arrange meetings on Sundays and to inform the GM in advance; on the other, they encouraged the GM to fix a time slot for committee members' meetings. The GM attended the meeting for only half an hour. After he left, many members were outraged: 'We do not want to be window-dressing [the factory] and get nothing from taking part in the game.' They knew it was a game because the factory needed the committee to convince buyers that their work practices were good.

One month later, representatives from one of the factory's main clients arranged a visit the factory to meet with the committee members. One week before the meeting was due to take place, the GM called up the members and warned them not to reveal the reality of life in the factory. In return, he promised that the factory would offer a special bonus for those who had worked there for more than six months. At the meeting with the GM, Deng and Ma were the two most outspoken and rebellious members. The next day, one of his colleagues and good friends told Ma that their divisional head had said the factory was going to sack him. Ma had learned how to make models from a craftsman who had been a designer in the factory for a year. This teacher had introduced him directly to plant A. In the afternoon, Ma received a phone message from his mentor: 'You should not cause so much trouble. Don't let me down!' Ma then went to talk with his divisional head, who warned him not to talk so much, or else the factory would dismiss him. At midnight, he went to his mentor's home and promised that he would not make trouble again.

A similar message was delivered to Deng. However, he remained determined to voice his concerns about wages to the client's representatives, and criticised Ma's treatment the day before the committee's meeting with them.

The next day, just one hour before the scheduled meeting time, Deng and Ma were sent by the factory's 'Chinese-side' director to the office of the local government joint-stock company that owned the industrial estates, where the two men were asked about their work in the committee. Meanwhile, the GM called in a member who had been promoted to be a group leader and had not attended committee meetings for a period of time and asked him to attend the meeting with the clients. It was then agreed that the management would not attend the meeting.

At the meeting, the group leader member immediately told the clients that all the factory's salaries were paid in accordance with the law. The other members were more subdued than at any previous meeting. Deng and Ma, who arrived late because of their earlier engagement, presented some positive achievements of the committee, which were endorsed by many other members.

One month after the meeting, it was the Chinese New Year festival. The GM convened a meeting with the committee members to present a small gift to each of them and promised pay rises in those divisions which had the lowest salaries. However, the overall standard of wages, especially in plant B, remained lower than the minimum legal rate.

After the New Year, it was estimated that about 150 workers quit their jobs. Ma found a job in another factory where the wage was even lower, but he thought he would have more opportunities to learn skills. Deng also planned to resign and go to another city to work with his younger brother. But the factory suddenly transferred Deng from plant B to plant A, so his salary increased from 16.50 yuan to more than 20 yuan per day. He was criticised by other members as 'self-interested', because he was either absent or kept a low profile in every meeting after his transfer.

It was unclear whether the wage adjustment after the New Year was an indirect concession to the committee or simply a strategy to retain workers in the face of the high turnover rate at the factory. The trainers did not intervene in the operation of the committee once the project ended two months after the New Year. The committee, although called for meetings by the managers from time to time, seemed to be increasingly passive. In the words of the workers, it was 'a flower vase' – meaning a mere decoration.

Limitations of the welfare committee

As is clear from the above description of its activities, the committee's achievements were very limited. After the training team withdrew, its most active member quit and others were placated by promotion, it became dysfunctional. In terms of its functions in the workplace, it was not much different from many other trade unions and workers' committees in China's private sector (Pun, 2005a; Sum and Pun, 2005; A. Chan, 2006b). It should be noted that, unlike the trade union project A. Chan (2007) evaluated, the local ACFTU branch did not intervene in the welfare committee, but the fates of the workplace democratic representative bodies seemed to be very similar. My experience in other projects and wide discussion with trainers in other organisations confirmed that the sustainability of the committee or trade union is always a problematic issue.

To be sure, some models and projects were more successful than others, in terms of the impacts of training and elections on the immediate improvement of wages and working conditions. For example, in one project, the factory management urged the trainers to delay the schedule of a lecture on the Labour Law and labour rights so that it could increase wages to the minimum rate beforehand. The factory was worried about workers' outrage once they were told their legal rights by experienced trainers, especially when TNC clients were present. However, it was generally hard to sustain a committee upon the withdrawal of the external support from a labour NGO amid pressure from management on its active members.

Factors handicapping the welfare committee

First, patron–client relations between the local state (and local villagers) and the business, which are structurally embedded in the legacy of the socialist state, hinder workers' activism. This was especially apparent in the special meeting arranged for Deng and Ma on the date they met the TNC clients. Local villagers, especially the cadres and Party members who act as managers or directors in the villagers' joint-stock company, benefited from the rental income from the factories. Some of the cadres or their relatives also gained extra salaries for acting as directors in one of the factories. For grassroots state departments, including the labour station at the residential district (*Jiedao*, equal to town) level, and the LSSB at district (*Qu*, equal to county) level, their incomes are dependent on the local state budget. Before 1995, there was a single tax system in China, with all of the tax income sent to the central state and then redistributed to the local level. Under this system, the taxes collected by the local state revenue department did not contribute directly to the local budget. As a result, the local state officials were reluctant to collect taxes, which led to loss of national revenue. The central government then introduced a dual tax system by separating national and local tax. The national tax is dependent on the value-added in the production chain, while the local tax is dependant on gross profit. The new system encouraged provinces and cities to compete for foreign or domestic private investment at the expense of lower environmental and labour standards. The tax reform in 1995 can be seen as a symptom of the internal contradiction of the state. In other words, as socialist ideology eroded, the capacity of the central government to control its subordinates weakened. It also explains why the rule of law is hard to realise in China (Lee, 2007a); the difficulty of implementing the Labour Law and Trade Union Law in the private sector is just one example of this. The scenario was even worse when one considers the many cases of hidden interest-exchange and corruption that were prevalent in the country.

Second, as global capitalism is expanding rapidly in China, the workers, especially those who are young or more skilled, find that quitting is a better way to secure their interests than lobbying within their current company. For example, Ma moved to another factory rather than staying where he was and trying to find a collective way to improve his situation. Although the manager neither punished nor dismissed him, Ma felt pressure within the factory. The extent and nature of the shortage of labour have been discussed in previous chapters, and there was further evidence of it in this case. In the Star factory, hundreds of workers quit after Chinese New Year and in the peak season. As at the Uniden, Sun and Moon factories, in response to labour shortages and rising labour costs, Star set up two subsidiary plants in the provinces of Jiang Xi and Jiang Su. The expansion of capitalism is a double-edged sword for workers' activism. Although it can encourage confidence in workers such as Ma, it also makes quitting a common strategy, which is detrimental to sustainable organisation in the workplace. Those with a weak market position, for example Hong and Deng, were too vulnerable to resist threats or co-option from the management. Hong was in her late thirties and the main breadwinner of a family with two sons at school. Her husband, whose wage was one-third lower than hers, worked in a garment factory as a general auxiliary worker. Deng was a slightly disabled man with low skill levels. It was too costly for either of them to lose their job. Chinese workers are engaged in the struggle of voice, exit and loyalty, in the terms of Hirschman (1970). Labour market and family status were two significant factors influencing workers' choice of strategy. After voice, Ma chose to exit; while Hong and Deng stayed out of loyalty. In any case, voice has become a more common strategy for migrant workers than ever before.

Third, the personal network is prevalent and exploited by factories as a control strategy. According to State Council research (SCRO Project Team, 2006), 60.37 per cent of migrant workers in the country acquire their jobs through personal networks of kinship and locality. They are often introduced into factories by senior staff. As we have seen, Ma was introduced by his mentor, a craftsman in the factory, and benefited from that mentor's personal relations so that he could work in plant A. Later, the mentor was a key person used by the manager to put pressure on Ma. After the New Year, the GM manipulated a by-election of three committee members organised because of the promotion or resignation of previous members. I had a deep discussion with one of the new members, who had been very outspoken and active in the meeting, and learned that both of his parents had worked in the factory for a long time. Hong, who had been in the factory for more than ten years herself, wanted to bring her husband into the factory, but he was rejected by the GM because of his age and lack of skills. Deng was introduced to the factory by his aunt, who still worked in the factory.

Walder (1986) explained the institutionalisation of an interpersonal-dependent culture as a way of controlling the workplace in communist China through his powerful concept of 'communist neo-traditionalism'. Although the mode of production and personal relationships in the workplace are totally different in FIEs compared to SOEs, the personal network of patron–client relations was embedded in both pre-capitalist culture and state-socialist traditions and is still prevalent in contemporary global factories. The culture could be eroded and phased out by reform of recruitment practice and rationalisation of management, as we saw in the Sun and Moon factories. Similarly, in the Star factory, personal introduction alone was insufficient to provide a labour supply. The factory hung out a banner in its grounds to advertise job vacancies throughout the year.

Fourth, workers' solidarity is dislocated by the management strategy of 'divide and rule'. Wage scales differed from plant to plant, division to division, and even from one worker to another. There were lots of interest differences between workers in plants A and B, between experienced workers and new workers on the production line, and between supervisors and committee members. The group leaders hated the activities of the committee because, when the members left their workshops to attend meetings, they had to replace them on the production line. The trainers suggested that the factory should employ 'substitute workers' to resolve the conflict, but that was rejected by the GM, although both the committee members and group leaders supported the suggestion. As will be explained below, the effect of a petition for higher wages in the handmade division was weakened by the failure of workers from other divisions to add their signatures. A base of solidarity was hard to identify and articulate in the day-to-day experience of workers. Workers will act together only when they perceive that their own interest is in line with those of others (Fantasia, 1988). To most of the workers, the primary reason for them to stay in work was to earn a living and escape hardship in rural villages. In the case of Deng, although he had a strong sense of justice, he was placated after being transferred to plant A. As human beings, workers always struggle between the material factor of self-interest and the moral factor of social justice (Kelly, 2002). But, to be sure, it will take time and struggle experience before a stratum of workers that is able to commit to class interest emerges.

Fifth, the external support for workers is weak. While the committee was reliant on the support and advice of the trainers, the trainers' role was restricted. First, the NGO worked in the factory only on a project basis. Without external funding and permission from the factory, the trainers could not provide long-term support. Moreover, if the trainers firmly stood up for the interests of the workers, the factory would not allow long-running involvement of the NGO. More structurally, NGOs in China do not have a legal right to represent workers and facilitate the establishment of workplace organisation independently from their employers. TNCs are even in a paradoxical position regarding their support of workers (Pun, 2005a) because of the fundamental conflict of interest over price. At an informal dinner after an MSI conference on 13 November 2005, a supplier manager complained that full compliance with the code would increase costs: 'The market is highly competitive. A little rise in price would make us lose the order.' In response, an ethical trade manager of a TNC stressed price pressure in their merchandising practice: 'Price is powerful! We should balance quality, price and ethics.' According to the Trade Union Law and the newly implemented Labour Contract Law, the role should be played only by the higher-level ACFTU branches.

To conclude, the potential of the welfare committee was limited because of the power imbalance between workers and management. Workers were divided and inexperienced and lacked external support, so they preferred individual ways of living and means of struggle. These characteristics made them too vulnerable to resist the management's pressure and co-option. The management, by contrast, could exploit the locality interest networks in the community and the factory to pressurise the workers, as we saw in the Sun factory before 2004.

Impacts of the welfare committee

Despite their fundamental weaknesses, though, the training project and welfare committee had some positive effects on the workers' experience.

First, there was the announcement that wages were to be raised in the manager's meeting with committee members before the New Year, even though the increase did not satisfy the workers or bring the factory up to legal and CSR code standards. The factory routinely withheld a proportion of wages during the New Year holidays to prevent workers leaving the factory without notice: seven days for plant A and twenty-five days for plant B. The GM, in this meeting, also announced that the figure for plant B would be reduced to ten days. A bonus of between 50 and 200 yuan had already been promised to workers who had served for more than six months.

Second, the food was improved (slightly) as a result of the demands of the committee. The manager asked the members to monitor and participate in the food purchase each morning. The factory paid five yuan per day to whichever member did this. However, some of the members were reluctant to take their turn. After the New Year, the canteen provided three dishes instead of the previous two, although it was still mostly vegetables.

Third, the greatest achievement, which was appreciated by both the manager and the workers, was a National Day cultural party. This event was proposed by the committee members and supported by the management. Five thousand yuan was spent on the party, which was attended by 300 workers. The ordinary workers genuinely seemed to enjoy it and truly appreciated the work of the committee in organising it.

As these 'concessions' from the management were quite insignificant, the achievements of the committee should not be overestimated. Furthermore, while the committee campaigned on all of these issues, other factors – the labour shortage, external resources from the TNC and the management's aim to boost productivity – also contributed to these 'achievements'. However, during the training, workers staged at least three collective protests, all of which were very effective in pressing the management and so were positive moments in the workers' experience.

A strike was staged soon after a talk on Labour Law had been delivered by the NGO trainers. A routine management abuse was delayed payments, between twenty and forty-five days, depending on plant and division. Workers were told by the trainers that it was illegal for the factory to delay payments for more than seven days. It was the first time that workers had heard this information and a discussion began. The factory's financial officer was forced to announce that the company would improve its payment practice, and as a first step the electronics and handmade divisions (which were forty-five days overdue) would be paid on the same day as the sewing division (thirty days overdue). However, that promise was not kept. Naturally, the workers in the electronics and handmade divisions divisions were frustrated and agitated. On the date when the sewing division was paid, they stopped working but remained in their workshops. The GM went to the workshops and asked all of the 150 strikers to queue up on the ground floor. 'He reprimanded us and asked if we wanted to work or not. No one answered. But then some of us began to move [back to the workshop]. That's how our short strike ended,' one of the committee members recalled. The problem was not resolved until the factory reduced the overdue days from forty-five to twenty for all divisions in plant B fifteen months later.

During the committee training, a number of anonymous workers filed a complaint to the district LSSB about the factory's infringement of the Labour Law on delayed wage payment and long working hours. The GM called a meeting with the committee to discuss the issue. He invited members to express the workers' grievances, and members voiced four areas of discontent. First, workers had to attend a morning assembly every day. The assembly was not counted as working time, but the workers were subjected to a penalty if they were late for it. Second, there was little choice of food and the hygiene was bad. Third, if workers could not finish their work targets during normal working hours, they had to work overtime without payment. Fourth, penalties in the factory were generally heavy. The result of the meeting was encouraging. The GM promised to change the regular morning assembly from a daily basis to a weekly basis and to provide more food options.

At the end of the formal training programme, Deng and another committee member from the handmade division of plant B, where the wage rate was the lowest in the factory, organised a petition in their division to ask for a pay rise. More than thirty workers signed the petition. They handed it to the GM at the final training session. The move forced the manager to make a promise on wages in the meeting to the effect that most workers in this division would be granted a pay rise from the next month onwards. Those who earned 10 yuan per day would have this increased to 13, and similar rises from 12 yuan to 13.5 or 14, 13 to 14 or 14.50, 14 to 15, 15 to 16, and 16 to 16.50 would also be implemented. (Those on a daily wage of between 17 and 20 yuan would not be given a rise.) This victory encouraged the committee members to plan a factory-wide survey to give voice to other workers' wage concerns. But as we have seen, the GM stopped this by putting pressure on Hong.

From all of this, we can see that the welfare committee did have some long-term impact. On the workers' side, through the training, meetings and activities of the committee, they learned their legal rights and gradually developed their organisational capacity. They progressed from an unorganised strike that achieved nothing, to a collective complaint which gained a non-wage concession, to a well-organised, tactical petition which brought pay rises. However, when this step-by-step process of organisation advanced towards the factory-wide wage survey in the name of the committee, it was halted by pressure from the manager. Afterwards, internal conflict arose and workers' confidence collapsed.

On the part of the management, it agreed to establish a committee for a number of reasons. First, the presence of a committee could show clients that 'good practice' was employed in the factory (pictures of committee events were always shown when clients came to do their factory audits). Second, the committee organised social activities that increased the workers' sense of belonging, productivity and willingness to stay in the factory. This point was repeatedly expressed by the GM in his meetings with clients, trainers and committee members. Third, the committee could express ordinary workers' concerns that otherwise would go to the LSSB or give rise to a strike. However, the management still wanted to place the committee entirely under its control, rather than allow it to function as a real representative body of workers that would be able to challenge management, which had been the aim of the external trainers.

In these respects, the welfare committee model was not much different from traditional state-socialist workplace trade unionism. What made the externally imposed committee different from a traditional trade union was the knowledge and expectation of workers. As we saw in the cases of the Uniden, Sun and Moon factories, even though there was a trade union committee in each factory, most of the ordinary workers did not know it existed or had little expectation of it. In the words of a female worker in the Moon factory, her understanding of a labour union (*Gonghui*) was that 'labourers gathered together in a meeting'. In the Star factory, however, the labour laws, ordinances, CSR codes and other labour rights, along with the organising skill to achieve these rights, were delivered to workers in classroom-based lectures and small-group workshops as well as informal contact between trainers and workers. With all of these expectations and knowledge in mind, as soon as ordinary workers thought that the committee was unable to protect their rights and interests, they would lose faith in it; and as soon as the committee members' attempts to voice the workers' rights and interests were hindered, they also felt frustrated, lost confidence and retreated to the individual strategy of quitting.

State, trade union and NGOs

As Chang and Wong (2005) suggested, the Western-based consumer movement and its attached CSR projects wanted to create opportunities for workers to organise on the ground. In this sense, international civil society played a role in linking workers' struggle in their workplace and community with the moral movement in the West. However, in China, official trade unions continued to act as a Party-state apparatus and were reluctant to work with international organisations in workplace organisation, while the independent NGOs which worked closely with international civil society also were not ultimately immune from the leverage of the Party state. Social and political developments since the labour shortage and wave of strikes beginning in 2004 imposed new challenges on both the official trade union and independent NGOs.

Pun (2009) suggested three kinds of legal status of labour NGOs in the PRD. Some survived under a 'patronised' partner such as the ACFTU or a university institution; some were registered as a business unit; while the rest operated without any registration. The example of the Chinese Working Women Network (CWWN), which was set up as early as 1996 as the first labour rights NGO in the PRD by a group of scholars, students, social workers and feminists in Hong Kong, shows that there is no legal channel for the group to achieve registration in the mainland. CWWN sought different state departments at provincial and municipal levels to affiliate to under their umbrella. Finally, a joint project by the name of the 'Nan Shan Women Worker Service Center' was launched by CWWN and the district trade union federation. CWWN's early work focused on empowering women workers in their service centres or workers' dormitories by providing legal and gender education. CWWN paid the trade union a service fee in exchange for the union officials being on-duty in the centre. The rise of the anti-sweatshop movement and CSR in the West as well as the general concern over development and poverty in China created more opportunities for NGO activism in the PRD from the late 1990s. In 2003, a newspaper reported that ten labour NGOs[4] had emerged in the PRD within one year and most of them were funded by foreign foundations (*Zhongguo Jingyingbao*, 5 December 2003). Like the CWWN service centre, some of the labour NGOs were initiated by Hong Kong-based NGOs, while the others were set up by mainland intellectual activists or workers who built connections with the foreign foundations at a later stage. Sponsored by TNCs, MSIs, charities and international trade unions, labour NGOs extended their activities from community-based service centres to factories by trade union or workers' committee training and social audit projects, public spaces in industrial zones (e.g. a mobile van project) and hospitals (e.g. an industrially injured workers' network). In 2004, CWWN cooperated with a local branch of the Chinese Communist Youth League to set up a new service centre and its projects were expanded to include a women workers' cooperative shop, a women's 'health express' mobile van, an OHS community education centre, an industrial injured workers' network, a factory workers' committee training programme and a legal advice hotline.

However, 2005 was a turning point for foreign-funded labour NGOs in the PRD. From that year, the government strengthened monitoring and constraints on the work of NGOs.[5] The NGOs' semi-official working partners, the ACFTU district branch and the Youth League in the case of CWWN, withdrew from the partnership after being subjected to pressure by the state. Those which registered as a business unit were also challenged on the grounds that the non-commercial nature of their activities did not comply with the terms stipulated in their registration. Some were forced to close while others continue to run under stricter monitoring from the local state. These survival difficulties of labour NGOs further undermined continued support for workers' committees under the CSR project.

On the other hand, the state also intervened more actively in both CSR practices and workplace organisations. In 2005, China announced its own CSR standard, CSC9000T, initially only for the textile industry, which is similar to the internationally accepted SA8000 standard (A. Chan, 2006b). Since 2006, the ACFTU, supported by the state authorities, launched a historic unionisation campaign, beginning with giant TNCs like Wal-Mart (A. Chan, 2006a; 2007). Usually local town-level Party-state officers go to factories to ask the management to set up trade unions. This is not legally compulsory, but the factory managers generally find it hard to resist such direct state pressure. When I interviewed a factory owner in the Long Gang district of Shenzhen, where the Star factory is situated, he complained of pressure from the residential district (*Jiedao*) government which pressed the factory to form a trade union and a Party Committee. From the middle of 2006, officials from the residential district government went to the factory to talk with its executive manager. The response from the factory was to set up a Party Committee in late 2006, although it resisted establishing a trade union. However, by the middle of 2007, the pressure from the state for unionisation was increasing. The factory owner said in December 2007:

> They [the residential district government officers] came to visit us many times. They said that it was the government's policy to request enterprises like ours, with more than 1,000 workers, to set up a trade union. The [residential district] secretary-general also phoned our managing director to talk over the issue. We are within their sphere (*Zai Tamende Dipan*), so it was very hard [to refuse.] . . . Now the government does not fear rich people, they fear poor people. China is different from other countries. In the West, it is the rich people who influence politics and the government fears the rich. Now, in China, it is the rich who fear the government and the government fears the poor. The poor have a high potential to threaten social stability and social order. The government now is mostly afraid of losing control. But they do not fear the boss. Some years ago, the government tried its best to attract foreign capital. Now it gets lots of money. Tax revenue has been quite sufficient. . . . The country itself has too much capital and savings. So they do not care if foreign capital moves out.

The government officers told him that a relative of the boss could not be appointed to the trade union chair. Even so, a factory director was assigned to be the chair, which in the understanding of the factory owner did not violate the state directive.

The policy of the local ACFTU is '*have* [a trade union] first' and '*be like* [a trade union] later'. This strategy can certainly achieve the unionisation rate target set by the higher level of the trade union, but it rarely provides successful union representation. Alongside forcefully pushing workplace unionisation, the SZMFTU also became more active in the community. In October 2007, it held a meeting with sixteen labour 'civil agents' (*Gongmin Daili*[6]) and NGO activists to show appreciation for their projects and discuss the possibility of integrating their work into community-based trade union legal rights centres. However, one condition that some of the activists could not accept was that they would not be allowed to contact overseas media or receive foreign funding.

Concluding remarks

As we have repeatedly seen in the cases presented in this book, unstable labour relations in China today make a stable representative mechanism in the workplace essential. High turnover of staff, wildcat strikes and administrative complaints, as well as the escalating number of labour disputes, create a problem for the state and trouble for employers. The state needs a trade union to mediate labour–management disputes, the employers need a trade union to improve productivity and stabilise the high labour turnover rate and stoppages, and the workers need a trade union to express their grievances. The traditional socialist trade unions cannot perform these functions as the workers do not trust a union that is in the hands of the management. Therefore, democratisation of workplace organisation is necessary.

However, as the Star factory case and other similar projects revealed,[7] democratisation is by no means sufficient to make workplace organisation effective. The management–labour relationship is highly imbalanced. While workers are extremely divided and inexperienced, management exploits personal interest networks inside and outside the production regime to divide and control workers. So, to achieve effective workers' organisation, external support is essential. Support from NGO trainers, MSIs and TNCs was insufficient as all of the CSR projects were short-term and both NGOs and MSIs do not have solid legal and ultimately political power in the authoritarian regime of China. Moreover, the business interests of TNCs often run contrary to workers' organising power. A. Chan (2007: 15) put it this way:

> Even in societies that have well-established trade unions and trade union cultures, much time and effort are needed to set up workplace trade unions and after that to ensure they have the competency to bargain with management. Moral and practical support and prolonged training by higher-level trade union organs are normally needed.

Accordingly, Chan (2007: 15) argued for 'the necessity for trade union involvement' in the CSR projects. However, the ACFTU is still resistant to working with overseas-sponsored NGOs to prevent independent labour organisation, and there is no sign of successful workplace organisation, as we saw in Shenzhen. The barriers to workplace organisation were indeed beyond the factory and embedded in the development of state, economy and society.

China is experiencing dramatic social and economic change today. Workers' wildcat forms of struggle and unstable labour relations in the workplace are impacting on both state policy and ACFTU strategy (Clarke and Pringle, 2007). A campaign is ongoing from the ACFTU with strong state support to set up workplace trade unions in FIEs. As A. Chan (2006a; 2007) pointed out, the active strategy and method of organising trade unions in Wal-Mart superstores was unprecedented. The new Labour Contract Law (2008) also enhances both workers' individual rights and the power of workplace trade unions. All of these reforms provide a new context for workers' activism and organising capacity.

Thus, the transition of China into global capitalism is very different from the West. The legacy of socialism guaranteed a strong state-manipulated trade union and weak civil society, resembling the older generation of East Asian NICs in the 1970s, especially South Korea and Taiwan. Thus, the potentials and limitations of workplace organising capacity followed the path of social and economic development in the later capitalist countries. The attempt of international civil society to reshape workplace relationships in China cannot succeed without a strong national and local foundation. The complexity of state–trade union–NGO relationships in contemporary China defies the optimistic elaboration of the new social movement unionism thesis on a 'global solidarity' in the new millennium (Waterman, 1999; 2001). To be sure, independent labour NGOs can play a supportive and stimulating role in workers' activism. However, more attention should be paid to the development of the state development strategy, which is in turn shaped by labour–management conflict and the power balance in the workplace and the community.

7 Conclusion

Workers' struggle and the changing labour regime in China

Introduction

> The new international labour studies was different from and could not be reduced to industrial relations, trade union studies, labour history or the sort of technical studies carried out by bodies like the ILO. . . . Within peripheral capitalist countries scholars were concerned with the process of proletarianisation, the nature of workers' struggles.
>
> (Cohen, 1991: 10)

This study has examined the formation and transformation of migrant workers' struggles and industrial conflicts in China, specifically in its first SEZ, Shenzhen. I drew fruitful insights from a wide range of labour studies traditions before deciding to focus on the nature of migrant workers' struggles and the historical process of class formation, inspired by the paradigm of 'new international labour studies' (Cohen, 1991). In Chapter 1, I laid out my research puzzle on the potential and limitations of the new working class during China's integration into global capitalism over the past three decades. By reviewing the previous literature on China labour studies, a key question emerged: what is the specificity of labour politics in China? Post-structuralist, culturalist and political economy-orientated institutionalism provided various answers. I tried to break through the limits of orthodox disciplines and undertake a coherent scholarship by connecting local politics with global force (Burawoy *et al.*, 2000) and micro-empirical reality with grand theories (Strangleman, 2005).

Inspired by the labour history tradition, Chapter 2 provided a review of labour conflicts in Shenzhen from 1979 to 2004 as a background to my ethnographic engagement from 2005 to 2008.

In Chapter 3, I drew insights from gender, culture and community studies to explore the social process of a migrant workers' settlement community, Militant village in Shenzhen, and its impact on the labour process and power relations on the shop floor. Apart from the extensive scope of social relations – gender, place and its attached gangsterism, age and skill – special consideration was paid to the formation of industrial masculinity as a prelude to the investigation of the role of male skilled workers in strikes.

In Chapter 4, a strike in the Sun factory, a Taiwanese-invested enterprise in Militant village, and its influence on its sister factory in the neighbouring city of Hui Zhou, was studied at length. My discussion started from the workplace industrial relations tradition with its insight into industrial conflict, but ended with a critique of the limits of the application of the tripartite institutional analysis: trade union, management and the state in China's global factories. Alternatively, I suggested that 'unorganised' workers in the industrial conflicts should be regarded as a 'collective' player in analysis of the development of workplace industrial relations in China.

Although stressing the role of workers, I did not intend to downplay the function of institutions. So, in Chapter 5, I brought a perspective of legal institutionalism to the study of the labour regime with the cases of the Moon factory and its sister factory, also in Shenzhen, concentrating on the wage issue. I suggested that wage politics is a contested terrain for workers, management and the state, and so an essential topic to explore. I argued that the workers' struggle had pressed the state to provide a new legal context, which, in turn, imposed limits on management. However, the inability of the workplace trade union or an alternative organisation to play its primary role of representing the workers impeded the transition of the labour regime (which I called 'contested despotism') into 'hegemony' in the wider context of political economy (Burawoy, 1979).

The question of workplace representation was studied in Chapter 6 through the case of the Star factory, where international civil society attempted to experiment with a model of democratic workplace representation in China.

Now, in this concluding chapter, the puzzles laid out in Chapter 1 will be linked with the findings and discussions of Chapters 2 to 6.

Emerging patterns of workers' protests

As shown in Chapters 2 to 6, one of the most significant developments in labour relations has been taking place since 2004. This view is shared by the research findings of CLB, an independent labour NGO based in Hong Kong (CLB, 2005b; 2007). CLB published two 'China Labour Movement Observation Reports', with a 2005 version covering 2000 to 2004 and a 2007 edition covering 2005 and 2006. These reports were based on nationwide macro-analysis of official statistics, official and academic documents, media-reported cases and journalists' articles. The 2005 report highlighted the labour surplus and employment pressure in the country:

> The sources from the CCP Propaganda Department and the MOLSS showed that . . . from 2001–5 . . . the city and town population which was seeking employment reached as high as 22 to 23 million each year, but the new jobs created each year only accounted for 7 to 8 million. Meanwhile, 150 million of surplus labour power was waiting to be transferred.
>
> CLB (2005b: 4)

But the 2007 report highlighted a labour *shortage* and the changing form of labour protests in 2005 and 2006:

> From 2003, a phenomenon of labour shortage emerged in the eastern coastal region. . . . The SOE reform which culminated in privatisation had basically finished. . . . In the post-reform enterprises, the wages, welfare and working conditions had lost any significant difference with the FIEs and POEs. . . . The previous SOE employees (urban employees) in the post-reformed enterprises also started to strive for their own rights and interests through strikes. And the basic demands of the urban employees and peasant workers were towards convergence as most of them involved directly [demanding] a wage rise and improvement in working conditions. This is because there is no significant difference between the post-reformed previous SOE and FIE and POE in terms of their management strategies and employment conditions, with the employment conditions in some [former SOEs] being even worse than the latter.
>
> CLB (2007: 4, 9)

These reports confirmed my analysis in Chapter 1: that the protests of laid-off SOE workers and pensioners would lose their significance as a sustainable means of social transformation in China and this agency would potentially be replaced by the new working class.[1]

By concentrating on local cases, ethnographic study may fail to grasp a general national picture, which orthodox industrial relations and labour movement studies may prefer. It was not my intention to provide a national account of patterns of workers' strikes. Rather, I saw Shenzhen as a pioneer in workers' struggle. This city is most prone to labour conflicts, as the number of cases handled by its labour dispute arbitration committees reportedly accounted for one-tenth of the total national figure (*Nanfang Ribao*, 28 October 2004). But the CLB (2007) report affirmed that the characteristics of the migrant workers' struggles in Shenzhen were shared to some extent by protests in factories with different ownerships and in other areas.[2]

As far as the city of Shenzhen was concerned, I adopted a multi-case method (Elger and Smith, 2005) to explore the similarities and differences between labour relations over time. My selection of cases before 2004 was based on the availability of resources and informants; the cases after 2004, namely the Uniden, Sun and Moon factories, however, were selected from among a dozen strike cases. My decision to explore these cases in-depth was because of their level of militancy and influence among the workers' community. All three cases happened in large FIEs and were well known among workers in Shenzhen, or at least in the district of Bao An. Rather than being typical cases, they were among the vanguard form of labour protest, which is ideal to explain and predict the scope and limits of industrial conflict and organisation in China.

In order to make comparison possible and highlight the significance of the impact of the labour market and economic expansion on workplace struggles (Franzosi, 1995), I borrowed the phrase 'wave of strikes' from Taylor *et al.* (2003:

175), who described strikes in the FIEs of southern China in the early 1990s as 'the third wave of strikes' in the history of the People's Republic. The strikes of the Uniden, Sun and Moon factories all occurred within a new wave of strikes from 2004 to 2005 due to the further expansion of global production into China after the country's WTO entry in 2001. The strikes in this wave were characterised by the enforcement of the minimum wage and social insurance. In August 2007, the Moon factory struck during a similar wave of strikes that forced the city government to raise the minimum wage in October that year, although its duration and scale were shorter and smaller than the 2004–05 wave due to the prompt response of the state. The strikes in Uniden, Sun and Moon were organised by different groups of workers, but workers learned from each other and accumulated experience as a collective. In fact, a cross-factory informal network was well developed among workers, especially those from the same province and at the skilled and supervisory levels. In light of this, I attempted to track a historical trend from the strike cases presented in this book.

Although cases of strikes were reported in the region as early as the 1980s, their impact and scale were considerably less than the waves of strikes that have occurred since 1993. A series of commonalities was evident across the pattern of strikes from 1993 to 2007. First, the timing of strike waves was directly related to the expansion of global capitalism and state intervention in production and reproduction of the labour force. Second, issues of discontent that were deeply embedded in the labour process were hard to resolve through existing formal channels. Third, a specific issue that went against workers' interests invariably ignited the strikes. Fourth, some hidden leaders, usually supervisory and skilled workers, acting behind the scenes were important components of the strikes. Fifth, violence or gangster activism usually forced other workers to strike or show discontent towards factory management. Sixth, each strike had a knock-on effect in other factories.

However, detailed analysis also shows evidence of significant developments:

1   The workers' demands became increasingly radical, from within the limit of the law to beyond the law. In 1993 and 1994, when management responded to the workers' wage demands by increasing food, accommodation and other fees, workers did not resist these acts as they were legal (AMRC, 1995). In 2004 and 2005, however, workers demanded real implementation of the minimum wage without any deductions. In 2007, strikers asked for a reasonable and decent wage as well as a proper working and living environment.

2   The workers learned from past experience and from each other, so their struggle became strategically more sophisticated over time. From 1993 to 1994, the strikers contained themselves within the complex of the factory (AMRC, 1995). In 2004 and 2007, workers began to walk onto the highway to attract media and public attention and state intervention. In the Sun factory case in 2004, workers transferred struggle experiences to the new factory in another city. In the Moon factory in 2007, two factories within the same company coordinated with each other to stage a joint strike.

3   The shortage of labour increased the confidence of workers (Franzosi, 1995). Despite the fact that the supply of migrant workers seemed to be unlimited in the early 1990s (Lee, 1998), the further expansion of global capitalism into China promptly pushed up the demand for labour (Lewis, 1954). One of the key characteristics of the 2004 and 2007 strikes was large-scale quitting following the strikes. Workers could easily find another job soon. Edwards and Scullion's (1982) study suggested that quitting itself is a form of industrial conflict. This study showed quitting, an individual form of struggle, increased in parallel with striking, a collective form. Although workers' wages were mostly raised after the strikes, their discontent with the management remained. Skilled workers in particular were not in 'unlimited supply' when the economy was in the process of rapid growth (Lewis, 1954).

4   The high staff turnover rate aggravated the effect of the shortage of labour and lowered productivity. Strikes further strengthened rank-and-file workers' confidence and increased the conflict between them and management. 'Voice' and then 'quit' or 'voice' became common ways to express discontent, borrowing terms from Hirschman (1970). This new pattern of workplace conflict brought a big challenge to the management, whose first concern was productivity, and the state, which was keen to maintain social order and a favourable investment environment. The emerging patterns of workers' protest had forced the state to improve labour protection (e.g. new labour legislation and a higher minimum wage rate) and management to adopt new business strategies (e.g. production relocation to other parts of China and outsourcing). But the workers' struggle strategy also changed over time due to changing legal, social, economic and political contexts.

5   The skilled and supervisory staff played a significant leading role in workers' struggle. In Uniden, the role of the engineers in the R&D department was highlighted. In the Sun and Moon factories, the leading and organising role rested on skilled and supervisory staff, some of whom were attached to place-of-origin-based community gangsters. Their privileged status in the labour market, production and community had provided them with much more workplace, market and (to a lesser extent) associational powers than ordinary workers (Wright, 2000). This provided them many organising resources which the ordinary workers lacked, as we saw especially in the Moon factory case.

6   The challenge from workers' protest forced the government to improve workers' legal protection. The speech of Labour Minister Li Bo Yong (quoted in Chapter 2) in response to the 1993–94 strikes was clear evidence of this. In response to the 2004–05 wave, a Labour Contract Law was legislated in 2007 to strengthen workers' individual and collective rights, alongside a Dispute Mediation and Arbitration Law and an Employment Promotion Law. At the local level, the legal minimum wage was dramatically increased after the 2004–05 strikes. The capacity of the workers' strikes to push up the legal minimum wage was more precisely demonstrated by the Moon factory case in 2007.

7   While workers and intellectuals in the early 1990s tried to organise inde-
    pendent trade unions, which continued to be strictly prohibited by the Party
    state, both the strikers and civil society had adopted a more pragmatic way
    to address the issue of FOA. In the Uniden case, a trade union, under the
    umbrella of the ACFTU, was one of the key demands of the workers involved
    in the strike. In fact, they sought advice from the higher-level trade union and
    received a positive response that they had the right to establish a union in
    their factory. And to a lesser extent, workers in the Sun and Moon factories
    also demanded the establishment of a trade union. However, the unions
    established after those strikes were highly manipulated by the management.
    Workers in the Moon factory demanded the inclusion of rank-and-file
    representatives on the union committee, but they were not successful. By
    contrast, the factory responded by promising to hold regular meetings with
    front-line supervisors.

Dynamics and limitations of workers' protests

Lee argued that 'Chinese workers can hardly be described as having much
marketplace, workplace, or associational bargaining power' (Lee, 2007a: 24).
Alternatively, I have argued that Chinese migrant workers have significantly
enhanced their 'marketplace bargaining power' and 'workplace bargaining power'
with the development of capitalism. Their wage standard, for example, has been
significantly increased. There are two explanations for this: first, the shortage
of labour (workers' 'marketplace bargaining power'); and second, the wave of
strikes (workers' 'workplace bargaining power'). The high turnover rate and the
consistent nature of resistance in the workplace are new forms of workers' struggle
which reshape the class power balance. By highlighting the rising capacity of
workers, the research presented here counters the simple pessimistic thesis
of 'working-class crisis' under globalisation.

However, workers' associational power, and so a labour movement, is still
fundamentally weak. The workplace trade unions did not play their primary role.
Without a representative body in the workplace to channel the interests of workers,
the latter understandably staged other forms of protest – from quitting and
complaining to stoppages, strikes and demonstrations – to express their grievances.
This has made workplace relationships highly unstable. From the wide-ranging
discussions in this book, especially in Chapter 6, a series of factors can be
identified as obstructions to effective workplace organisation.

First, as the economy was still in rapid expansion, 'voice' and then 'exit' were
more common than 'voice' and 'stay' as workers found it easy to find another job
with similar or sometimes better pay. Here the labour market exerted a dual effect
on workers' activism. It encouraged protest but not necessarily organisation.
Capital's capacity to relocate and outsource production also weakened workers'
marketplace, workplace and associational power. In all of the main cases in this
book – Uniden, Sun, Moon and Star – the management relocated part of their
production out of Shenzhen.

Second, the *Hukou* system, which separated the production and reproduction of labour, also made stable workers' community and workplace organisation hard to achieve. Chinese New Year was still a peak time for workers to quit their jobs, go home, and then look for a new job after the holiday. Although in Chapter 3 I showed that workers tended to stay for a long time in both the Sun factory and Militant village. This had made the factory and the village pioneers in terms of the militancy and duration of workers' struggle. Chapter 3 also pointed out that a number of older migrant workers returned to their villages under the state initiative to cancel the agriculture tax, indicating the availability of collective land in the villages, a legacy of the socialist *Hukou* system, which still provides a means of living for at least some migrant workers. More significantly, the reproduction of the new generation of labour occurred in the rural villages, rather than the urban areas. Xiao Ying and Xiao Lin, for example, had to leave their child at home with their parents. Within the factory, the personal network rooted in the traditional society is prevalent and exploited by the factory as a control strategy, in some cases through the interaction of gender, locality and its associated gangsterism.

Third, there were no powerful external institutions ready to provide support to workplace organisations and their activists. Although ordinary workers had little awareness of the trade union, some skilled and supervisory staff were much more conscious of association. In fact, strikers (or, more precisely, the leaders of the strikes) tried to form or reform workplace trade unions throughout the strike cases from 1994 to 2007 that are presented in this book. International civil society also put great effort into facilitating effective workplace organisations, either trade unions or alternatives committee, from 2000, while the ACFTU itself pushed some of its workplace affiliates to experiment with direct elections (A. Chan, 2006b; Howell, 2006). However, there was no single successful workplace organisation which was able to promote workers' interests seriously in a sustainable way. The fundamental issue was management's manipulation of workplace organisations (Clarke *et al.*, 2004; CLB, 2008). In this study, in Uniden and the Moon and Star factories, active and independent union and welfare committee members all came under pressure from management. A legal framework for negotiation was available, but the right to strike was not recognised after it was omitted from the revised 1982 version of the constitution. Even in the new wave of the unionisation campaign after 2006, as was discussed in Chapter 6, the SZMFTU and local state were more interested in the establishment of workplace trade unions to fulfil political and administrative targets, rather than activating workplace representation. The Trade Union Law reform in 2001 had enhanced the unions' representative and mediating role, while at the same time tightening control of higher-level trade unions over their affiliates to pre-empt independent trade unionism (F. Chen, 2003a). However, the reality is that while the workplace trade union was manipulated by management, the higher level of the trade unions as a part of the Party state did not have much leverage over workplace organisation without support from the state and the cooperation of management. It does not function as a class organisation to represent and be monitored by the workers. The role of the local state was even more ambiguous, considering its patron–client relations with business. Labour NGOs might play a role, but their weak political and legal foundation undermined their freedom to operate in China. Their existence was under constant state monitoring. The Party state was especially sensitive to intervention from international civil society in the country's labour politics. Grassroots labour NGOs, however, mostly depended on overseas funding to survive.

In short, the economic conditions and the legacy of state socialism (by *Hukou* and socialist trade unionism) have resulted in the separation of production from reproduction of labour and the ACFTU from its rank-and-file members. Recalling the grand theory competition on the uniqueness of labour politics in China that I reviewed in Chapter 1, here I prefer a political economy and institutional account while paying full attention to the cultural factors, as I will discuss in the following section.

Class relations, class identity and class struggle

Scholars who have studied migrant workers' protest in modern China from a culturalist perspective have tended to downplay the existence of class-consciousness by emphasising non-class identities like place, gender and skill (Honig, 1986; Hershatter, 1986; Perry, 1993). Their approach has continued to influence ethnographic studies in contemporary China (Yu, 2006; Lee, 2007a; 2007b).

In her recent book, Lee (2007a) privileged 'citizenship' over 'class' identity for migrant workers and implied that laid-off state workers were more class conscious, although the former was within and the latter was outside a capitalist class relation. In Chapter 1, I commented that she abstracted 'class' from its historical context and material base. This abstraction made her include 'class' as one of the discourses among workers in protests: 'the discourse of class, Maoism, citizenship, and legality as the repertoire of standards of justice and insurgent identity claims' (Lee, 2007a: 29). But as this study has shown, the language of class is not a reliable basis on which to make a judgement of class-consciousness and class behaviour. For example, in the Sun factory, workers generally distinguished each other by their provincial identities – *Si Chuan Ren* (Sichuan people) and *Waishengren* (people from other provinces) – and called their boss *Taiwan Lao* (Taiwanese guy), as opposed to their self-identity as mainland Chinese. In the Moon factory, the workers called themselves *Tongbao* (fellow countrymen), as opposed to their German manager. But after supervisory and skilled workers returned to work on the second day of the strike, production position identities, *Zhiyuan* and *Yuangong*, were employed to denounce the 'betrayal' by the former and consolidate solidarity among the latter. No single mention of *Gongren* (worker) or *Gongren Jieji* (working class) was used. But workers in factories in the community sourced by other capital, including those owned by local mainland Chinese bosses, followed their example of striking with similar demands. Obviously, these workers would not perceive that their strike was against the Taiwanese or the Germans, but against their boss. While class as a discourse or language cannot explain this spread of the strike in the community, class as social relations can. The purpose of studying the usage in discourses of terms such as Si Chuan people, mainland people, *Tongbao*, *Yuangong* (employee), *Zhiyuan* (staff) and *Zhiyuangong* (staff and employees) in the protest is to explore how a basis of solidarity is constructed or deconstructed in a specific context. However, as an analytical tool, the 'subjective' basis of solidarity in term of workers' self-identification is by no means able to transcend or replace 'objective' class interests rooted in class relations. As Clarke (1978) illuminated, class relations and their political and ideological forms cannot be separated from each other in class analysis, but the concept of class as a social relation should be analytically prior to the latter.

The significance of the 'subjective' base of solidarity was evidenced by the development of strikes in 2007 from those in 2004 and 2005. In the earlier wave of strikes, in which workers' demands basically related to enforcement of their legal rights, the language of legality provided a bottom line and a base of solidarity for the supervisory, skilled, semi-skilled and ordinary workers: 'The Sun factory violates the Labour Law and does not raise wages!' one banner proclaimed. However, in the 2007 strike, workers' demands had gone beyond the law and asked for a 'reasonable', rather than a 'legal', wage. So the earlier base of solidarity was lost. Workers then were divided by the management through its strategy to give supervisory and skilled staff more concessions. Some supervisors then tried to persuade ordinary workers to return to work, while the ordinary workers had a strong sense of being 'betrayed'. From then on, a base of solidarity was based on production position: *Yuangong* emerged to consolidate solidarity in the strike. This does not suggest that workers in the Sun factory had more of a citizenship identity while their counterparts in the Moon factory had an ordinary worker (*Yuangong*) identity. In fact, they were under the same class relations as their boss but developed a different base of solidarity in a different context.

One may contest that the 'betrayal' of *Zhiyuan* hinted at the ambiguous role of the middle-range staff, which did not necessarily support the 'class interest', so the strike was not a class action. The question of class action will be discussed below, but for this case, I understood this phenomenon in a specific, local context.

First, leaders in the strike were all victims of revenge and victimisation by the management during or after the strike. There were no legal and institutional supports for this range of activists. In the Uniden case, some engineers stood firmly for the interests of ordinary workers or class interests, but their leaders were victimised and finally dismissed. In this sense, after some of the supervisory and skilled workers went back to work, it was understandable that the hidden leaders of the strike, who were machinery repairers, did not stand up to push forward the strike.

Second, the management's divisive strategy was unsuccessful because the strike continued. The more significant moment for the collapse of the strike was when the factory announced that workers could resign immediately while those who returned to work would get extra pay. It was a concession from the management and so a material gain for workers as many of them were already in the queue for permission to resign or were planning to resign. In fact, allowing so many workers to leave immediately did considerable harm to the factory.

Even during a strike organised by a trade union in the West, some workers go back to work earlier than the others. But as a strike is not legally recognised in China, a picket line is impossible. The weakness of wildcat strikes in China is due more to organisational and institutional issues, and of course an experience constraint, rather than consciousness.

Considering the possible positive insights of cultural and identity studies exploring how solidarity is created or collapsed (Fantasia, 1988), in this study full attention was paid to these aspects of 'identities': place of origin, gangster, gender, skill and age. Although the traditional boundaries of these 'intra-class divisions' are usually exploited by management to divide and pacify workers, they can function in the interests of workers when their structural power is increased, as we saw in the case of the Sun factory. These traditional values also helped to articulate justice behind workers' collective action (McAdam, 1988). The sense of 'injustice' and confidence that had developed from industrial masculinity was one of the prominent factors accounting for workers' enthusiasm in the protests. Moreover, as time goes by, with common experience of social life, workers' traditional attachments have the potential to be transformed into a more open cross-provincial, class-based network in the community (Sargeson, 2001).

After connecting the class relations in China's global factory with workers' identity and intra-class division, a dilemma remained about the relationship between class organisations and class struggle. In the West, the Marxist tradition of labour studies generally linked class organisations with class struggle or class action, while industrial relations studies also took for granted a tripartite institutional analysis: union, management and the state. Katznelson (1986: 20) defined 'class action' as actions 'that are organized and through movements and organisations to affect society and the position of class within it'. Similarly, Burawoy (1979: 179) referred to 'class struggle' as the struggle between union and management. Under these definitions, there is no class action or class struggle in China. However, developments in NICs, such as South Korea (Koo, 2001), showed that a workers' independent trade union was a result rather than a precondition of workers' collective mobilisation. In China, the workers' struggle has brought considerable challenges to both management and the state. As shown in this study, workers' collective actions were able to improve wages as well as welfare and working conditions by directly gaining concessions from management, and indirectly pressing the central state, local authority and the ACFTU to improve their regulations and policies. Therefore, I suggested that 'unorganised workers' in industrial conflicts as a collective should be regarded as an independent party in analysis of the transformation of industrial relations in China, and credited for its capacity to force concessions from state legislation, legal enforcement and management. As far as class action or class struggle is concerned, we should distinguish between different levels of class or struggles for clarification.

Katznelson (1986) offered a four-layered framework for analysing class formation: class structure, class organisation, class disposition and class action.

He defined 'class action' as 'classes that are organized and that act through movements and organizations to affect society and the position of class within it' (Katznelson, 1986: 20). In this framework, as class organisation is ineffective in contemporary China, workers' collective actions that by-pass the ACFTU are not class actions. However, within a capitalist class structure, workers in China have shown some degree of class disposition or class-consciousness. For example, strikers in the Sun factory raised the slogan in their demonstration: 'For our common interests'. This is not to suggest that the class-consciousness of migrant workers was mature. Instead, I put it into a historical context to see how it changed over time, inspired by Thompson's (1963/1980) historical approach. If we compare the worst case of a strike in the 1980s (in which only twenty-one workers stopped work without any voice) with the well-planned 2007 strike in a similar geographical area, a historical advance was very apparent. As a development and critique of Thompson's (1963/1980) UK-centred approach, Katznelson indicated that a better framework of class formation was a historically and internationally comparative one. However, his notion of class action was still Western-centred and less useful to study class formation in countries like China. The reason for this is that the condition of class organisation is too complicated in the non-Western world to bind class action with class organisation.[3]

Burawoy (1979: 179; 242–43) also provided categories for workplace class struggle: economic, political and ideological. For him, 'economic class struggle' reshapes 'the distribution of economic rewards'; 'political class struggle' is concerned with 'the relations in production'; and 'ideological class struggle' is concerned with 'the relations of production' in the whole economy. In this categorisation, workers' workplace struggle in China today is well within the sphere of 'economic class struggle', given its capacity to obtain class-based material benefits and reshape economic distribution in society through collective action. However, 'ideological class struggle' is basically non-existent, while 'political class struggle' is defensive and passive, rather than proactive and persistent.

As the class-organisation-centred approach showed its limitations and contradictions in grasping the development of class relations in China, I referred to workplace struggle in China as 'class struggle without class organisation'. To underpin the positive dynamics of the economic class struggle is not to suggest a labour movement or 'class-for-itself' had emerged in China. On the contrary, the limitation of the class struggle in China is due to its concentration on the economic aspect and the existence of traditional and structural obstacles that prevented it from giving rise to political and ideological struggles. I have identified the barriers to the rise of the political struggle in the workplace in my discussion of weak workers' associational power. Here, I would add one point regarding the difficulty of the ideological struggle. Ideological struggle needs an imagination of social relations beyond capitalism. This imagination was especially feeble among migrant workers due to the history of Chinese 'socialism'. Their experience of Maoism and 'socialism' was not the same as that of the urban workers under the urban–rural separation policy of *Hukou*. The resources of the rural regions were mobilised to support urban construction in Mao's era. The poverty and backwardness of the rural villages is still remembered by many migrant workers. It was a dream for many of them to live in a city, such as the first generation of migrant workers like Lian, whose story was presented in Chapter 2, and the new generation of working couples, such as Xiao Lin and Xiao Ying, whose struggles were illustrated in Chapter 3. When *Dagong* was not a good choice, the only way out was to run a small business, rather than imagining other, more progressive ideas. An ideological struggle has a much longer way to go for Chinese workers behind the changing economic, social, legal and political contexts that may create opportunities for the exercise of a political struggle in the workplace, as I will discuss in the final section.

Labour challenge and the changing labour regime

A main theme of this book is that workers' workplace struggle has exerted significant challenges to central and local state authorities as well as global capital in the context of an expanding economy. Capital responded to these challenges by work intensification, production rationalisation and expansion, relocation and outsourcing. The local state reacted by better enforcement of the labour regulations and steady enhancement of the minimum wage, while the central state initiated a new round of labour legislation to improve protection of workers' rights and interests. The ACFTU was under strong pressure from the Party state to reform itself by extending its coverage in the workplace, although there have been very few successful examples of effective workplace trade unionism so far. The new labour NGOs also arose in the 1990s to provide workers with legal education and assistance, although they did not have a sound legal basis to help them survive in China.

In this scenario, the main barrier to a 'class-for-itself' in China was the state manipulation of the ACFTU and management's manipulation of its workplace organisations, while the effective strategy to relocate and expand production and separation of production and reproduction by the *Hukou* system also played a role.

However, there were also some positive developments for a more stable workers' community and organisation. *Hukou* and the production relocations had dual effects on workers' activism. On the one hand, availability of job opportunities in other cities or factories, and other survival means in workers' home villages, encouraged workers' struggle by 'voice' and 'exit' or just 'exit'. On the other hand, they made a stable labour force, urban community and ultimately workers' organisation more difficult to achieve. However, although the turnover rate was very high, many workers returned to their factories some months later, while management had to abandon or loosen its policy of denying re-entry to those who had left the factory without permission because of the difficulty of hiring other workers. Most workers found that pay and conditions were more or less the same in other factories. One explanation for the labour shortage in the PRD was that workers had flowed into the YRD. However, as we saw in Chapter 5, the minimum wage rate had been formulated with reference to other cites with similar economic development levels.

Militant village also demonstrated the possibility of a more stable worker community and network. Like Xiao Ying and Xiao Lin, many workers left the community but returned after a period of time. Their return to the village was motivated by the familiar social network and lifestyle that were available there. Like many others, Xiao Ying's dream to run a business was broken while her working life in the factory next to the Sun factory continued after a short disruption. For millions of young migrants, *Dagong* is the only way to make a living. More significantly, skilled workers were more stable, staying in a factory with more marketplace and workplace bargaining power, while their associational power was dislocated in the form of informal networks or sometimes gangsterism.

This book is being finished in the aftermath of the thirtieth anniversary of Deng Xiao Ping's 'reform and open door' policy of 1978. No momentous celebrations were organised by the Party state. Hardly surprising, as the government faced the challenge of rising domestic inflation and a declining global economy. On 2 June 2008, the Shenzhen government held a joint press conference with its subordinate SZMLSSB to announce the new minimum wage for the year from 1 July: 1,000 yuan inside the SEZ and 900 yuan outside. In addition to the rising wages in competitive cities, attention was paid to the escalating national inflation rate (*Nanfang Ribao*, 3 June 2008). The new wage rate in Shenzhen keeps its main competitor, Shang Hai, whose minimum wage is 960 yuan, in second place nationally. Along with a mounting wage standard, three labour ordinances, namely the Labour Contract Law, the Employment Promotion Law and the Labour Dispute Mediation and Arbitration Law, which were legislated in 2007, provide a new legal framework for workers' rights and interests. However, the global economic crisis constrained both workers' material aspirations and the state's reformist efforts in respect to workers' rights.[4] As Marx (1963: 15) noted: 'Men make their own history, but they do not make it just as they please; they do not make it under circumstances chosen by themselves, but under circumstances directly encountered, given and transmitted from the past.'

Nevertheless, without considerably more associational power, I would not put workers' struggle in a framework of a labour movement, considering its weakness to mount a political and ideological challenge to the state and capital. Instead, I apply the notion of 'a changing labour regime', which was also used by Lee (1999) when referring to the SOE reform, to sketch the changing power relations in the global factories and beyond. As despotism still prevails and the state's intervention and workers' collective actions are more and more potent, I refer to it as 'contested despotism', which has the potential to give way to a new form of factory regime. The underlying drivers of the factory regime transition come from two fronts, capitalist competition and class struggle (Burawoy, 1979). Here I reconstruct Burawoy's concept to bring in Chinese workers' collective actions that bypass the official trade union as the economic class struggle. To what extent can workers' activism continue to reshape the labour regime in changing economic, legal and political contexts? It depends on the dynamic relationship between state regulation, management strategy and workers' collective struggle, while the possibility of effective workplace trade unionism remains a central issue.

Stories of the Chinese migrant workers' struggles reveal that work, factory and working class are far from 'ended' (Gorz, 1980; Rifkin, 1995). Instead, they are reconstructed in different spaces and different forms. In fact, the public concern in the West with Chinese labour conditions has recently changed from the 'race to the bottom' effect on both wages and consumer prices (e.g. *The Economist*, 30 September 2004) to the suggestion that rising wages in China will lead to the stagnation of the Western economy (*Financial Times*, 12 June 2008). Although the locations of production and forms of employment have dramatically changed since the 1970s, the basic logic of the accumulation of global capitalism remains unchanged (Harvey, 1990; Cohen, 1991; Wood *et al.*, 1998). A new agenda for social scientists is to understand how class struggle unfolds in different local contexts, and how the pattern of the struggle changes over time.

Notes

1 Introduction

1 For a review and critique of this thesis see Strangleman (2007).
2 They introduced me as a 'reporter' to their friends and workmates and emphasised that I was a person who could help them by discovering problems in the factory. It took some time for me to clarify that was not the case.
3 The 'linguistic turn' in social science has exerted a profound effect on labour studies. The dominance of class analysis among the old generation of labour studies was said to be a project of 'modern discourse' (Cannadine, 1999; Day, 2001; Skeggs, 2004; Thiel, 2007: 230). Under its influence, the new researchers turned to study workers' identity(ies) by their language and communication. This Western trend also dominates the literature of Chinese labour studies (Lee, 2007b). If not fully rejected, class was downplayed as one of the multifaceted identities of workers. This approach risks a pragmatic pluralism.
4 But at the same time, she also pointed out: 'the "new working class" . . . is often deformed, or even killed, at the moment of its birth' by state mechanisms (Pun, 2005c: 20).

2 Labour conflict in Shenzhen

1 Data from this section to the section 'Strike Tide in 1993–94' was used in the author's MA dissertation (C. Chan, 2005).
2 A pseudonym is used here and for all other interviewees.
3 Throwing stones and bricks is common in villagers' disputes in eastern Guang Dong.
4 This case was documented by Wong (1989), a trade unionist in Hong Kong. The information was provided by SKIZFTU in Wong's fieldwork in Shenzhen.
5 This section is based on W. Y. Leung (1988). Leung had been a labour organiser and researcher since the early 1980s in Hong Kong.
6 The strike cases concerned were rarely elaborated in either newspaper or labour organisation publications. Several labour activists in Hong Kong claimed that it was after 1992, when the media widely reported labour abuse and strike cases, that they began to conduct fieldwork in the PRD and initiate local and global education campaigns on labour rights in China. Their explanation and the relative scarcity of documentation of the early stage situation provide a clue to the placid labour relations in this period.
7 A woman journalist, Luo Jian Lin, who had worked and lived with workers in a factory in SKIZ, recorded this strike story in *Special Economic Zone Literature Herald*, February 1987. The newspaper was closed for political reasons later in 1987, but the story was translated and documented by W. Y. Leung (1988). Part of the information in this section was also cited in AMRC (1995). AMRC is a labour rights campaign and research organisation in Hong Kong.

8 *Gongyun Yuekan* (1994), AMRC (1995) and the Hong Kong Christian Industrial Committee's newspaper cuttings archives. Examples of media reports include *Nanfang Gongbao* (3 January 1994).

9 Apart from scholars (e.g. Taylor *et al.*, 2003), labour activists in Hong Kong who conducted fieldwork in Shenzhen and Zhu Hai during this period also portrayed the strikes as 'tidal waves' (*Bagong Chao*), to denote the wave-by-wave, knock-on effect of the strikes.

10 The first and second waves were both in the 1950s.

11 According to *Guang Dong Statistical Yearbook* (1991), cited in Liu *et al.* (1992), the average monthly salary was 359 yuan in Shenzhen and 304 yuan in Zhu Hai, followed by Guang Zhou, the provincial capital city, with 295 yuan.

12 According to Yang Fan, a researcher from the Chinese Academy of Social Sciences, the inflation rate in 1992 and 1993 was 13 per cent, and it rose to 20 per cent in 1994. This was a historic peak, surpassing the previous highest level of 18.9 per cent in 1988 (W. Y. Leung, 1998: 79).

13 The stories were recorded in three labour organisation publications: *Gongyun Yuekan* (1994), AMRC (1995) and Shek and Leung (1998). According to the authors and editors, they were based on newspaper reports and on-site visits to workers. I also referenced some news reports in Hong Kong newspapers when writing this section.

14 An anonymous labour activist conducted interviews with the strikers in 1994 and recorded this story in AMRC (1995: 37–38). An informal interview was conducted with this activist to cross-check and clarify some of the information before this section was written.

15 Field notes from talking with a researcher on mainland Chinese labour in Hong Kong.

16 The factory supplied products for Italian brand Chicco. Details refer to case thirteen in A. Chan (2001).

17 See the ACFTU bulletin *Zhongguo Gongyun* (1994: 8–9), or case thirteen in A. Chan (2001) for a detailed account.

18 For a more in-depth study of migrant workers' communities in Beijing, see Zhang (2001).

19 'Arbitrated Collective Labour Disputes' in Table 2.3 refers to cases involving thirty employees or more.

20 A quotation from Deng, 'Stability has priority over all other things' (*Wending Yadao Yiqie*), became a propaganda slogan after 1989 and was accompanied by another, 'Only development is the great truth' (*Fazhan Cai Shi Dalaoli*), to dominate the political discourse after 1992.

21 The data with detailed sources and short description was produced by Parry Leung, who has worked in independent labour NGOs in Hong Kong and researched into labour conditions in the PRD since 2000. An interview with him found that the data was produced from his wide scanning of NGO publications and media research using the search engine of the internet database Wisenews. The author is indebted to Leung's sharing of his research data.

22 Ibid. Some cases had more than one reason, so the total figure in this table is more than sixty-three (the number of reported collective actions).

23 The term 'new generation of peasant workers' (*Xin Yidai Mingong*), despite its ambiguity, has been used in the media since 2004 to explain the 'shortage of labour' and labour protest in the country.

3 Community and shop floor culture

1 Chong Qing was the biggest city of Si Chuan province until it was designated as a municipality directly administered by central government with a status equal to a province in 1997. Migrants from Chong Qing continued to identify themselves as Si Chuan people after the reform of the administration.

2 The survey was conducted by the project team for 'research on the problem of peasant workers under urbanisation' (Ren and Pun, 2007).

3 The information was collated from several newspaper reports.

4 Author's estimate.

5 Si Chuan had supplied most migrant workers to the coastal provinces before Chong Qing was made administratively independent from the province in 1997. The position of largest migrant supplier was then taken by He Nan province. However, as already noted, historical, geographical and cultural approximation means workers from Si Chuan and Chong Qing still identify themselves as *Laoxiang*.

6 *Jiacai* was a common event in Mao's era when commune members of a production team came together to celebrate or relax after a period of hard work or at festivals.

7 Commonly, in the factories in southern China, if a worker wanted to leave the production line for a while, for example to visit the bathroom, she or he had to get an off-duty permit from the supervisor. On fast-moving assembly lines, the line supervisor or a spare worker would fill in the position to avoid disruption to production. To avoid many workers being excused at the same time, usually there was only one permit per production line.

4 Strikes and changing power relations in the workplace

1 My visits to the dormitories with workers showed that control in the dormitory blocks was even more strict than on the shop floor. There was a security guard sitting on the stair entrance of each floor. See Pun (2005a and 2005b) for workers' dormitory life and Smith and Pun (2006) and Pun and Smith (2007) for a portrait of dormitory control and resistance.

2 According to Tilly (1984: 1), 'proletarian' refers to 'people who work for wages, using means of production over whose disposition they have little or no control'.

3 A similar phenomenon happened after a strike in the Moon factory in 2007, as will be shown in Chapter 6, although social insurance was not an issue there. But the concerns over work intensification and autonomy were exactly the same in the two factories.

4 It is illegal to buy and sell land in China, but reform has made it possible to buy and sell a lease to use land.

5 Information from an interview with the owner of a medium-sized factory in the town of Bu Ji, Shenzhen, close to the territories of Hui Zhou, in May 2006. The owner told me that the Hui Zhou government often invites factories in Shenzhen to relocate or set up a new factory in their city.

6 *Laowu Bumen* refers to a specially designed government institution based in the LSSB that facilitates the outflow of migrant workers. Usually the institutions in inland provinces sign contracts with large enterprises in the coastal cities to supply labour.

7 According to orthodox economists, as soon as demand for labour increases, wages will rise, assuming labour supply is constant. Lewis (1954) argued that demand for labour will increase as a result of economic growth in developing countries, but wages will not rise immediately. As a result, there is a period of low pay *and* labour shortage, as was seen in China.

5 Workplace conflict, legal institution and labour regime

1 The committee was run as a shareholding institution for SOEs, including those that were privatised but in which the city authority still held some shares.

2 The demanded wage standard related to workers' monthly income, including overtime but not extra subsidies such as for accommodation and night shift work.

3 Here only the wage demand of ordinary manual workers was listed and the basic salary referred to the monthly wage for eight hours per day, five days per week. Their overtime pay would be calculated on the basis of this rate. The basic salary of ordinary workers

in most of the factories was no more than the legal minimum rate: 710 yuan at the time of strike. So the strikers' demand was 100 yuan above the legal minimum.

6 International civil society, Chinese trade unionism and workplace representation

1 Anita Chan conducted in-depth evaluation into this case. See A. Chan (2007). The above information was also drawn from interviews with trainers of Hong Kong-based NGOs and reference to their training reports.
2 Interview, 11 March 2006.
3 The peasants with *Hukou* in rural villages were all allocated a piece of farmland after the reform in 1978. Rapid industrialisation from the early 1990s dramatically transformed the farms into industrial land. The industrial zones were all developed by village governments and rented out to FIEs and POEs until the mid-1990s, when larger factories were allowed to build industrial complexes by 'renting' a piece land. In reality, this entailed paying a lump sum for a thirty-year lease. The urbanisation policy granted the rural population the status of citizenship, and the villages were then renamed 'communities'. The communities also settled some migrants, who gained the status of permanent citizenship by purchasing a house or getting a proper job within their territories under a quota system run by the state. However, the new citizens were not entitled to the rental income of the land and industrial estates. Share companies were set up to collect the rents and other incomes and distribute them to previous villagers.
4 It was estimated that there were over sixty labour NGOs in Guang Dong province in 2007.
5 This policy change might be explained by the suggestion that the revolutions in several former Soviet republics gave rise to worries in the Chinese government that foreign-funded NGOs would be pushed by anti-communist forces to stir up social unrest (K. M. Chan *et al.*, 2005).
6 According to the law, workers can be represented in court by a trade union or their relatives under the system of 'civil agent' (*Gongmin Daili*). Some workers with legal experience and practical knowledge chose to earn a living by helping other workers in legal cases against their employers. They helped prepare documents and even represented claimants in court and charged a service fee. As a service fee is widely regarded as improper, they are sometimes termed 'black lawyers'.
7 Including the TNC-facilitated trade union election project, described by A. Chan (2007).

7 Conclusion

1 By 'new working class', here I mean not only migrant workers in FIEs, on which this study focuses, but urban and migrant workers in enterprises with other ownership forms.
2 For instance, the CLB report quoted a journalist's article on a strike wave of migrant workers in Da Lian, a coastal metropolitan city in northeastern China. The strike was led by workers in a Japanese-owned factory in July 2005 and the strikers successfully achieved a wage rise after the intervention of the trade union and the government. The strike then extended to more than ten other Japanese-owned factories in the city (Zhan, 2005).
3 In many developing countries, there are multiple trade union syndicates with different political orientations. In South Korea, for example, the Federation of Korean Trade Unions now competes with the rising Korean Confederation of Trade Unions. Both camps claim to represent working-class interests, although their strategies towards the state and capital are often oppositional. So which camp can be said to take 'class

action'? If the answer is 'both', then there might be two kinds of class action that are oppositional to each other. This phenomenon also exists in other East Asian NICs like Taiwan and Hong Kong.

4 The impact of the global economic crisis on labour activism and workplace relations in China is outwith the scope of this book, but it merits a new research project.

Bibliography

Books, periodicals and research papers

ACFTU (1995) *Shekou Moshi* (Shekou Model). Beijing: ACFTU Policy Research Institute. [In Chinese]

Acker, J., Barry, K. and Esseveld, J. (1991) 'Objectivity and truth: problems in doing feminist research.' In M. Fonow and J. Cook (eds) *Beyond Methodology: Feminist Scholarship as Lived Research.* Bloomington: Indiana University Press: 133–53.

Althusser, L. and Balibar, E. (1970) *Reading Capital.* Translated by B. Brewster. London: New Left Books.

Aminzade, R. (1981) *Class, Politics, and Early Industrial Capitalism:A Study of Mid-Nineteenth-Century Toulouse, France.* Albany: State University of New York Press.

—— (1993) 'Class analysis, politics, and French labor history.' In L. R. Berlanstein (ed.) *Rethinking Labor History.* Chicago: University of Illinois Press: 90–113.

AMRC (1995) *Zhujiang Sanjiaozhou Gongren Quanyi Zhuangkuang* (Condition of Workers' Rights in the Pearl River Delta). Hong Kong: Asia Monitor Resource Centre. [In Chinese]

Aronowitz, S. and Cutler, J. (eds) (1998) *Post-work: The Wages of Cybernation.* London: Routledge.

Aronowitz, S. and DiFazio, W. (1994) *The Jobless Future: Sci-tech and the Dogma of Work.* Minneapolis: University of Minneapolis.

Au, L. Y. (2005) 'The post MFA era and the rise of China.' *Asian Labour Update,* 56. Hong Kong: Asia Monitor Research Centre: 14–19.

Bai, N. S. and Song, H. Y. *et al.* (2002) *Huixiang Haishi Jingcheng? Zhongguo Nongcun Waichu Laodongli Huiliu Yanjiu* (Return Home or Entering a City? Research on the Return of Rural Migrant Labour Force in China). Beijing: China Financial and Economic Press. [In Chinese]

Bauman, Z. (1998) *Work, Consumerism and the New Poor.* Buckingham: Open University Press.

Bélanger, J., Edwards, P. K. and Haiven, L. (1994) *Workplace Industrial Relations and the Global Challenge.* Ithaca: ILR Press.

Benson, J. (2003) *The Working Class in Britain: 1850–1939.* London: I. B. Tauris.

Berlanstein, L. R. (1992) *The Industrial Revolution and Work in Nineteenth-Century Europe.* London and New York: Routledge.

—— (ed.) (1993) *Rethinking Labor History.* Chicago: University of Illinois Press.

Bourdieu, P. *et al.* (1999) *The Weight of the World: Social Suffering in Contemporary Society.* Translated by P. P. Ferguson *et al.* Cambridge: Polity Press.

Braverman, H. (1974/1998) *Labor and Monopoly Capital.* New York: Monthly Review Press.

Brewer, J. (2000) *Ethnography.* Buckingham: Open University Press.

Bryman, A. (2004). *Quantity and Quality in Social Research.* London: Allen and Unwin.

Burawoy, M. (1979) *Manufacturing Consent: Changes in the Labor Process under Monopoly Capitalism.* Chicago: The University of Chicago Press.

—— (1985) *The Politics of Production.* London: Verso.

Burawoy, M. and Verdery, K. (1999) *Uncertain Transition: Ethnographies of Change in the Postsocialist World.* Lanham and Oxford: Rowman & Littlefield.

Burawoy, M. *et al.* (2000) *Global Ethnography: Forces, Connections, and Imaginations in a Postmodern World.* Berkeley: University of California Press.

Burnham, P. (2001) 'Marx, international political economy and globalization.' *Capital and Class*, 75: 103–12.

Cai, Y. S. (2002) 'The resistance of Chinese laid-off workers in the reform period.' *The China Quarterly*, 170: 327–44.

Cannadine, D. (1999) *The Rise and Fall of Class in Britain.* New York: Columbia University Press.

Casey, C. (1995) *Work, Self and Society after Industrialism.* London: Routledge.

Castells, M. (1997) *The Information Age, vol. 2: The Power of Identity.* Oxford: Blackwell.

Chan, A. (1993) 'Revolution or corporatism? Workers and trade unions in post-Mao China.' *The Australian Journal of Chinese Affairs*, 29: 31–61.

—— (2000) 'Globalization, China's free (read bonded) labour market, and the Chinese trade unions.' In C. Rowley and J. Benson (eds) *Globalization and Labour in the Asia Pacific Region.* London: Frank Cass: 260–81.

—— (2001) *China Workers under Assault: Exploitation and Abuse in a Globalizing Economy.* New York: M. E. Sharpe.

—— (2003) 'A "race to the bottom": globalisation and China's labour standards.' *China Perspectives*, 46: 41–49.

—— (2006a) 'Organising Wal-Mart: the Chinese trade unions at a crossroads.' *Japan Focus*, 8 September. Online. Available: http://japanfocus.org/products/details/2217 (accessed 8 June 2008).

—— (2006b) 'Realities and possibilities of Chinese trade unionism.' In C. Phelan (ed.) *The Future of Organised Labour: Global Perspectives.* Oxford: Peter Lang: 275–304.

—— (2007) 'Corporate facilitated trade union elections in Chinese factories – an evaluation.' Paper presented at the conference on Fair Trade, Corporate Accountability and Beyond: Experiments in Globalising Justice, 19–20 December, Law School, University of Melbourne.

Chan, A. and Robert, J. S. R. (2003) 'Racing to the bottom: industrial trade without a social clause.' *Third World Quarterly*, 24 (6):1011–28.

Chan, C. K. C. (2005) 'Labour disputes in China's Pearl River Delta: 1979–94.' MA dissertation, Sociology Department, University of Warwick.

—— (2009) 'Strike and workplace relations in a Chinese global factory.' *Industrial Relations Journal*, 40 (1): 60–77.

Chan, K. M., Qiu, H. X. and Zhu, J. G. (2005) 'Chinese NGOs strive to survive.' *Social Transformations in Chinese Societies*, 1: 131–59.

Chang, D. O., Siwari, P. and Shepherd, E. (eds) (2004) *A Critical Introduction to Corporate Labour Codes of Conduct.* Hong Kong: Asia Monitor Resource Centre.

Chang, D. O. and Wong, M. (2005) 'FDI and labour in China: the actors and possibility of a new working class activism.' In E. Shepherd and D. O. Chang (eds) *Asian*

Transnational Corporation Outlook 2004: Asian TNCs, Workers and the Movement of Capital. Hong Kong: Asia Monitor Resource Centre: 107–54.

Chang, K. (2004) *Lao Quan Lun: Dangdai Zhongguo Laodong Guanxi De Falu Tiaozheng Yanjiu* (The Theory of Workers' Rights: Research on the Legal Regulation of Labour Relations in Contemporary China). Beijing: China Labour and Social Protection Press. [In Chinese]

Chen, F. (2000). 'Subsistence crisis, managerial corruption and labor protest in China.' *The China Journal*, 44: 41–63.

—— (2003a). 'Between the state and labour: the conflict of Chinese trade unions' double identity in market reform.' *The China Quarterly*, 176: 1006–28.

—— (2003b) 'Industrial restructuring and workers' resistance in China.' *Modern China*, 29 (2): 237–62.

—— (2006) 'Privatization and its discontents in Chinese factories.' *The China Quarterly*, 185: 42–60.

Chen, G. H. (2004) 'An analysis of income distribution in China.' Online. Available: http://www.opentimes.cn.to/laigao/2004/0222{hy}03{hy}002.htm (accessed 25 November 2004). [In Chinese]

Chen, H. (2006) *1979–2000 Shenzhen Zhongda Juece He Shijian Minjian Guancha* (Shenzhen Big Decisions and Issues from 1979–2000: A Non-governmental Perspective). Wuhan: Changjiang Wenyi Chubanshe. [In Chinese]

Clarke, S. (1978) 'Capital, fractions of capital and the state: "neo-Marxist" analyses of the South African state.' *Capital & Class*, 5: 32–77.

—— (1991) *Marx, Marginalism and Modern Sociology: From Adam Smith to Max Weber*. London: Macmillan.

—— (2005) 'Post-socialist trade unions: Russia and China.' *Industrial Relations Journal*, 36 (1): 2–18.

—— (ed.) (1996) *Labour Relations in Transition: Wages, Employment and Industrial Conflict in Russia*. Cheltenham: Edward Elgar.

Clarke, S., Fairbrother, P. and Borisov, V. (1995) *The Workers' Movement in Russia*. Aldershot: Edward Elgar.

Clarke, S. and Lee, C. H. (2003) 'The significance of a tripartite consultation in China.' *Asia Pacific Business Review*, 9 (2): 61–81.

Clarke, S., Lee, C. H. and Li, Q. (2004) 'Collective consultation and industrial relations in China'. *British Journal of Industrial Relations*, 42 (2): 255–81.

Clarke, S. and Pringle, T. (2007) 'Labour activism and the reform of trade unions in Russia, China and Vietnam.' Paper presented at ESRC Non-governmental Public Action Labour Workshop, November. Online. Available: http://www.warwick.ac.uk/fac/soc/complab studs/russia/ngpa/ (accessed 16 February 2008).

Clarke, S. *et al.* (1993) *What about the Workers? Workers and the Transition to Capitalism in Russia*. London: Verso.

CLB (2005a) *Deadly Dust: The Silicosis Epidemic among Guangdong Jewellery Workers*. Hong Kong: China Labour Bulletin.

—— (2005b) *Zhongguo Gongren Yundong Guancha Baogao 2000–2004* (Speaking Out: The Workers' Movement in China 2000–2004). Hong Kong: China Labour Bulletin. [In Chinese]

—— (2007) *Zhongguo Gongren Yundong Guancha Baogao 2005–2006* (Speaking Out: The Workers' Movement in China, 2005–2006). Hong Kong: China Labour Bulletin. [In Chinese]

—— (2008) 'Are trade union and labour officials in Guangdong beginning to take their responsibilities seriously?' *ACFTU Analysis and Commentary*, 28 February. Online. Available: http://www.clb.org.hk/en/node/100211 (accessed 28 June 2008). Hong Kong: China Labour Bulletin.

Cockburn, C. (1983) *Brothers: Male Dominance and Technology Change*. London: Pluto Press.

Cohen, R. (1980) 'Resistance and hidden forms of consciousness among African workers.' *Reviews of African Political Economy*, 19: 8–22.

—— (1987) *The New Helots*. Oxford: Open University Press.

—— (1991) *Contested Domains: Debates in International Labour Studies*. London: Zed.

Collier, R. B. (1999) *Paths toward Democracy: The Working Class and Elites in Western Europe and South America*. Cambridge: Cambridge University Press.

Cooke, F. L. (2005) *HRM, Work and Employment in China*. London: Routledge.

Dawley, A. (1976) *Class and Community: The Industrial Revolution in Lynn*. Cambridge, MA, and London: Harvard University Press.

Day, G. (2001) *Class*. London: Routledge.

deMarrais, K.B. (ed.) (1998) *Inside Stories: Qualitative Research Reflections*. New Jersey: Lawrence Erlbaum.

Deng, X. P. (1992) 'Zai Wuchang, Shenzhen, Zhuhai, Shanghai dengdi de tanhua yaodian.' (The main points of speeches in Wuchang, Shenzhen, Zhuhai, Shanghai, etc.). Online. Available: http://www.njmuseum.com/zh/book/cqgc_big5/dxpnxjh.htm (accessed 18 December 2004). [In Chinese]

Denzin, N. K. and Lincoln, Y. S. (1998) 'Introduction: entering the field of qualitative research.' In N. K. Denzin and Y. S. Lincoln (eds) *The Landscape of Qualitative Research: Theories and Issues*. London: Sage.

Deyo, F. C. (1989) *Beneath the Miracle: Labor Subordination in the New Asian Industrialism*. Berkeley: University of California Press.

Dienel, E. and Crandall, R. (1978) *Ethics in Social and Behavioral Research*. Chicago: University of Chicago Press.

Edwards, P. K. (1986) *Conflict at Work: A Materialist Analysis of Workplace Relations*. Oxford: Basil Blackwell.

—— (2000) 'Late twentieth century workplace relations: class struggle without classes.' In R. Crompton *et al.* (eds) *Renewing Class Analysis*. Oxford: Blackwell: 141–64.

Edwards, P. K. and Scullion, H. (1982) *The Social Organization of Industrial Conflict: Control and Resistance in the Workplace*. Oxford: Blackwell.

Edwards, R. C. (1980) *Contested Terrain: The Transformation of the Workplace in the Twentieth Century*. London: Heinemann.

Elger, T. and Smith, C. (2005) *Assembling Work: Remaking Work Regimes in Japanese Multinationals in Britain*. Oxford: Oxford University Press.

Engels, F. (1969) *The Condition of the Working Class in England*. Chicago: Academy Chicago.

Fantasia, R. (1988) *Cultures of Solidarity: Consciousness, Action and Contemporary American Workers*. Berkeley: University of California Press.

Feng, T. Q. (2001) 'Laodong guanxi de bianhua he zhongguo gonghui de jiben tezheng.' (The changing labour relations and basic characteristics of the Chinese trade union). *Hong Kong Journal of Social Science*, 21 (Winter): 67–98. [In Chinese]

Fox, A. (1966) *Industrial Sociology and Industrial Relations: An Assessment of the Contribution which Industrial Sociology Can Make towards Understanding and Resolving Some of the Problems Now Being Considered by the Royal Commission*. London: HMSO.

Franzosi, R. (1995) *The Puzzle of Strikes: Class and State Strategies in Postwar Italy.* Cambridge: Cambridge University Press.

Friedman, A. (1977) *Industry and Labour.* London: Macmillan.

Freidson, E. (1984) 'The changing nature of professional control.' *Annual Review of Sociology,* 10: 1–20.

Frobel, F., Heinrichs, J. and Kreye, O. (1980) *The New International Dvision of Labour.* Cambridge: Cambridge University Press.

Gallagher, M. E. (2005) *Contagious Capitalism: Globalization and the Politics of Labor in China.* Princeton and Oxford: Princeton University Press.

Gluck, S. B. and Patai, D. (1991) *Women's Words: The Feminist Practice of Oral History.* New York: Routledge.

Gorz, A. (1980) *Farewell to the Working-Class: An Essay on Post-industrial Socialism.* London: Pluto.

Gould, R. V. (1995) *Insurgent Identities: Class, Community, and Protest in Paris from 1848 to the Commune.* Chicago: Chicago University Press.

Gouldner, A. W. (1954) *Wildcat Strike: A Study in Worker–Management Relations.* New York: The Antioch Press.

Haggard, S. K. (1983) *Pathways for the Periphery: The Newly Industrializing Countries in the International System.* Ann Arbor.: University Microfilms International.

Harvey, D. (1990) *The Condition of Postmodernity: An Enquiry into the Origins of Cultural Change.* Oxford: Basil Blackwell.

—— (2001) *Spaces of Capital.* New York: Routledge.

Hayter, T. and Harvey, D. (1993) *The Factory and the City: The Story of the Cowley Automobile Workers in Oxford.* London: Mansell.

Hershatter, G. (1986) *The Workers of Tianjin, 1900–1949.* Stanford: Stanford University Press.

Hirschman, A. O. (1970) *Exit, Voice and Loyalty: Response to Decline in Firms, Organizations, and the States.* Cambridge, MA: Harvard University Press.

Hobsbawm, E. J. (1968) *Labouring Men: Studies in the History of Labour.* London: Weidenfeld and Nicolson.

—— (1984) *Worlds of Labour: Further Studies in the History of Labour.* London: Weidenfeld and Nicolson.

Hodson, R. (2001) *Dignity at Work.* Cambridge: Cambridge University Press.

Holloway, J. (2002) 'Class and classification: against, in and beyond labour.' In A. Dinerstein and M. Neary (eds) *The Labour Debate: An Investigation into the Theory and Reality of Capitalist Work.* Aldershot: Ashgate: 27–40.

Honig, E. (1986) *Sisters and Strangers: Women in the Shanghai Cotton Mills, 1919–1949.* Stanford: Stanford University Press.

—— (1993) 'Regional identity, labour, and ethnicity in contemporary China.' In E. J. Perry (ed.) *Putting Class in Its Place: Worker Identities in East Asia.* Berkeley: University of California Press.

Howell, J. (1993) *China Opens Its Doors: The Politics of Economic Transition.* Hemel Hempstead: Harvester Wheatsheaf.

—— (2006) 'New Democratic Trends in China: Reforming the All-China Federation of Trade Unions.' Institute of Development Studies, Working Paper 263, University of Sussex.

Hurst, W. and O'Brien, K. J. (2002) 'China's contentious pensioners.' *China Quarterly,* 170: 345–60.

Hutchison, J. and Brown, A. (eds) (2001) *Organising Labour in Globalising Asia.* London: Routledge.

Hyman, R. (1989) *Strikes*. Basingstoke: Macmillan.

Izraelewicz, E. (2005) *Dang Zhongguo Gaibian Shijie* (When China Changes the World). Translated by X. L. Fei and H. X. Yao. Beijing: China CITIC Press. [In Chinese]

Jiang, K. W. (1996) 'Gonghui yu dang-guo chongtu: bashi niandai yulai de zhongguo gonghui gaige' (Conflicts of trade unions and Party state: Chinese trade union reform since the 1980s). *Hong Kong Journal of Social Science*, 8 (Autumn): 121–58. [In Chinese]

Jiang, X. (2004) *Woguo Zhong Changqi Shiye Wenti Yanjiu* (Research on Medium- and Long-Term Unemployment Problems in China). Beijing: Renmin University of China Press. [In Chinese]

Katz-Fishman, W., Scott, J. and Modupe, I. (2002) 'Globalization of capital and class struggle.' In B. Berberoglu (ed.) *Labor and Capital in the Age of Globalization: The Labor Process and the Changing Nature of Work in the Global Economy*. New York: Rowman and Littlefield: 179–94.

Katznelson, I. (1986) 'Working-class formation: constructing cases and comparison.' In I. Katznelson and A. R. Zolberg (eds) *Working-Class Formation: Nineteenth-Century Patterns in Western Europe and the United States*. Princeton: Princeton University Press: 3–41.

Katznelson, I. and Zolberg, A. R. (eds) (1986) *Working-Class Formation: Nineteenth-Century Patterns in Western Europe and the United States*. Princeton: Princeton University Press.

Kelly, J. (2002) *Rethinking Industrial Relations: Mobilization, Collectivism and Long Waves*. London: Routledge.

Kim, S. K. (1997) *Class Struggle or Family Struggle? The Lives of Women Factory Workers in South Korea*. Cambridge: Cambridge University Press.

Koo, H. (2001) *Korean Workers: The Culture and Politics of Class Formation*. Ithaca: Cornell University Press.

Lambert, R. (2002) 'Labour movement renewal in the era of globalization: union responses in the South.' In J. Harrord and R. O'Brien (eds) *Global Unions: Theory and Strategies of Organized Labour in the Global Political Economy*. London: Routledge: 185–203.

Lee, C. K. (1998) *Gender and the South China Miracle: Two Worlds of Factory Women*. Berkeley: University of California Press.

—— (1999) 'From organized dependence to disorganized despotism: changing labour regimes in Chinese factories.' *The China Quarterly*, 147: 44–77.

—— (2000a) 'Pathways of labor insurgency.' In E. J. Perry and M. Selden (eds) *Chinese Society: Change, Conflict and Resistance*, London: Routledge: 40–61.

—— (2000b) 'The revenge of history: collective memories and labor protests in north-eastern China.' *Ethnography*, 1 (2): 217–37.

—— (2002a) 'From the specter of Mao to the spirit of the law: labor insurgency in China.' *Theory and Society*, 31: 189–228.

—— (2002b) 'Revisiting the South China miracle.' *Labor Studies Journal*, 27 (2): 61–64.

—— (2004) 'Made in China: labor as a political force?' Discussion paper at Mansfield Conference, 18–20 April, University of Montana, Missoula. Online. Available: http://www. umt.edu/mansfield/Ching%20Kwan%20Lee%20paper.pdf (accessed 23 November 2004).

—— (2007a) *Against the Law: Labor Protests in China's Rustbelt and Sunbelt*. Berkeley: University of California Press.

—— (ed.) (2007b) *Working in China: Ethnographies of Labor and Workplace Transformation*. London and New York: Routledge.

Leidner, R. (1993) *Fast Food, Fast Talk: Service Work and the Routinization of Everyday Life*. Berkeley: University of California Press.

Leung, P. (2005) 'Jinnian zhongguo zhusanjiao gongren jiti xingdong ziliao souji' (The data collection of workers' collective actions in China's Pearl River Delta in recent years). Unpublished research data, Hong Kong University of Science and Technology. [In Chinese]

Leung, W. Y. (1988) *Smashing the Iron Rice Pot: Workers and Unions in China's Market Socialism*. Hong Kong: Asia Monitor Resource Centre.

—— (1998) 'The politics of labour rebellions in China: 1989–94.' PhD thesis, University of Hong Kong.

Lewis, W. A. (1954) 'Economic development with unlimited supply of labour.' *The Manchester School*, 22 (May): 139–91.

Lin, F. (1998) 'What is the future of employment relationship in the Pearl River Delta – an examination of the current reform of employment relations and legislation.' In J. Y. S. Cheng (ed.) *The Guang Dong Development Model and Its Challenges*. Hong Kong: City University of Hong Kong Press: 211–50.

Liu, P. W., Wong, Y. J., Sung, Y. W. and Lau, P. K (1992) *Zhongguo Gaige Kaifang Yu Zhujiang Sanjiaozhou De Jingji Fazhan Yanjiu Baodao* (A Study Report on Economic Development of the Pearl River Delta and China's Reform and Openness). Hong Kong: Nanyang Commercial Bank. [In Chinese]

Marx, K. (1963) *The Eighteenth Brumaire of Louis Bonaparte*. New York: International Publishers.

—— (1967) *Capital: Volume I*. New York: International Publishers.

—— (1977) *Selected Writings*. Edited by D. McLellan. Oxford: Oxford University Press.

—— (1980) *Marx's 'Grundrisse'*. Selected, edited and translated by D. McLellan. London: Macmillan.

—— (1982) 'Poverty of philosophy.' In A. Giddens and D. Held (eds) *Class, Power and Conflict*. Berkeley: University of California Press: 35–37.

May, T. (1997) *Social Research: Issues, Methods, and Process*. Buckingham: Open University Press.

Mazur, J. (2000) 'Labor's new internationalism.' *Foreign Affairs*, January–February: 79–93.

McAdam, D. (1988) 'Micromobilization contexts and recruitment to activism.' *International Social Movement Research*, 1: 125–54.

Meng, X. (2000) *Labour Market Reform in China*. Cambridge: Cambridge University Press.

Mills, C. W. (1959) *The Sociological Imagination*. New York: Oxford University Press.

Moody, K. (1997) *Workers in a Lean World*. London, New York: Verso.

Munck, R. (1988) *The New International Labour Studies: An Introduction*. London. New Jersey: Zed Books.

—— (2002) *Globalisation and Labour: The New 'Great Transformation'*. London and New York: Zed Books.

Munck, R. and Waterman, P. (eds) (1999) *Labour Worldwide in the Era of Globalization* New York: St. Martin's Press.

Narayan, K. (1993) 'How native is a "native" anthropologist?' *American Anthropologist*, 95: 671–86.

Nee, V. and Stark, D. (1989) *Remaking the Economic Institutions of Socialism*. Stanford: Stanford University Press.

Nelson, D. (1975) *Managers and Workers: Origins of the New Factory System in the United States 1880–1920*. Wisconsin: University of Wisconsin Press.

Nelson, J. M., Tilly, C. and Walker, L. (eds) (1999) *Transforming Post-communist Political Economies*. Washington, DC: National Academic Press.

Ng, S. H. and Warner, M. (1998) *China's Trade Unions and Management*. London, New York: Macmillan/St. Martin's Press.

O'Leary, G. (ed.) (1998) *Adjusting to Capitalism: Chinese Workers and the State*. Armonk: M. E. Sharpe.

Olson, M. (1971) *The Logic of Collective Action*. Cambridge, MA: Harvard University Press.

Ostercher, R. J. (1986) *Solidarity and Fragmentation: Working People and Class Consciousness in Detroit, 1875–1900*. Urbana: University of Illinois Press.

Padilla, F. M. (1992) *The Gang as an American Enterprise*. New Brunswick: Rutgers University Press.

Pearson, R. and Seyfang, G. (2001) 'New hope or false dawn? Voluntary codes of conduct, labour regulation and social policy in a globalizing world.' *Global Social Policy*, 1 (1): 49–78.

Perry, E. (1993) *Shanghai on Strike: The Politics of Chinese Labor*. Stanford: Stanford University Press.

—— (1997) 'From native place to workplace: labor origins and outcomes of China's *Danwei* system.' In X. B. Lu and E. Perry (eds) *Danwei: Changing Chinese Workplace in Historical and Comprative Perspective*. New York: M. E. Sharpe: 42–60.

—— (ed.) (1996) *Putting Class in Its Place: Worker Identities in East Asia*. Berkeley: University of California Press.

Polanyi, K. (1957) *The Great Transformation*. Boston: Beacon Press.

Pollert, A. (1981) *Girls, Wives, Factory Lives*. London: Macmillan.

Pun, N. (2005a) 'Global production, company codes of conduct, and labor conditions in China: a case study of two factories.' *The China Journal*, 54: 101–13.

—— (2005b) 'Global production, company codes of conduct, and labor conditions in China: a case study of two factories.' Working paper, Hong Kong University of Science and Technology.

—— (2005c) *Made in China: Women Factory Workers in a Global Workplace*. Durham, NC: Duke University Press.

—— (2009) 'The making of a global dormitory labour regime: labour NGOs and workers' empowerment in South China.' In R. Murphy (ed.) *Labour Migration and Social Development in Contemporary China*. London: Routledge: 154–70.

Pun, N. and Chan, C. (2008) 'The subsumption of class discourse in China.' *Boundary 2*, 35 (2): 75–91.

Pun, N. and Ren, Y. (forthcoming) 'Nongmingong de yinyu: wufa wancheng de wuchan jieji guocheng' (The metaphor of peasant workers: the impossible to finish process of proletarianisation). *21 shi ji*. (21st Century.) Hong Kong: Chinese University of Hong Kong. [In Chinese]

Pun, N. and Smith, C. (2007) 'Putting transnational labour process in its place: the dormitory labour regime in post-socialist China.' *Work, Employment and Society*, 21: 1, 27–45.

Ren, Y. and Pun, N. (2007) 'Nongmingong laodongli zai shengchan zhong de zhengfu quewei' (The state function gap in the reproduction of peasant workers' workforce). *Zhongguo Shehui Kexue Neikan* (Internal Journal of Chinese Social Science), April: 105–20 [In Chinese]

Richards, A. (1996) *Miners on Strike: Class Solidarity and Division in Britain*. Oxford: Berg.

Rifkin, J. (1995) *The End of Work: The Decline of the Global Labor Force and the Dawn of the Post-Market Era.* New York: Putnam.

Ross, R. F. S. and Chan, A. (2002) 'From North–South to South–South: the true face of global competition.' *Foreign Affairs*, September–October: 8–13.

Sargeson, S. (1999) *Reworking China's Proletariat.* London: Macmillan.

—— (2001) 'Assembling class in a Chinese joint venture factory.' In J. Hutchison and A. Brown (eds) *Organising Labour in Globalising Asia.* London: Routledge: 48–70.

Scott, J. (1990) *A Matter of Record.* Cambridge: Polity.

Sewell, W. H., Jr. (1980) *Work and Revolution in France: The Language of Labor from the Old Regime to 1848.* New York: Cambridge University Press.

—— (1993) 'Toward a post-materialist rhetoric for labor history.' In L. R. Berlanstein (ed.) *Rethinking Labor History.* Chicago: University of Illinois Press: 15–38.

Shek, P. K. and Leung, T. (1998) 'Export processing zones in China.' In AMRC (ed.) *We in the Zone: Women Workers in Asia's Export Processing Zones.* Hong Kong: Asia Monitor Resource Centre: 191–241.

Silver, B. J. (2003) *Forces of Labor: Workers' Movements and Globalization since 1870.* Cambridge: Cambridge University Press.

Skeggs, B. (2004) *Class, Self, Culture.* London: Routledge.

Smith, C. and Pun, N. (2006) 'The dormitory labour regime in China as a site of control and resistance.' *International Journal of Human Resource Management*, 17 (8): 1456–70.

Solinger, D. (1993) *China's Transition from Socialism? Statist Legacies and Market Reforms, 1980–90.* Armonk and London: M. E. Sharpe.

—— (1999) *Contesting Citizenship in Urban China: Peasant Migrants, the State, and the Logic of the Market.* Berkeley: University of California Press.

Somers, M. R. (1997) 'Deconstructing and reconstructing class formation theory: narrativity, relational analysis, and social theory.' In J. R. Hall (ed.) *Reworking Class.* Ithaca: Cornell University Press: 73–106.

Stark, D. and V. Nee (1989) 'Toward an institutional analysis of state socialism.' In V. Nee and D. Stark (eds) *Remaking the Economic Institutions of Socialism.* Stanford: Stanford University Press: 1–31.

State Council Research Office (SCRO) Project Team (2006) *Zhongguo Nongmingong Diaoyan Baogao* (A Research Report on Peasant Workers in China). Beijing: Zhongguo Yan Shi Chubanshe. [In Chinese]

Steinberg, M. (2003). 'Capitalist development, the labor process, and the law.' *American Journal of Sociology*, 109 (2): 445–95.

Strangleman, T. (2005) 'Sociological futures and the sociology of work.' *Sociological Research Online*, 10 (4). Online. Available: http://www.socresonline.org.uk/10/4/strangleman.html (accessed 3 October 2007).

—— (2007) 'The nostalgia for permanence at work? The end of work and its commentators.' *The Sociological Review*, 55 (1):82–103.

Sum, N. L. and Pun, N. (2005) 'Globalization and paradoxes of ethical transnational production: code of conduct in a Chinese workplace.' *Competition and Change*, 9 (2): 181–200.

Tam, S. M. M. (1992) 'The structuration of Chinese modernization: women workers of Shekou industrial zone.' PhD dissertation, University of Hawaii.

Taylor, B., Chang, K. and Li, Q. (2003) *Industrial Relations in China.* Cheltenham: Edward Elgar.

Thiel, D. (2007) 'Class in construction: London building workers, dirty work and physical cultures.' *The British Journal of Sociology*, 58 (2): 227–51.

Thompson, E. P. (1963/1980) *The Making of the English Working Class*. Harmondsworth: Penguin.

—— (1967) 'Time, Work-Discipline, and Industrial Capitalism.' *Past and Present*, 38: 56–97

—— (1978) 'Eighteenth Century English Society: Class Struggle without Classes?' *Social History*, 3: 133–65.

Thrasher, F. M. (1927) *The Gang: A Study of 1,313 Gangs in Chicago*. Chicago: The University of Chicago Press.

Tilly, C. (1978) *From Mobilization to Revolution*. New York: McGraw-Hill.

—— (1984) 'Demographic Origins of the European Proletariat.' In D. Levine (ed.) *Proletarianization and Family Life*. New York and London: Academic Press: 1–85.

Walder, A. G. (1986) *Communist Neo-traditionalism: Work and Authority in Chinese Industry*. Berkeley: University of California Press.

Wang, K. (2008) 'A hanging arena of industrial relations in China: what is happening after 1978.' *The Employee Relations*, 30 (2): 190–216.

Wang, S. G. (2000) 'The social and political implications of China's WTO membership.' *Journal of Contemporary China*, 9 (25): 373–405.

Waterman, P. (1999) 'The new social unionism: a new union model for a new world order.' In R. Munck and P. Waterman (eds) *Labour Worldwide in the Era of Globalization*. New York: St. Martin's Press: 247–64.

—— (2001) *Globalization, Social Movements, and the New Internationalisms*. London: Continuum.

Weinstein, D. and Weinstein, M. A. (1991) 'Georg Simmel: sociological flaneur bricoleur.' *Theory, Culture and Society*, 8: 151–68.

Whitehouse, L. (2003) 'Corporate social responsibility, corporate citizenship and the global compact: a new approach to regulating corporate social power?' *Global Social Policy*, 3 (3): 299–318.

Willis, P. (1979) 'Shop-floor culture, masculinity and the wage form.' In J. Clarke *et al.* (eds) *Working Class Culture*. London: Hutchinson: 185–98.

Wong, H. (1989) 'The changing international division of labour: migration of labour and capital in the Zhujiang delta region.' MA dissertation, Sociology Department, University of Warwick.

Wood, E. M., Meiksins, P. and Yates, M. (eds) (1998) *Rising from Ashes? Labor in the Age of 'Global' Capitalism*. New York: Monthly Review Press.

Wright, E. O. (2000) 'Working-class power, capitalist-interests, and class compromise.' *American Journal of Sociology*, 105 (4): 957–1002.

Xie, Q. S. (1997) 'Guangzhou shi de waisheng mingong shequn – zhongguo minjian Shehui de zaixian' (Cross-province migrant workers' community: the re-emergence of Chinese civil society). *Chinese Social Science Quarterly (Hong Kong)*, 18–19 (Spring–Summer): 197–202. [In Chinese]

Yu, J. R. (2006) *Zhonguo Gongren Jieji Zhuangkuang – Anyuan Shilu* (The Plight of China's Working Class – An Analysis of Anyuan). Hong Kong: Min Jing Chubanshe. [In Chinese]

Yin, Y. Q. and Yang, Z. H. (2004) *Ju Bian: 1978 Nian–2004 Nian Zhongguo Jingji Gaige Licheng*. (Great Transformation: The Process of Chinese Economic Reform 1978–2004). Beijing: Dangdai Shijie Chebanshe. [In Chinese]

Zhan, Y. H. (2005) 'Dalian ri qi bagong shijian diaocha' (A survey of workers' strikes in Japanese firms in Dalian). *Feng Huan Zhou Kan*, 203: 28–31. [In Chinese]

Zhang, L. (2001) *Strangers in the City: Reconfigurations of Space, Power, and Social Networks within China's Floating Population*. Stanford: Stanford University Press.

Statistics and other documents

ACFTU (1994) *Zhongguo Gongyun* (China Labour Movement). Beijing: ACFTU. [In Chinese]

Gongyun Yuekan (Labour Movement Monthly) (1994) volume 127. Hong Kong: Hong Kong Trade Union Education Centre. [In Chinese]

Guang Dong Provincial Statistics Bureau (1991) *Guangdong Tongji Nianjian* (Guang Dong Statistical Yearbook). Beijing: China Statistical Publishing House. [In Chinese]

Ministry of Commerce (various years) 'Foreign direct investment in China.' Online. Available: http://english.mofcom.gov.cn/ (accessed 27 October 2007).

MOLSS (2004) *Report*. Beijing: Ministry of Labour and Social Security. Online. Available: http://www.molss.gov.cn/new2004/0908a.htm.

National Bureau of Statistics of China (2000; 2005) *China Statistical Yearbooks 1999*; *2004*. New York: Praeger.

National Bureau of Statistics of China (various years) *Zhongguo Laodong Tongji Nianjian* (China Labour Statistical Yearbook). Beijing: China Statistical Publishing House. [In Chinese]

Shenzhen Municipal Government (2008) 'General information: overview.' Online. Available: http://english.sz.gov.cn/gi/200708/t20070824_229880.htm (accessed 25 July 2008).

Shenzhen Municipal Statistics Bureau (2006) 'Population.' Online. Available: http://www.sztj.com/pub/sztjpublic/szgk/rk/default.html (accessed 25 June 2007). [In Chinese]

Shenzhen Municipal Statistics Bureau (various years) 'Standard of minimum wage.' Online. Available. http://www.cn12333.com/writ_view.asp?id = 2272 (accessed 2 July 2008). [In Chinese]

SZMLSSB (2006) 'Shenzhen shi gongbu 2006 niandu zuidi gongzi biaozhun' (The city of Shenzhen announced the standard of the minimum wage for 2006). Online. Available: http://www.lm.gov.cn/gb/salary/2006–{06/05}/content_118530.htm (accessed 27 June 2008) [In Chinese]

Index

Note: Page numbers followed by 'm' , 'n' or 't' refer to maps, notes or tables respectively.

accommodation 83, 84, 111, 127; rent increases 126; *see also* dormitories
ACFTU: *see* All China Federation of Trade Unions (ACFTU)
age: discrimination 66, 72, 107, 137, 156; division of labour based on 46, 64, 66, 127; profile in Hui Zhou factory 112; social groups among workers based on 46, 53, 59, 60
All China Federation of Trade Unions (ACFTU) 7, 16, 34, 35, 144, 154, 175; banning Hong Kong trade union trainers 148; resistant to working with overseas NGOs 162–3; unionisation campaign 34, 42, 161–2, 163
Aminzade, R. 9
AMRC (Asia Monitor Resource Centre) 26, 28, 30, 32, 33, 34, 167, 179n
arbitration 7, 11, 14, 36–7; institutionalisation of 22, 24, 143; in labour disputes 1993–2004 36t; problems for workers in pursuing 36
Au, L.Y. 6, 22

Bai, N.S. 21, 22
bargaining power, workplace and marketplace 120, 141–2, 168, 169
Bélanger, J. 4
Benson, J. 46, 48
Berlanstein, L.R. 9, 79
Braverman, H. 4
Brown, A. 5, 146, 147
bullying in workplace 71, 72–3, 81
Burawoy, M. 4, 10, 23, 122, 143, 144, 145, 165, 173, 174, 176
Burnham, P. 2, 3

business, running a small 51–3
Business Weekly 6

Cai, Y.S. 8, 13, 22
Canon strike 31
capitalism: crisis of Western 1; and labour regimes 143–4; *see also* global capitalism
Castells, M. 4, 8
Chan, A. 3, 4, 6, 7, 10, 11, 22, 34, 36, 83, 150, 154, 162, 163, 170, 179n, 181n
Chan, C. 20
Chan, C.K.C. 121
Chang, D.O. 147
Chang, K. 18, 28
Chen, F. 8, 14–15, 22, 33, 170
Chen, G.H. 6
Chen, H. 19
China Labour Bulletin (CLB) 36, 37, 144, 165, 166, 170
China News Net 5, 6
China Youth News 26
Chinese Labour Movement Observation Reports 165–6
Chinese Working Women Network (CWWN) 160
Clarke, S. 7, 16, 36, 144, 146, 148, 150, 163, 170, 171
class-consciousness 10, 119, 171; formation of 46, 48, 146; of laid-off state workers 15; strengthening of 16, 174
class formation 9–11, 15–17, 171–5
class struggle 7–8; and changing labour regime 13–17, 143–5, 175–7; leading role of artisans and skilled workers 93–4; and wage levels 118, 142

CLB (*China Labour Bulletin*) 36, 37, 144, 165, 166, 170
Cockburn, C. 61, 78
codes of conduct 147–9, 156–7
Cohen, R. 2, 3, 4, 10, 118, 164, 177
Collier, R.B. 9
The Communist Manifesto 2–3
community culture, migrant workers':
cross-provincial peer groups 60–1;
gangsters in 52–9; industrial
masculinity in 62–3; interactions with
indigenous locals 57; locality of Sun
Factory 47–8; men's social lives 59–61,
62; a migrant couple's experiences
48–53; place-of-origin networks 35,
52–3, 54, 59–60; sexual activity 61–2;
a woman's experience 51–3; women's
social lives 61–2
complaints, worker 25–6, 96–8, 107, 129;
reluctance to file 72–3
Cooke, F.L. 7, 18, 21, 22, 34, 150
corporate social responsibility (CSR)
10–11, 16, 147–8, 160, 162; China's
standard 161
CWWN (Chinese Working Women
Network) 160

Dawley, A. 18, 48
democracy movement 22
Deng, X.P. 5, 20, 21, 22
Deyo, F.C. 1
dismissals: as a cause of collective action
38t; with a change of department
superintendent 69, 75, 98; on grounds
of age 107; in low season 66; of
'skilled' workers 95, 99; in strikes
25–6, 32, 38, 41, 86, 90, 115, 116;
threats to 'drop from on high' to claim
compensation 99–100; without
severance compensation 38, 98
Dispute Mediation and Arbitration Law
168
dormitories: cost of living in 84, 111, 115,
127; living conditions 127, 136;
management control of 61, 84, 111,
115, 127, 180n; protest development in
13–14, 27, 33, 88, 134, 160; social
networks 47; a strike issue at Moon
Factory 135; unpopularity 47
drug smuggling 52–3

The Economist 5, 177
Edwards, P.K. 16, 109, 168

Edwards, R.C. 143
Elger, T. 166
Employment Promotion Law 2007 143, 168
The End of Work 2
'end of work' thesis 2, 5
environment allowances 83, 85, 99, 101

Fantasia, R. 109, 119, 156, 173
Farewell to the Working Class 2
femininity, industrial 73, 79
fights among workers 60–1, 74, 76–7
financial crisis, global 176
Financial Times 177
fines: factory 37, 96; workers' 32, 67, 68, 95, 96
first generation migrant workers 71–2
food: deductions for cost of 115, 126, 128,
132, 167; disputes over quality 38, 84,
114–15; eating at home 59, 84; outside
factories 60, 84, 127–8; preferences
reinforcing place-of-origin clusters 59;
separate canteens for managers and
workers 63, 114; welfare committee
seeks to improve 157, 158
foreign direct investment (FDI) 22, 23
Fox, A. 4
Franzosi, R. 23, 119, 166, 168
freedom of association (FOA) 147–9
Freidson, E. 94
Friedman, A. 118, 142
Frobel, F. 2, 3

Gallagher, M.E. 18, 36
gangsters: and control of informal
economy 52–9; maintaining relations
with 52, 58–9; management attempts to
get rid of 95, 99, 106; place-of-origin
networks 52–3, 54–6; privileged
positions in workplace 75–6, 85;
similarities to US gangsters in 19th
century 53–4, 79; 'skilled' workers
connected to 71, 75–6, 77, 95, 99;
strike leadership 86, 88, 91; structure
58–9; and workplace influence and
control 70–4, 78, 79, 82, 106, 119
gender: divisions in the workplace 64,
65–6, 65t, 67, 138; divisions in
workplace 112; industrial masculinity
as a process of gendering 78–9; and
management control of workers 78;
social groups based on 60, 61–2
global capitalism 3, 4, 8–9, 10; differences

between Chinese and Western transition to 163; expansion into China 8, 13, 43, 120, 143, 144, 155, 168
'global solidarity' 147, 163
globalisation 1, 2–3, 117, 155; and Chinese migrant workers 5–6
Gorz, A. 2, 3, 8, 177
Gouldner, A.W. 9, 81, 119
gross domestic product (GDP) 6, 21

Haggard, S.K. 10, 34
Harvey, D. 3, 48, 117, 177
Hayter, T. 48
Hershatter, G. 46, 119, 171
Hirschman, A.O. 155, 168
Hobsbawm, E.J. 79, 80, 146
Hodson, R. 46, 79
Holloway, J. 53
Honig, E. 46, 57, 119, 171
Household Registration System (*Hukou*) 6, 48, 170, 175
Howell, J. 10, 34, 170
Hui Zhou plant: *see* Sun Factory Hui Zhou plant
Hukou system 6, 48, 170, 175
Hurst, W. 8, 13, 22
Hutchison, J. 5, 146, 147
Hyman, R. 9, 93, 119

identities, self 171–2
industrial femininity 73, 79
industrial injuries 12, 14, 73, 111; insurance 82, 96, 100
industrial masculinity 62–3, 74–9, 173
industrial relations studies 4–5, 173
industrial sociology 4–5
informal economy 51–9, 79
internal contracting 102–5
Izraelewicz, E. 6

Jiang, K.W. 29, 34
justice in labour protests, a sense of 77, 79, 120, 173

Kader toy factory 25–6
Katz-Fishman, W. 3
Katznelson, I. 9, 16, 79, 146, 173, 174
Kelly, J. 119, 120, 156
Kim, S.K. 10
Koo, H. 8, 173
Kuai Pao 30

Labour and Social Security Bureau (LSSB) 34, 73, 129, 140; dealing with complaints after Sun Factory strike 96, 97; involvement in a resignation dispute 49–50; and Sun Factory strike 87, 88, 90; and Sun Mei strike 31–2; and Uniden strike 39, 40; and Yong Feng strike 32, 33
Labour Contract Law 2007 143, 157, 163, 168
Labour Dispute Mediation and Arbitration Law 2007 143
Labour Law 1994 7, 18, 94; internet forum discussion of 136, 137; limitations of 35–7; problems in implementing 155
labour market: age discrimination 66, 72, 107, 137, 156; gangsters role in 53–4, 79–80, 119; impact on industrial conflict 141–2, 155, 166–7, 169; reform 18, 20–3; uneven bargaining power 141–2; *see also* labour shortages
labour movement: in China 16–17, 19, 174, 176; in developing countries 9–10
labour reform 20–3
labour regime: Burawoy's categories for 143–4; class struggle and China's 13–17, 143–5, 175–7; 'contested despotism' in reshaping China's 17, 123, 143, 176; legal institution context 122, 143
labour shortages 23, 118; among skilled workers 23, 79, 118, 168; CLB Report 2007 on migrant workers 166; influencing 'voice' and 'exit' strategies 82, 142, 155, 168, 169, 175; at Moon Factory 137–8, 139; SCRO Project report 43; at Sun Factory 105–6, 111–12, 117, 118; and uneven bargaining power 141–2; wage increases in response to 120, 122–4, 169
labour studies 3–5, 10, 173
Lambert, R. 10
Against the Law 14
Lee, C.H. 36
Lee, C.K. 6, 7, 8, 13, 14, 18, 19, 21, 22, 34, 46, 109, 118, 119, 122, 123, 141, 142, 143, 155, 168, 171, 176, 178n
Leung, P. 35, 38
Leung, T. 21, 31, 179n
Leung, W.Y. 13, 22, 25, 26, 28, 29, 31, 178n, 179n
Lewis, W.A. 118, 141, 168, 180n
Lin, F. 36

Liu, P.W. 29, 179n
locality, politics of: in a migrant
    community 47–8, 53–60; in workplace
    46, 64–5, 68–74, 118, 119, 143, 155;
    see also place-of-origin networks
The Logic of Collective Action 120
LSSB: *see* Labour and Social Security
    Bureau (LSSB)

machine repairers: gender and age 67;
    impact of internal contracting on
    102–3; privileges of 75, 129, 138;
    promotion to 74–5; strike leadership
    131, 172
Marx, K. 2–3, 7–8, 119, 176
Marxism 7–8; crisis of labour studies 3–5;
    understanding of globalisation 2–3
masculinity, industrial 62–3, 74–9, 173
Mazur, J. 3
McAdam, D. 120, 173
Meizhi Haiyan strike 37
Meng, X. 18
Militant Village: *see* community culture,
    migrant workers'
minimum wage: capacity of strikes to push
    up 32–3, 125–6, 168, 169; comparing
    Hui Zhou and Shenzhen 110;
    consultation conference 125;
    enforcement of 7; increases in response
    to shortage of labour 122–4, 169;
    management strategies to deal with
    rises in 108, 126; pay below 7, 32–3,
    83; in Shang Hai 123, 125, 140, 176; in
    Shenzhen 107, 110, 123–5, 124t, 140,
    176; and worker demands beyond
    125–6, 167
Moon Factory: accommodation 127;
    background to 126–7; basis of worker
    solidarity 134, 135, 171, 172;
    grievances 128, 129, 130; increased
    production targets 128–9, 138, 139–40;
    labour shortages 137–8, 139;
    mechanics 75, 138; overtime
    restrictions 129, 131; piece-rate policy
    128; recruitment 137, 142; restriction
    of resignation rights 128–9, 131, 135;
    segregation on basis of production
    position 127, 128, 130, 134, 135, 144;
    self-identities 171; wages 127, 128,
    131, 139, 140; working conditions 127,
    128, 129, 130–1, 138; *see also* Moon
    Factory strike
Moon Factory strike 131–6; collapse of

136; evidence of pre-planning 136,
    137; knock-on effects of 138–40;
    leadership 131, 132–3, 136, 138;
    management tactics to end 134–6;
    pamphlet 134, 135; public letter posted
    in workshops 131, 132; refusal to select
    worker representatives 133; and rush of
    resignations after 135–6, 172–3;
    spreads to a sister factory 136–7;
    supervisory staff return to work 134;
    and trade union issue after 138–9,
    141–2; uneven bargaining power in
    141–2; *Yuangong* continue to strike
    134–5, 141; *Zhiyuan* betrayal of
    Yuangong 135–6, 139, 171, 172
Munck, R. 2, 5, 10, 147

Nee, V. 9, 10
Nelson, D. 79, 84, 94
Nelson, J.M. 10
new international labour studies 4, 10
newly industrialised countries (NICs) 1, 3,
    10, 163
non-government organizations (NGOs)
    156, 160–3, 170–1, 175

O'Brien, K.J. 8, 22
O'Leary, G. 10
Olson, M. 120
open door policy 19–20, 176; historical
    review 21–3
ordinary workers: and gangster control of
    workplace 70–4; ignorance of trade
    unions 138–9, 141, 159; management
    control of 64, 76, 78, 94–5, 118, 128–9,
    143; role in strikes 91–3, 119, 120, 133,
    134–6, 141; sense of betrayal by skilled
    workers 135–6, 138, 139, 171, 172
Ostercher, R.J. 53
overtime: discontent over restrictions on
    95, 115, 129, 131; disputes concerning
    25–6, 85, 87, 132; high levels of 83, 96;
    legal rates for 33, 83; without payment
    158

Padilla, F.M. 53, 80
patron-client relations 154–5, 156
Pearson, R. 11, 147
People's Daily 29
Perry, E. 10, 46, 53, 80, 93, 171
place-of-origin networks: in gangs 52–3,
    54–6; in migrant communities 35,
    52–3, 54, 59–60; in recruitment

practices 68–9, 155–6; in the Sun
factories 63–5; in Sun factories 65t, 74,
117; and workplace control 70–4, 75–6,
119, 155–6
Polanyi, K. 10
'politics of production' 23, 122
Pollert, A. 61
Poverty of Philosophy 7–8
Pringle, T. 144, 146, 163
promotion practices 69, 70, 71, 74–5, 98
Pun, N. 8, 9, 11, 13, 14, 15, 18, 19, 21, 22,
46, 47, 48, 148, 154, 156, 160, 180n

recruitment: at Hui Zhou plant 111–12,
117, 118; introduction fees 68–9, 74,
106; at Moon Factory 137, 142;
outsourcing 105–7; and place-of-origin
networks 68–9, 155–6; and problem of
retention 142; at Star Factory 155–6; at
Sun Factory 68–9, 74, 106–7
resignation: laws 100, 113; at Moon
Factory 128–9, 131, 135–6, 172–3;
preferred way to secure individual
interests 155; problem of obtaining
wages due 49–51, 129; restrictions on
right to resign 49, 128–9, 142; at Star
Factory 153, 155; at Sun Factory
100–2; 'voice' and 'exit' strategies 82,
142, 155, 168, 169, 175
Richards, A. 48
Rifkin, J. 2, 4, 177
Robert, J.S.R. 3, 6
Ross, R.F.S. 3

San Mei strike 31–2, 42
Sanyo strike 26–8, 33
Sargeson, S. 8, 10, 13, 14, 46, 173
Scullion, H. 109, 168
security guards 58, 77–8, 114, 115, 180n
Sewell, W.H. 9
sexual activity 61–2
Seyfang, G. 11, 147
Shang Hai: minimum wage in 123, 125,
140, 176; strike study in 1920s 93–4
She Kou Industrial Zone Federation of
Trade Unions (SKIZFTU) 25, 26, 27,
28, 33
Shek, P.K. 21, 31, 179n
Shenzhen: economic growth 21; formation
of modern 19–20; history of labour
reform 20–3; labour shortage statistics
23; map 21m; minimum wage 107,
110, 123–5, 124t, 140, 176; prone to

labour conflicts 166; social insurance
for migrant workers 97, 100
Shenzhen Municipal Federation of Trade
Unions (SZMFTU) 25, 26, 124, 162,
170
shop floor culture 63–74, 116–17
Silver, B.J. 3, 4
skilled workers: 'false' gang-connected 71,
75, 76, 77, 95, 99; high turnover of
155, 168; hiring in Hui Zhou factory
112; horizontal tensions between 74,
77, 82; labour shortage among 23, 79,
118, 168; leadership in disputes 43, 86,
88, 89, 91, 94, 119, 167; management
assaults on power of 94–5, 99, 102–4;
militancy and industrial masculinity
among 79, 119; predominantly men 62,
67, 112; privileged positions of 67, 75,
119, 168; relationship with security
guards 77; role in class struggle 93–4;
shirking among 75–6, 85, 99, 117;
social lives 62, 84; *see also* machine
repairers
SKIZFTU: *see* She Kou Industrial Zone
Federation of Trade Unions
(SKIZFTU)
Smith, C. 9, 13, 14, 18, 47, 166, 180n
social insurance 96–8, 100–2
social movement unionism 4–5
Solinger, D. 10
Song, H.Y. 21, 22
South Korea 1, 8–9, 163, 173, 181n
Southern Metropolitan Daily 48, 54, 123,
124
Special Export Zones (SEZ) 20, 21
Star Factory: background 149–50; delayed
payment abuse 158; factors
handicapping the welfare committee
154–7, 161; impact of global capitalism
on 155; impact of welfare committee
157–9; management agreement for a
welfare committee 159; operation of
welfare committee 151–3; recruitment
155–6; resignations 153, 155; strike
158; training welfare committee
members 150–1, 156; wages 151, 156,
157, 158–9; worker solidarity 149, 156
Stark, D. 9, 10
state: regulatory role in workplace
relations 107–8, 109, 143–4, 163, 168,
170–1, 175; repressive apparatus of 34;
strike interventions 27–8, 31–2, 33, 40,
120, 160–1

State Council Research Office (SCRO) 43
state-owned enterprises (SOEs) 6, 8, 21,
    22; class-consciousness of laid-off
    workers in 14–15; protests 8, 13, 22,
    166
state socialism 10; legacy for trade unions
    28–9, 33–4, 42–3, 171; and patron-
    client relationships 154–5, 156
Steinberg, M. 122, 140, 143
Strangleman, T. 4, 5, 164, 178n
strikes: in 1920s Shang Hai 93–4; in 1980s
    24–9; 1992-4 29–30; 1993-4 30–5;
    2004-7 35–43; at Canon 31; capacity to
    push up minimum wage 32–3, 125–6,
    140, 168, 169; cross-factory networks
    167; developments in staging of 167–9;
    dismissals in 25–6, 32, 38, 41, 86, 90,
    115, 116; emerging patterns of labour
    protests 167; individual self-interest in
    120; leadership 93–4, 119; at Meizhi
    Haiyan 37; moving beyond issues of
    legality 167, 172; ordinary workers'
    role in 91–3, 119, 120, 133, 134–6,
    141; and radicalisation of workers
    34–5; right to strike 7, 27–8; at San
    Mei 31–2, 42; at Sanyo 26–8, 33; at
    Star Factory 158; state interventions
    27–8, 31–2, 33, 40, 120, 160–1; at
    Uniden 38–42; wages a central issue in
    141–2; 'wave of strikes' 166–7; at Ya
    Pu Luo 32; at Yong Feng 32–3, 41–2;
    see also Moon Factory strike; Sun
    Factory strike
Sum, N.L. 11, 154
Sun Factory: accommodation 83, 84;
    background 47; basis of worker
    solidarity 119, 171, 172; bullying 71,
    72–3, 81; discipline and punishment
    66–7; 'false' skilled workers 71, 75–6,
    77, 95, 99; fights among workers 75–6;
    gangster influence and control 70–4,
    78, 79, 82, 106, 119; gender bias 64,
    65–6, 65t, 67; induction of new
    workers 106–7; industrial masculinity
    74–9; internal contracting 102–5;
    management targetting of 'skilled'
    workers 95, 99, 102–4; management
    team 63; place-of-origin networks
    63–5, 65t, 74, 82, 117; promotions 69,
    70, 71, 74–5, 98; radical strategies to
    obtain severance compensation
    99–100; recruitment 68–9, 74, 105–6;
    resignations 100–2; security guards

77–8; self-identities 171; shirking work
    75–6, 85, 99; social insurance 82, 96–8,
    100–2; time-rate and piece-rate work
    66–7; trade union 108; treatment of
    veteran workers vs. temporary workers
    66–7, 68; wages 66–7, 70, 83, 108;
    working conditions 81, 82–4
Sun Factory Hui Zhou plant:
    accommodation 111; assembly line
    111, 118; canteen food dispute 114–15;
    labour shortages and recruitment
    111–12, 118; strikes 114–16; transfer
    of workers' experience from old
    factory 109, 114, 116, 118, 119–20;
    wages and subsidies 109–10, 115; work
    culture 116–17; workers' views on old
    factory 112–14; working conditions
    110–11
Sun Factory strike 85–93; background to
    82–5; detention of workers 86; five
    days of 85–90; and further department-
    based strikes 98–9, 104; at Hui Zhou
    plant 114–16; incident leading to 84–5;
    industrial relations after 93–109, 120;
    knock-on effect 93; lack of media
    reports 90; leadership 85, 86, 88, 89,
    91, 99, 172; legacy of 108–9; LSSB
    involvement 87, 88, 90; management
    control mechanisms after 94–5, 99,
    102–4; non-participants 91–3, 119;
    reasons for joining 85, 93; state
    involvement in labour relations after
    107–8, 109; treatment of worker
    representatives 86, 87, 88, 89, 90;
    workers' discontent after 95–6;
    workers' involvement 91; working
    conditions prior to 81, 82–4
superintendents: background 70; and
    control of workers 70; dealings with
    gangsters 71, 72; favouring friends and
    relatives 69, 73, 75–6, 98; gender and
    place-of-origin of 65t; management
    strategies to curb power of 95, 102–4;
    promoting workers 70, 74–5, 98;
    recruitment practices 68, 69, 70–1; strike
    support 91; wages 70; work culture
    63–4
supervisors: bargaining power 141, 142,
    168; 'betrayal' of ordinary workers
    135–6, 138, 139, 171, 172; bullying
    workers 72–3; control of ordinary
    workers 70, 74; dealing with mechanics
    75, 77; gender and place-of-origin of

65t; management strategies to curb power of 95, 99, 102–4, 106; promotion 69, 70; recruitment practices 69–70; relations with gangsters 71, 78; strike involvement 86, 88–9, 91, 98, 116, 119, 168; wages 83, 110, 127; work culture 63–5

SZMFTU: *see* Shenzhen Municipal Federation of Trade Unions (SZMFTU)

Tam, S.M.M. 48
tax system 154–5
Taylor, B. 7, 18, 30, 166, 179n
Taylorism 118
Thompson, E.P. 11, 15–16, 18, 79, 94, 128, 174
Thrasher, F.M. 53, 79
Tilly, C. 94, 120, 180n
township or village enterprises (TVEs) 18, 21, 33
Trade Union Law 2001 155, 157, 170
trade unions: absence of freedom of association a problem for 146–7; ACFTU campaign for 34, 42, 161–2, 163; affiliation to ACFTU 7; business 10; factors obstructing organisation of effective 169–71; factory owner's views on pressures to set up 161–2; in FIEs 33, 34, 42, 161–2, 163; ignorance of 108, 138–9, 141–2, 159; independent 22; management control of 34, 108, 125, 146, 147, 162, 169; pilot training project 148–9; relationship with state and NGOs 160–2, 163, 170–1; set up for CSR social audits 147–8; similarities with welfare committees 159; state socialist legacy 28–9, 33–4, 42–3, 171; strike attempts to set up 32, 33, 37–8, 39–40, 41–2, 138–9; *see also* All China Federation of Trade Unions (ACFTU); Shenzhen Municipal Federation of Trade Unions (SZMFTU)
transnational corporations (TNCs) 3–4, 162; corporate codes of conduct 147–9, 156–7

Uniden strike 38–42, 172

Verdery, K. 10

wage deductions: for absences from work in protest 50–1; for failing to meet targets 72, 73, 95; for living expenses

32, 84, 111, 115, 127; protests over 14, 31, 32–3, 37t, 38t; for social insurance 82, 96

wages: central to collective action 141–2; changing Western concerns over 177; in comparison to Mexico and US 5–6; enhanced bargaining power leading to increases in 116, 120, 122–4; at Hui Zhou plant 109–10, 115; knock-on effect of Sun Factory strike 93; levels as a result of class struggle 118, 142; at Moon Factory 127, 128, 131, 139, 140; resignation and problems in obtaining 49–51, 129; at Star Factory 151, 156, 157, 158–9; state policy and 107–8; at the Sun Factory 66–7; at Sun Factory 83, 108; superintendents 70; supervisors 83, 110, 127; welfare committee attempt to address 151–3; *see also* wage deductions

Wal-Mart 42, 47, 84, 163
Walder, A.G. 156
Wang, S.G. 22
Waterman, P. 5, 10, 147, 163
welfare committee: achievements 157–9; factors handicapping 154–7, 161; management reasons for agreeing to 159; members' training 150–1, 156; operation 151–3; similarities with trade unionism 159
Whitehouse, L. 11, 147
Willis, P. 78
women: CWWN 160; introduction fees 69; one woman's experience in a migrant community 51–3; physical and mental trauma in workplace 73; protests of 13–14, 26; sexual activity 61–2; skill segregation 65–6, 65t, 67, 75, 78; social lives 61–2; standing up for their rights 49, 50, 115, 129, 133; subordination of 62; timidity of 62
Wood, E.M. 1, 2, 3, 177
worker solidarity 14, 94, 109, 119–20, 172, 173; 'global solidarity' 147, 163; industrial masculinity and 62–3; at Moon Factory 134, 135, 171, 172; at Star Factory 149, 156; at Sun Factory 119, 171, 172
workers' subjectivity 9, 11, 28, 142, 172
working conditions 29–30, 43, 44, 54, 79; exhausting workload 51, 74, 79, 128, 129, 138; in Hui Zhou plant 129; knock-on effects of strikes on 93; and

labour rights' campaigns 34–5; in Moon Factory 127, 128, 129, 130–1, 138; petition to management 130; and provision of drinking water 132, 135, 136; strikes to improve 32, 166; in Sun Factory 81, 82–4; use of toxic chemicals 51, 83, 130, 135
World Trade Organisation (WTO) 23
Wright, E.O. 81, 119, 168

Xie, Q.S. 29, 35, 47

Ya Pu Luo strike 32
Yong Feng strike 32–3, 41–2
Yu, J.R. 22, 171

Zhu Hai Municipal Federation of Trade Unions (ZHMFTU) 31, 32
Zolberg, A.R. 9, 79, 146

New eBook Library Collection

Taylor & Francis eBooks
Taylor & Francis Group

eFocus on China

30 day free trials available!

Highly topical, this new cutting-edge collection includes everything you need to know about modern day China. The collection features a special selection of 100 core titles taken from our current repository of over 350 eBooks on China.

The collection adopts a **multi-disciplinary approach** to Chinese studies spanning subject areas such as:

- Economics
- Business
- Politics
- Law
- International Relations
- Security
- Sociology
- Media and Culture
- Philosophy
- Religion.

Also within the collection you will find some **key works of reference** including:

- The Routledge History of Chinese Philosophy
- Encyclopedia of Contemporary Chinese Culture
- A Dictionary of Chinese Symbols
- Encyclopedia of Chinese Film
- Dictionary of the Politics of the People's Republic of China

Contributions from renowned authorities, the very best in academia...

Including **Mark Selden**, Cornell University, USA; and **Stan Rosen**, University of South California, USA.

eFocus on China is available as a subscription package of 100 titles with 15 new eBooks per annum.

Recommend this package to your librarian today!

Order now for guaranteed capped price increase.

For a complete list of titles, visit: **www.ebooksubscriptions.com/eFocusChina**
www.ebooksubscriptions.com

For more information, pricing enquiries or to order a free trial, please contact your local online sales team:

UK and Rest of the world

Tel: +44 (0) 20 7017 6062
Email: online.sales@tandf.co.uk

United States, Canada and South America

Tel: 1-888-318-2367
Email: e-reference@taylorandfrancis.com

eBooks – at www.eBookstore.tandf.co.uk

A library at your fingertips!

eBooks are electronic versions of printed books. You can store them on your PC/laptop or browse them online.

They have advantages for anyone needing rapid access to a wide variety of published, copyright information.

eBooks can help your research by enabling you to bookmark chapters, annotate text and use instant searches to find specific words or phrases. Several eBook files would fit on even a small laptop or PDA.

NEW: Save money by eSubscribing: cheap, online access to any eBook for as long as you need it.

Annual subscription packages

We now offer special low-cost bulk subscriptions to packages of eBooks in certain subject areas. These are available to libraries or to individuals.

For more information please contact webmaster.ebooks@tandf.co.uk

We're continually developing the eBook concept, so keep up to date by visiting the website.

www.eBookstore.tandf.co.uk